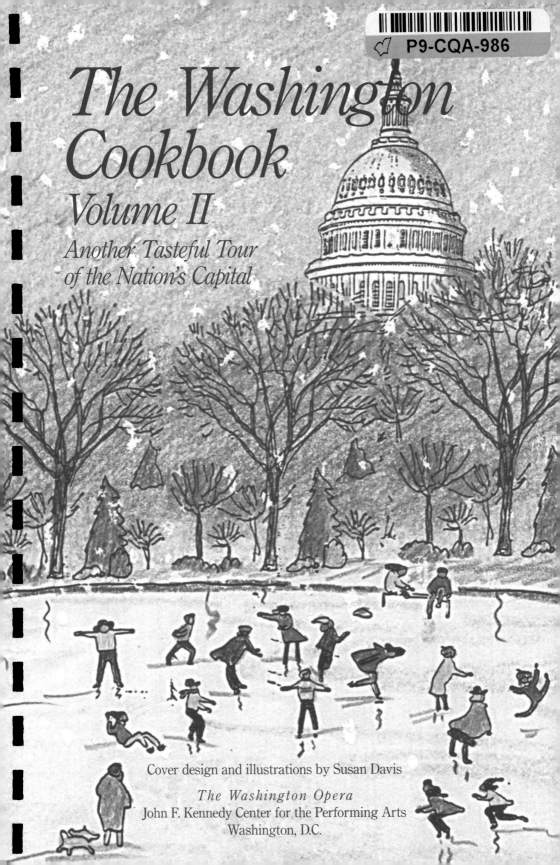

The Washington Cookbook
Volume II
Another Tasteful Tour of the Nation's Capital

Cover design and illustrations by Susan Davis

The Washington Opera
John F. Kennedy Center for the Performing Arts
Washington, D.C.

For Additional Copies
of Volume I or Volume II

Call 202/416-7800 or 1-800/87-OPERA.
Monday through Friday, 10 a.m.–5:30 p.m. Eastern Time.
$12.50 per copy, plus shipping and handling.

Shipping and Handling Fees

1 copy	$3.50
2–3 copies	$5.00
4–5 copies	$7.50
6–10 copies	$8.50

We accept MasterCard and Visa.

ISBN 0-9610542-1-2
Printed in the United States of America
by The McArdle Printing Company, Inc.
Upper Marlboro, Maryland

The Washington Opera's

exciting plans for the future unfold, the Company is happily "cooking on all burners." What better time to introduce Volume II of *The Washington Cookbook!*

When Volume I made its debut in 1982, little did our Women's Committee dream that its brainchild would go through three printings and become a well-thumbed reference book in capital kitchens. The feedback has been fabulous! In answer to your requests, The Washington Opera takes you on another tasteful tour of the nation's capital.

Working with their usual dedication, members of the Women's Committee have compiled an entirely new volume of recipes, again generously contributed by Washington notables. My compliments to the chefs who sliced, diced, baked, and mixed it up for The Washington Opera.

In Volume II, you'll find plenty of food for thought. Our contributors have lightened up with delicious diet and health-conscious recipes and added more quick-fix and easy entertaining suggestions for busy cooks. Among the cherished family recipes and exciting new inspirations, you'll discover a big, wide, wonderful world of internationally-flavored specialties.

Opera is a feast for the senses, and our new *Washington Cookbook* will satisfy every taste. We can all thank the Women's Committee for gathering these culinary delights for the benefit of The Washington Opera.

Bon appétit,

Christine F. Hunter

Christine F. Hunter
Chairman, Executive Committee

Our thanks and appreciation

to the multitude of friends here in Washington and across the country who made this book possible. Among those who shared their favorite recipes, you will find the First Lady, members of the diplomatic corps and of Congress. In addition, you will find contributions from professionals in the world of cuisine including chefs of the area and of the Washington Chapter of Les Dames d'Escoffier. Les Dames is a professional organization of women with careers in food and wine which has assisted many qualified women to achieve their career goals through scholarship awards. Their recipes are identified by their symbol throughout.

In this second volume of the *The Washington Cookbook* we have attempted to produce a collection of recipes that includes some new ideas, some challenges and some fun. We wish that space had allowed us to include every recipe we received. We hope you will enjoy reading, using and perhaps adapting to your own tastes the recipes you will find. As a wise friend once said, "A recipe is really something to start with."

Committee

Paula Jeffries, Chairman

Marnell Bruce	Katie Hunnicutt
Elena Schupp Darden	Pauline Innis
Sally Davidson	Sarah T. Minikes
Mary Welby Garrison	Anne Shultz
Nancy Geltman	Dorothy Wexler
Anne Green	Mary Wheeler

The Women's Committee of The Washington Opera
and the supportive staff of The Washington Opera

Contents

The Washington Opera. A Brief History.

In 1956 a new voice sang out—an opera company made its debut in the nation's capital. Today, 39 years later, The Washington Opera performs to standing-room audiences and has achieved world-class status.

Without the lavish government support given to the opera companies in other world capitals, The Washington Opera has earned its high position in the musical world with its excellent performances, the number and quality of its new productions, the development of its two-theater concept, its discovery and nurturing of important young American talent, its use of English Surtitles and, not least, the international collaboration system it has pioneered with leading foreign companies.

Under the leadership of Martin Feinstein, General Director since 1980, the company has grown from a total of 16 performances of four operas with rented sets, to some 65 performances of seven operas. The Company has averaged 98% attendance since the 1985–86 season. In spite of this remarkable sales record, the company must still raise nearly 40% of its total budget through contributions from individuals, corporations, foundations and fund raising endeavors such as *The Washington Cookbook.*

In June of 1994 The Washington Opera announced that Placido Domingo, world-renowned tenor and conductor, will become Artistic Director of the company effective July 1, 1996. With Mr. Domingo's appointment, the curtain goes up on another exciting chapter of operatic history-in-the-making.

Appetizers

ARTICHOKE DIP

1 14-ounce can artichokes,
  chopped
1 cup Parmesan cheese
¾–1 cup mayonnaise
2 garlic cloves, chopped
1 teaspoon curry powder

3 tablespoons lemon juice
Pinch of chili powder
1 tablespoon breadcrumbs
Paprika
French bread

Mix artichokes, cheese, mayonnaise, garlic, curry powder, lemon juice and chili powder in a food processor. Add breadcrumbs and a sprinkle of paprika and mix with a wooden spoon. • Place by heaping spoonfuls on rounds of French bread.

Mirta Londero

BARBI'S SPINACH DIP AND BREAD

1 pound round pumpernickel
  bread
2 cups sour cream
2 cups mayonnaise
1 small onion, chopped
2 1.4-ounce packages Knorr's
  vegetable soup mix

1 8-ounce can sliced water
  chestnuts (optional)
2 packages frozen chopped
  spinach, thawed and well
  drained

Two hours before serving, mix the sour cream, mayonnaise, onion, soup mix, water chestnuts (if desired) and spinach and refrigerate. Immediately before serving, hollow out bread and fill with dip. Toast center of bread and use as dipsters.

Senator Dale Bumpers
(Arkansas)

Jefferson Memorial

CAPONATA ON GARLIC TOAST — Makes 36

1 eggplant (1 pound)
1 tablespoon extra virgin
   olive oil
1 stalk of celery, diced into
   ¼-inch pieces (½ cup)
1 medium onion, diced into
   ¼-inch pieces (1 cup)
3 cloves garlic, minced
2 tablespoons sugar
¼ cup red wine vinegar
2 cups plain tomato sauce

¼ cup capers, rinsed and
   drained
3 tablespoons currants
Salt and pepper to taste
2 tablespoons pine nuts,
   toasted (optional)
1 thin firm loaf of French or
   Italian bread, sliced into
   36 ½-inch thick slices
3 cloves garlic, unpeeled
   and cut in half

Preheat oven to 400°. • With a paring knife make about 10 slits in skin of eggplant. Place on a sheet pan and place in oven to roast for about 30 minutes, or until very soft and beginning to collapse. When eggplant is cool enough to handle, remove skin with a sharp knife and discard. Dice flesh and put in a bowl. Set aside. • While eggplant is roasting, warm olive oil in a large saucepan over low heat. Add celery, onion and garlic, cover pan, and, stirring occasionally with a wooden spoon, cook until tender and beginning to brown, about 15 minutes. Stir in sugar and cook for a minute or so. Add vinegar, tomato sauce, red pepper flakes and eggplant. Stir well and increase heat to medium-low. Simmer, uncovered, for a few minutes, until it thickens and flavors meld. Transfer to a mixing bowl and stir in capers and currants. Season to taste with salt and pepper. Cover tightly and refrigerate until ready to serve. • Preheat oven to 375° and spread bread slices on sheet pan. Toast in oven until lightly browned, about 5 minutes. If using pine nuts, spread them on a small sheet pan and toast at the same time as toasting bread. Watch pine nuts closely to avoid burning. • While toast rounds are still warm, rub each with cut side of garlic clove. Spoon 2 tablespoons of eggplant mixture onto each round of toast, garnish with a couple of pine nuts and serve.

Lisa Cherkasky
Co-author of "The Artful Pie"

REFRIED BEAN DIP

3 avocados, chopped
2 tablespoons lemon juice
Salt and pepper to taste
1 cup sour cream
½ cup mayonnaise
1 package taco seasoning mix
2 cans jalapeño bean dip

3 tomatoes, peeled, seeded
  and chopped
2 4.25-ounce cans chopped
  black olives
8 ounces sharp cheese,
  shredded
4–5 scallions, chopped

Mix together the avocados, lemon juice, salt and pepper. In another bowl, mix sour cream, mayonnaise and taco seasoning. In yet another bowl, mix bean dip and tomatoes. In a large glass casserole, layer the bean dip mixture, avocado mixture and sour cream mixture. Top with olives, shredded cheese and scallions.

Dotty Wexler

TAPENADE DIP   Makes about 1 cup

½ cup black pitted
  Mediterranean olives
  (approximately 22)
1 garlic clove, mashed
1 tablespoon drained capers
4 anchovy fillets
1 egg yolk
1 teaspoon Dijon mustard
1 tablespoon lemon juice
1 6⅛-ounce can tuna fish,
  drained

¼ cup olive oil
1 tablespoon chopped fresh
  basil or parsley
Assorted raw vegetables, such
  as carrots, fennel, celery,
  cauliflower and broccoli
  florets, zucchini, snow
  peas, etc.

Place olives, garlic, capers, anchovies, egg yolk, mustard, lemon juice and tuna fish in blender or food processor and purée until smooth. While the motor is running, add the olive oil in a thin stream until it is absorbed by the purée. • Transfer to a serving bowl and garnish with basil. • Prepare the vegetables and arrange on a platter. Serve with the dip.

Mrs. Arthur Wexler

GREEN OLIVE TAPENADE   Makes 6 cups

5 cups stuffed Spanish olives	1 tablespoon minced anchovies
¼ cup chopped fresh garlic	(optional)
¼ cup fresh lemon juice	¼ cup extra virgin olive oil

Combine all the ingredients in a food processor and blend until coarsely chopped. • Serve at room temperature for maximum flavor. • This spread is recommended for earthy, crusty Italian bread. It can also be used to finish tomato-based sauces for pasta or any meat glaze. The tapenade will keep well refrigerated for up to a week.

Chris Comerford, Colonnade Chef
ANA Hotel, Washington, DC

ROASTED GARLIC AND   Serves 12
SUN-DRIED TOMATO TAPENADE

2 bulbs garlic, roasted	2 tablespoons finely chopped
4 ounces Calamata olives,	fresh rosemary
roughly chopped	4 tablespoons extra virgin
⅝ cup sun-dried tomatoes	olive oil
3 anchovy fillets, made into	1 tablespoon fresh lemon juice
a paste	Black pepper to taste
2 tablespoons chopped capers	Salt to taste

Preheat oven to 300°. • Slowly roast garlic for about half an hour, until garlic sugars release. • When garlic has cooled, squeeze into a mixing bowl. Add olives, sun-dried tomatoes, anchovy paste, capers and rosemary. Add olive oil and lemon juice and mix well. Adjust seasoning with black pepper and salt, if needed.

Chef Michael Patton
Assistant Chef Tom Blundell
1789 Restaurant

TARAMASALATA

Makes 2 to 3 cups

⅓ cup tarama caviar
    (Greek style carp roe)
⅓ cup lemon juice
½ medium onion, chopped
½ cup olive oil

½ cup corn oil
1 slice white bread, soaked in
    water and squeezed dry
¾ cup mashed potatoes
Pepper to taste

Blend tarama caviar and half of lemon juice in blender. Add onion, olive oil, corn oil and remaining lemon juice and blend. Add bread and blend. Add potatoes and blend. This may be refrigerated for up to 1 week or frozen. If frozen, defrost and blend in mixer before serving. • Serve with triangles of pita bread or cucumber spears.

Laine Forman
Laine Forman Caterers

BRIE AND BREAD

3 loaves of frozen unbaked
    French bread
Vegetable shortening
1 9-inch wheel of Brie

1 egg yolk plus 1 tablespoon
    of water (egg wash)
Slivered almonds

Leaving bread in package, defrost overnight in refrigerator. About 3 hours before serving, rub bread with vegetable shortening. Slice each loaf lengthwise into 3 strips and braid. • Grease large ovenproof pan or dish (a paella pan is perfect) and place Brie in center. Surround with braided bread. Paint all with the egg wash. Sprinkle slivered almonds on top of Brie. • Heat oven to 200°. Place a large pan of hot water on the lowest rack. Turn off oven. Place Brie and bread on rack above water, close door and let rise 1–2 hours or until double in size. Remove water and Brie and bread from oven. Heat to 350° and then bake Brie and bread about 30 minutes or until done. • Serve warm.

Barbara Kilcarr

The Willard Hotel

BRIE TART

"Two variations on a theme."

First Variation (Serves 8 to 10)
1 8-inch uncooked pie pastry
1 pound young Brie cheese
6 egg yolks, beaten
½ teaspoon saffron
⅔ teaspoon light brown sugar

⅜ teaspoon powdered ginger
Salt to taste (depends on age
   of Brie and whether you
   use rind, which is salty)

Second Variation (Serves 10 to 12)
1 8-inch uncooked pie pastry
½ pound young Brie cheese
½ cup heavy cream
3 eggs, lightly beaten
⅛–¼ teaspoon powdered
   ginger

⅛ teaspoon saffron
½ teaspoon brown sugar
Salt to taste (depends on age
   of Brie and whether you
   use rind, which is salty)

Bake pie pastry at 425° for 10 minutes. • Remove rind from Brie. (Optional: Cut rind into pieces about 1-inch square and sprinkle evenly on pie crust. This will give a stronger cheese flavor.) • Mix Brie with remaining ingredients except salt in a blender or with an egg beater. Add salt to taste. Mixture should be smooth. • Pour mixture into pastry shell and bake at 350° for 30–40 minutes or until set and brown on top.

Mrs. Garrison Norton

BRAZILIAN CHEESE PUFFS
(PAOZINHO DE QUEIJO)

"The State of Minas Gerais in Brazil produces wonderful cooks who created these delicious breads which are a classic in Brazilian cuisine."

1 cup light olive oil
2 cups milk
1 cup water
1 tablespoon salt

4 cups unsweetened tapioca
    flour (povilho azedo)
4 eggs, beaten
2 cups freshly grated Romano
    cheese

Bring to a boil the oil, milk, water and salt. Pour this mixture over tapioca flour, stirring constantly with a wooden spoon. Crush all lumps and mix well. Add eggs and blend well into dough. Add cheese and mix well. Roll into 1⅝-inch balls and place on a buttered cookie sheet. Bake at 350° for 35 minutes, until puffs are nicely browned.

Ms. Dorothea Elman Winston for
Mrs. Paulo Tarso Flecha de Lima
Wife of the Ambassador of Brazil

CHEESE CRISPIES

1 cup butter at room
    temperature
2 cups grated sharp cheddar
    cheese
1 teaspoon salt

¼ teaspoon cayenne pepper
2 cups flour
2 cups Rice Krispies cereal
Paprika (optional)

Preheat oven to 350°. • Mix butter and cheese. Add salt and red pepper. Gradually blend in flour until smooth. Add Rice Krispies and blend. • Form into balls the size of walnuts and place on ungreased baking sheet. • Dip a fork in water and flatten each with fork tines. • Bake for approximately 15 minutes, checking often. Do not over-brown. Sprinkle with paprika or additional cayenne pepper. • Serve warm or store in tightly covered tin. These can be frozen and reheated.

Mrs. Philip W. Pillsbury, Jr.

CHEESE STRAWS   Makes about 90 4-inch straws

"The warmer the weather, the easier they are to make."

1 pound extra sharp cheddar
   cheese (New York)
¼ pound margarine
2 cups sifted flour

½ teaspoon salt
¼ teaspoon paprika
¼ teaspoon cayenne pepper

Grate cheese and combine with margarine. Cover and allow to sit until mixture reaches room temperature. • Sift together flour, salt, paprika and cayenne and add to cheese mixture. Work with your hands until well mixed. • Preheat oven to 350°. Place mixture in a cookie press fitted with a star plate. Press out in rows onto ungreased cookie sheets, cut into 4-inch lengths, and bake for 10–15 minutes, until they look dried. These may be served warm. They may also be frozen and warmed when needed.

Mrs. Howell T. Heflin
Wife of the Senator from Alabama

*Kennedy Center,
home of The
Washington Opera*

CHILIES AND CHEESE

2 cans mild green chilies,
   chopped
3 cups grated cheddar cheese
3 eggs, beaten

4 tablespoons milk
Corn or tortilla chips or
   crackers

Preheat the oven to 350°. • Grease a 9 x 12 inch glass baking dish. Spread chilies on bottom of dish. Sprinkle cheese evenly over chilies. Mix egg with milk and pour over cheese. • Bake for 45 minutes. Cool slightly and cut into chunks. Serve on chips or crackers.

Ainslie Turner

DOME CHEESE SPREAD

2 pounds Cooper cheese or
   sharp cheddar cheese
   that has been aged
2 pounds Neufchâtel cheese

½ teaspoon minced garlic
½ teaspoon salt
Yellow food coloring
Dash of Tabasco sauce

Chop cheese and grind it in a food grinder. Stir in Neufchâtel and add other ingredients. Add food coloring and mix.

Chef Robert Traylor
The Dome Restaurant
Woods Hole, Cape Cod, MA

MY BOURSIN CHEESE

1 8-ounce package cream
   cheese
2 tablespoons butter
2 cloves garlic, crushed
½ teaspoon fresh lemon juice,
   or to taste

1 teaspoon oregano
½ teaspoon salt
½ teaspoon cayenne pepper
2 tablespoons fresh parsley
Crushed black pepper
   (optional)

Combine all above ingredients in a food processor with steel blade until thoroughly blended. Taste for flavor and seasonings. • Shape into a ball. May be rolled in crushed pepper. Place on serving dish and refrigerate overnight before serving.

Selma Jarow

PASTRY CHEESE BALLS

½ cup sharp cheese spread
   or grated American cheese
3 tablespoons butter
¾ cup flour

½ teaspoon salt
¼ teaspoon paprika
¼ teaspoon curry powder

Cream together cheese and butter. • Sift together flour, salt, paprika and curry powder and blend with cheese mixture. Pinch off pieces and roll into ¾-inch balls. • They should be chilled for 2 hours, but may be baked at once. Bake for 10 minutes in 400° oven. Serve hot.

Mrs. George W. Bush

SAGE DERBY CHEESE

1 8-ounce package of cream
   cheese
2 tablespoons sage

2 tablespoons chopped
   scallions
¼ teaspoon salt
2 tablespoons poppy seeds

Allow cream cheese to soften. Beat with sage, scallions and salt. Place in a round mold and cover tightly. Refrigerate. • Unmold and smooth with spatula. Lightly press with poppy seeds. Refrigerate. Serve with crackers.

Mrs. Philip W. Pillsbury, Jr.

BAKED OYSTERS ON THE HALF SHELL   Serves 12
WITH SWEET AND SOUR CABBAGE

24 oysters
3 tablespoons peanut oil
1 yellow onion, julienned
¼ head savoy cabbage,
   chopped
½ head napa cabbage,
   chopped

½ bunch bok choy, chopped
¼ teaspoon crushed
   red pepper
¼ teaspoon minced garlic
1 tablespoon champagne
   vinegar
¼ teaspoon sugar

Shuck oysters and remove from shells. Save shells. • In a skillet, heat oil to smoking point. Add onions and caramelize (by cooking, partially covered, very slowly for up to an hour). Add cabbages and quickly stir-fry. Add crushed red pepper and garlic to stir-fry. • Transfer mixture into a large bowl. Add vinegar, sugar and adjust seasoning. • When mixture has cooled, place a small amount in the bottom half of each oyster shell. Top with an oyster and additional cabbage mixture.

Chef Michael Patton
Assistant Chef Tom Blundell
1789 Restaurant

CRAB SPREAD

1 cup mayonnaise
2 8-ounce packages of cream
  cheese
2 6.5-ounce cans crabmeat,
  flaked

4 hard-boiled eggs, finely
  chopped
1 green pepper, finely
  chopped
1 pimento, chopped
½ teaspoon Tabasco sauce

Blend mayonnaise and cream cheese. Add remaining ingredients. Mix well.
Refrigerate for several hours before serving to blend flavors. Serve with
melba toast or crackers.

Belinda McKenzie

1789 MINIATURE CRAB CAKES · Serves 12

2 pounds crabmeat
1 tablespoon minced garlic
2 tablespoons chopped onion
1 teaspoon chili powder
½ teaspoon cayenne pepper
1 tablespoon Old Bay
  seasoning
1½ tablespoons chopped
  parsley

½ teaspoon salt
½ teaspoon white pepper
3 tablespoons oil
¼ cup fresh breadcrumbs
¼ cup Dijon mustard
⅛ cup mayonnaise
2 eggs

Preheat oven to 400°. • Pick crabmeat free of all shells and place in a mixing bowl. Set aside 1 cup to fold in later. • Combine onion with garlic, chili powder, cayenne, Old Bay seasoning, parsley, salt and pepper. Sauté in a little of the oil. Add to crabmeat. Fold in breadcrumbs, mustard, mayonnaise, and eggs. Mix well, but don't break up all lump meat. Fold in the remaining crabmeat. • Heat remaining oil in a skillet over medium-high heat. Carefully form crab cakes and place in pan to brown. Remove from pan and drain on paper towels. Transfer to a cookie sheet and heat in oven for approximately 5 minutes or until golden brown. Arrange on a warm platter and serve with mustard aïoli.

Whole-grain mustard aïoli:

3 egg yolks
1 cup extra virgin olive oil
⅛ cup fresh lemon juice

1 tablespoon crushed garlic
Salt and pepper to taste
1 tablespoon whole-grain
  Dijon mustard

In a food processor, whip egg yolks. Very slowly add half of the olive oil and half of the lemon juice. (Sauce will separate if added too quickly.) Add garlic to mixture and add rest of olive oil and lemon juice, until proper consistency is achieved. Season with salt and pepper.

Chef Michael Patton
Assistant Chef Tom Blundell
1789 Restaurant

GRAVLAX
(MARINATED SALMON)

1 3-pound piece of fresh
    salmon fillet, center cut,
    cleaned and scaled
1 bunch fresh dill
3 tablespoons coarse salt
3 teaspoons sugar

1 teaspoon white peppercorns,
    crushed
Dark bread
Slices of lemon
Capers
Chopped onions

Cut the salmon in half. Coarsely chop dill. Mix salt, sugar and pepper. Place
one piece of salmon, skin side down, in a large dish and coat with dill.
Sprinkle with all of the salt mixture. Place second piece of salmon, skin side
up, directly over first piece. Cover tightly with aluminum foil. Place something heavy on fish for weight and refrigerate for 3 days, turning salmon and
basting with accumulated juices each day. • When ready to serve, remove
salmon from marinade and wipe dry. Place salmon, skin side down, on a
wooden cutting board and carve into paper-thin diagonal slices. Serve with
dark bread, lemon slices, capers and finely chopped onion.

Mrs. Albert deP. d'Amecourt

POACHED FISH IN ASPIC
(RÍBA SALIVNÁYA)

Serves 8 to 12

*"Popular and colorful for special occasions. For Russians, sturgeon is the fish
of choice, but you may substitute the suggested fish as well."*

½ teaspoon salt
1 bay leaf
5 black peppercorns
5 allspice berries
1 carrot, peeled and cut
    into 1-inch chunks
1 stalk celery, chopped
1 medium onion, chopped
3 sprigs parsley

2 pounds sturgeon, red
    snapper or salmon fillets,
    skinned, boned and cut
    into 3 or 4 pieces
2 envelopes unflavored gelatin
Capers
2 lemons, peeled and thinly
    sliced
Parsley or dill

Pour 6 cups water into a 3-quart pot. Add salt, bay leaf, peppercorns, allspice, carrot, celery, onion and parsley and bring to a boil. Lower heat and
simmer, uncovered, for 30 minutes. Add fish and simmer for another 10 minutes, until fish is cooked. Do not overcook. Carefully remove fish with a spatula and cut into 12 or more serving pieces. Place in a single layer in a 2-inch
deep serving dish leaving space between pieces (see note). Remove carrot
pieces and set aside. Reserve fish broth and cool. • Soften gelatin in ¼ cup

cold water. Strain broth through a fine sieve, pressing vegetables to extract all liquid. Discard solids and return 4 cups broth to cleaned saucepan. Add gelatin and stir until dissolved. Set aside. • Cut carrot chunks into thin slices. Decorate fish with carrots, capers, lemon slices and parsley or dill. Carefully spoon aspic over fish so that decorations are not disturbed. Refrigerate for at least 3 hours or overnight. Serve with tartar sauce.

Tartar sauce:

2 egg yolks
1 teaspoon prepared mustard
1 cup olive oil
Salt and pepper
Sugar
Juice of 1 lemon

½ cup heavy cream
⅓–⅔ cup chopped cornichons
   (small French gherkins in
   vinegar)
1 bunch parsley, chopped

Mix egg yolks with mustard and stir until smooth. Add oil by drops and stir in the same direction until thick and creamy. Season with salt, pepper, sugar and lemon juice. Stir in cream and add cornichons and parsley.

NOTE: This dish may be assembled in a shaped mold. When ready to serve, unmold and garnish with a selection of the following: tomato, cucumber or dill pickle slices; caviar or pieces of crab; black olives or pimento.

Mrs. Vladimir Petrovich Lukin
Wife of the Ambassador of the Russian Federation

FRESH POTATO CHIPS

4 cups vegetable oil or lard
2 Idaho baking potatoes
Salt, black pepper and cayenne pepper

Heat 1–2 inches of oil in a wok or deep skillet. Scrub the potatoes well but do not peel them. Cut into thin slices (⅛ inch thick) and pat dry with paper towels. • When the oil is hot but not smoking (when a test slice of potato bubbles and floats on the top), add the potatoes a few slices at a time (to keep the oil hot) until they go limp. Remove with a slotted spoon and drain on paper towels. Let slices rest for 10 minutes or more. • Reheat the oil and refry the slices until they are crisp and browned, 2–4 minutes. Drain again on paper towels and season to taste. Eat immediately!

Mrs. Arthur Wexler

CRUNCHY COCONUT SHRIMP
WITH PINEAPPLE-JALAPEÑO SALSA

Serves 12

Shrimp:

24 large shrimp
½ cup flour
1 egg
¼ cup pineapple juice
¼ cup milk
1½ teaspoons salt

½ teaspoon baking powder
¼ teaspoon cayenne pepper
3½ cups vegetable oil
10 ounces unsweetened
   shredded coconut

Salsa:

1½ cups fresh pineapple
   chunks
3 tablespoons orange
   marmalade
1 tablespoon minced
   jalapeño pepper

1 tablespoon minced
   roasted red pepper
2 teaspoons fresh lime juice
1 tablespoon chopped fresh
   cilantro
Salt to taste

Shell shrimp, leaving tail intact. Slit along back and remove vein. • In a blender, combine flour, egg, pineapple juice, milk, salt, baking powder and cayenne pepper and blend at medium speed. Transfer batter to a mixing bowl. • Heat oil to 350° in a deep-fat fryer or medium-sized skillet. Dip shrimp in batter and shake off excess batter. Press shrimp into coconut and fry in small batches, turning once, until golden brown all over. Drain on paper towels. • To make salsa, pulse pineapple in a food processor until finely chopped. Place in a mixing bowl and stir in marmalade, jalapeños, roasted red peppers, lime juice, cilantro and salt. (The salsa may be made 1 day in advance. Bring to room temperature before serving.) To serve, arrange shrimp on a platter with salsa in a bowl on the side.

Chef Michael Patton
Assistant Chef Tom Blundell
1789 Restaurant

SMOKED SALMON LOAF

1 8-ounce package cream
   cheese, chilled
¼ pound thinly sliced smoked
   salmon

2 teaspoons capers (or to taste)
⅓ cup snipped fresh dill

Using a very sharp knife, cut cream cheese in four horizontal layers. Cover one slice of cream cheese with salmon and capers and repeat, ending with cream cheese. Gently pat the dill around the top and sides of loaf and wrap with plastic wrap. This will keep in the refrigerator for up to 2 days. Serve with rice crackers.

Mrs. Richard D. Van Winkle, Jr.

SHRIMP DIP

1 4.25-ounce can small shrimp,
   peeled and rinsed in cold
   water
1 8-ounce package cream
   cheese

½ cup finely chopped celery
½ cup finely chopped onion
½ cup mayonnaise
1–2 tablespoons lemon juice
Dash of cayenne pepper

Simply mix ingredients in the order listed in an attractive bowl. Cover and refrigerate until ready to serve. Serve with a variety of crackers or celery and other vegetable sticks.

Senator and Mrs. Paul Simon
(Illinois)

TEQUEÑOS   Makes about 60

4 cups flour
1½ teaspoons salt
1 heaping tablespoon butter
2 egg yolks

1 teaspoon sugar
1 cup water, approximately
1 pound semi-soft white cheese
Vegetable oil

Combine flour, salt, butter, egg yolks, sugar and enough water to make a soft dough. Set aside for a few minutes. • Cut cheese into strips 2½ inches long and ½ inch wide. • Divide dough into four parts. Roll each part as thin as possible, cut into ½ inch strips and wind around cheese so that cheese is completely covered. • Deep-fry in hot oil until golden brown and serve immediately.

Embassy of Venezuela

RILLETTES DE LAPIN
(PÂTÉ OF RABBIT)

Serves 6 to 8

"Beatrix Potter's Mr. McGregor was part of my real fantasy world, for when I was a child we waged war against the wild rabbits. In vain was the garden fortifed with ckicken wire, in vain did Old Metcalfe, the mole-catcher, set snares to catch them. The rabbits gambolled regardless on the front lawn. On fine mornings my mother would rise early to take a pot shot from the bedroom window with a rifle, but the rabbits had a sixth sense and off they would scamper just as she was taking aim. Now 40 years later and a thousand miles south in Burgundy, we again have an abundance of rabbits. These ones are tame, raised by our caretaker Madame Milbert, so rabbit can be on the menu any day at an hour's notice."

2 rabbits (about 5 pounds
    together), cut into pieces
3 onions, sliced
3 carrots, sliced
2 cloves of garlic, peeled
4–5 sprigs fresh thyme or
    2 teaspoons dried
Bouquet garni

2 cloves
1 teaspoon black peppercorns
2 cups white wine
Salt and pepper to taste
2½ cups veal stock
2 shallots, finely chopped
¼ cup dry vermouth

Place the rabbit pieces in a heavy casserole, layering with onions, carrots, garlic, thyme, bouquet garni, cloves and peppercorns. Pour the wine over all and marinate, covered, in the refrigerator for 12–24 hours. • Preheat oven to 350°. • Mix a little salt and pepper with stock and pour over rabbit. Shake the casserole to mix contents with wine, cover and set in a large pan filled with water. Bring water to a boil on top of stove. Place pan with water and casserole into oven and cook for 1¾–2 hours, until meat falls easily from the bones. • Allow to cool. • Lift out meat and remove bones. Shred the meat in a deep glass bowl with two forks. Stir in shallots and vermouth. • Skim fat from casserole liquid and boil until it has been reduced to 5 cups. Strain over the meat. Cover and chill until set. • Can be refrigerated for up to 3 days. Flavor mellows on standing.

Anne Willan, President
École de Cuisine, La Varenne

BLACK BEAN PÂTÉ   Serves 15 to 18

4 cups dried black beans
1 large onion, chopped
6 cloves garlic, peeled and
    chopped
1 3-inch piece of ginger,
    peeled and chopped

3 tablespoons butter or oil
1 cup sour cream
6 whole eggs
2 teaspoons salt
1 tablespoon black pepper
1 buttered loaf pan or tureen

Sort black beans and remove stones. Cook in rapidly boiling water for approximately 45 minutes, or until beans are soft. Drain in a colander until cool and as dry as possible. • Meanwhile, sauté onion, garlic and ginger in butter or oil until soft and transparent. Set aside to cool. • Transfer black beans to a food processor and pulse briefly, until beans are coarsely chopped. Add beans to onion mixture. Add sour cream, eggs, salt and pepper. Mix well. • Place mixture in loaf pan or tureen. Cover with buttered foil. Place the tureen in a larger baking pan filled with hot water that comes halfway up the sides of tureen. Bake at 350° for approximately 1 hour 20 minutes, or until firm. • Cool completely before slicing ¼ or ½ inch thick.

Sauce:

1 egg yolk
½ cup red wine vinegar
2 tablespoons Dijon mustard
4 scallions with tops

3 cloves garlic
1 teaspoon sugar
1½ cups olive oil
Salt and pepper to taste

In the bowl of a food processor, place egg yolk, vinegar, mustard, scallions, garlic and sugar. Process until well blended, adding olive oil in a slow steady stream through the feeder tube. Season with salt and pepper.

Garnish:

1 red bell pepper, cut into strips
16 ounces feta cheese, cut into cubes

To serve, fan two slices of black bean pâté on a plate, top with scallion sauce and garnish with red pepper slices and approximately 1 ounce of cubed feta cheese.

Alison Swope, Chef
David Hegedorn, Sous Chef
New Heights Restaurant

CAVIAR MOUSSE

1 package unflavored gelatin
2 tablespoons lemon juice
1½ tablespoons dry vermouth
2 teaspoons anchovy paste
5 hard-boiled eggs
¾ cup mayonnaise

1 teaspoon Worcestershire
  sauce
1 tablespoon grated onion
1 3½-ounce jar Danish
  lumpfish caviar
1 cup finely chopped parsley

Soften gelatin in lemon juice and vermouth. Place the bowl containing this mixture in a pan of simmering water to dissolve. When thoroughly dissolved, add anchovy paste and stir. Allow to cool. • Grate eggs and blend with mayonnaise, Worcestershire sauce and onion. Add gelatin mixture and blend thoroughly. Spread caviar on the top and fold in very gently. • Lightly oil a 2-cup fish mold and fill with mixture. Cover with plastic wrap and chill until firm. Unmold onto a platter 2–3 hours before serving and garnish with parsley. Serve with rounds of pumpernickel or rye bread.

Sarah Paula Garrison

SMOKED MACKEREL PÂTÉ

2 smoked mackerel
Juice of 1 lemon, strained
½ cup butter, heated until
  foaming

Salt and pepper to taste
1 cup heavy cream

Skin and bone mackerel and place in blender or food processor. Add lemon juice. While machine is running, add butter in a thin stream, omitting white residue. Add only as much butter as necessary to gently blend the mixture. • Transfer to a bowl and add salt and pepper. • Beat cream until stiff and fold delicately into mackerel mixture. Adjust seasoning, including additional lemon juice if a sharper flavor is preferred. Turn into a bowl, individual pots or mold. • Chill for several hours, covered, before serving.

Lady Denman
Wife of the Former Ambassador
to the European Economic Community

PHEASANT PÂTÉ

2 tablespoons olive oil
1–2 red onions, diced
1 cup shallots, diced
3–4 garlic cloves, minced
6 pheasants, skinned, boned, with sinew removed
3–4 pounds veal, membrane removed, cut into strips
2 tablespoons freshly cracked pepper

1 teaspoon ground pepper
1 tablespoon salt
1 tablespoon dried thyme
3 bay leaves
20 juniper berries
1 bottle port wine (750 ml)
Breadcrumbs (optional)
2–3 pounds thickly sliced bacon or fatback, cut into strips

In a skillet, heat oil and sauté onions and shallots over medium heat until almost transparent. Add garlic and sauté for 1 minute. • Place pheasant meat and veal in a large glass dish. Cover with sautéed mixture, cracked and ground peppers, salt, thyme, bay leaves, juniper berries and port wine. Marinate in refrigerator for 24 hours. • Preheat oven to 350°. Remove dish from refrigerator and, after removing bay leaves, place meats and marinade in a meat grinder and grind with large disc. Mix well. Change to medium disc and grind further. Adjust texture with bread crumbs, if necessary. • Spray terrine molds or loaf pans with non-stick coating and line with strips of bacon fat or fatback, allowing slices to overhang edges of mold. Press ground mixture into mold, packing tightly. Fold overhanging fat strips over top. • Place mold in a large shallow pan on oven rack. Add boiling water to shallow pan to reach halfway up side of mold. Bake for 1½ hours, or until liquid in mold runs clear. Do not overbake. Remove mold from oven and cool slightly. • Refrigerate for several hours. Before serving, unmold and slice thinly.

Senator and Mrs. Larry Pressler
(South Dakota)

COUNTRY PÂTÉ   Serves 12

1 pound ground lean pork
1 pound ground veal
½ cup finely chopped onions
½ cup finely snipped parsley
1½ teaspoons salt
½ teaspoon black pepper

1 tablespoon Worcestershire
  sauce
1 teaspoon chopped basil
  leaves
2 tablespoons dry sherry
4 eggs, lightly beaten
Small sour pickles

Preheat oven to 375°. • Blend all ingredients, except pickles, in a large mixing bowl. Turn mixture into an ungreased 9 x 5 x 3 inch loaf pan. Bake for approximately 1 hour, until loaf is set. • Cool in baking pan. Turn out of pan, wrap tightly in aluminum foil and refrigerate. • Cut into thin slices and serve with pickles.

Christine van Mulders

MEXICALI COCKTAIL QUICHE

¼ cup butter or margarine
5 eggs
¼ cup flour
½ teaspoon baking powder
Dash of salt

1 4-ounce can chopped green
  chili peppers or jalapeño
  peppers, drained
1 cup cottage cheese
½ pound Monterey Jack
  cheese, shredded

Melt butter. • Beat eggs lightly and add all other ingredients. Add melted butter and mix well. Pour into a greased 9-inch square pan. • Bake at 350° for 35–45 minutes. Cut into small squares. Serve warm or at room temperature.

Kay Mereness

BLACK OLIVE QUICHES   Makes 48 quiches

1 sheet Pepperidge Farm
  frozen puff pastry
1 8-ounce package cream
  cheese
2 eggs

2 cups chopped pitted ripe
  black olives
½ cup grated Swiss cheese
½ cup grated Parmesan
  cheese

Preheat oven to 350°. • Let pastry dough come to room temperature. Roll out one sheet and, using a small cookie cutter, cut about 4 dozen rounds of pastry. Line small-sized muffin tins with pastry rounds. • Combine cream cheese, eggs, olives, Swiss and Parmesan cheeses and mix well. • Fill pastry rounds with cheese and olive mixture and bake for about 30 minutes. The quiches will puff up beautifully. • Once baked, they may be frozen. Reheat (either thawed or frozen) in a 400° oven for 10–15 minutes.

Loni Landfield

COUNTRY HAM AND   Serves 8
CHEDDAR CHEESE SOUFFLÉS

4 tablespoons butter at room
  temperature
1½ cups milk
½ cup flour
¾ cup grated aged white
  cheddar cheese

8 tablespoons finely chopped
  country ham
4 egg yolks
Salt and white pepper to taste
3 egg whites

Using 1 tablespoon butter, grease bottom and sides of eight 4-ounce soufflé dishes. • Place milk in a saucepan, heat to a simmer and cool to lukewarm. Place flour in a mixing bowl and add lukewarm milk, stirring with a whisk. Return mixture to saucepan and cook, stirring, over medium heat until thick. Cool slightly and add remaining butter, cheese, ham and egg yolks. Mix thoroughly and season with salt and pepper. • Preheat oven to 350°. • Beat egg whites until stiff but not dry and fold into soufflé base. Fill dishes to the top and bake in a water bath until puffed and light brown. Serve immediately.

Susan McCreight Lindeborg, Chef
Morrison Clark Inn

MUSHROOM STRUDEL   Makes about 25 slices

10 ounces fresh mushrooms,   4 ounces cream cheese
  sliced   5 sheets phyllo pastry
1 clove garlic, minced   (sold frozen)
2 teaspoons dried thyme   4–6 tablespoons additional
1 tablespoon butter   butter, melted
Salt and pepper to taste

In a frying pan, sauté mushrooms, garlic and thyme in butter until mushrooms are soft. (Season with salt and pepper.) • Cut cream cheese into lumps

and add to mushrooms, stirring over low heat until mixture binds together. Remove from heat and set aside. • To make strudel, defrost phyllo dough and spread one sheet on cookie sheet or jelly roll pan and brush thoroughly with melted butter. Cover with a second sheet of phyllo dough and again brush with butter thoroughly. Repeat with remaining sheets of phyllo dough. • To assemble, place filling mixture in a mounded column the length of phyllo dough about one inch from the edge. Roll like a jelly roll and center on pan, seam side down. Fold both ends under to seal. • Brush top with melted butter and bake at 425° for approximately 15 minutes, until brown. • Cool slightly and cut into ½–¾ inch slices. Serve warm.

NOTE: Partially freezing the strudel after baking makes it easier to slice. It may be best if reheated before serving. Do not microwave.

Jean Ernst

ASPARAGUS STRUDEL WITH BEURRE BLANC   Serves 8

¾ pound asparagus, trimmed and cut into 1-inch lengths

2 medium leeks, white parts only, thinly sliced

1 tablespoon chopped shallots

1 cup plus 4 tablespoons unsalted butter, melted

½ pound Gruyère cheese, grated

2 ounces sliced almonds, toasted

3 eggs

2 tablespoons chopped fresh mint

2 tablespoons chopped fresh parsley

4 tablespoons chopped fresh dill

2 tablespoons snipped fresh chives

1 teaspoon salt

½ teaspoon pepper

½ teaspoon paprika

Dash of cayenne pepper

2 tablespoons fresh lemon juice

12 leaves of phyllo pastry, thawed

Beurre blanc:

6 tablespoons fresh lemon juice

¼ teaspoon thyme

1 pound butter

To serve:

Cooked asparagus spears, for garnish

Cherry tomato slices, for garnish

Blanch asparagus in boiling water for 3 minutes. Drain and pat dry. Place in a large bowl. • Sauté leek slices with shallots in 4 tablespoons butter until transparent. Add to asparagus. Add all other ingredients except the remaining 1 cup of melted butter and phyllo leaves. Preheat oven to 350°. • Brush a cookie sheet with melted butter. Lay 1 sheet of phyllo on work surface and brush with melted butter. Continue until you have 6 layers, buttering each thoroughly. • Place half of the asparagus mixture along one short end. Tuck in ends and roll jelly-roll fashion. Place on baking sheet. • Make a second strudel with remaining 6 sheets of phyllo. Place on baking sheet, leaving ample space between the rolls. Brush with remaining melted butter. Bake for 40–45 minutes, until golden. Cool slightly and cut into 2-inch slices. • To make beurre blanc warm lemon juice and thyme in a saucepan. Whisk in butter, one tablespoon at a time. To serve as a first course, pool a little beurre blanc on each plate. Arrange 2 slices of strudel, 3 asparagus spears and 3 slices of cherry tomato on top.

Mrs. W. Averell Harriman
U.S. Ambassador to France

PETROSSIAN BLINI   Makes 12

1¼ teaspoons dry yeast   1 cup flour
1 cup lukewarm milk   2 tablespoons melted butter
3 eggs, separated   2 tablespoons sugar
1 tablespoon corn oil   Crème fraîche or sour cream
½ teaspoon salt   Fresh salmon roe

Dissolve yeast in milk and set aside to proof. • Whisk together egg yolks and oil. Stir in yeast mixture and mix in salt and flour. Stir in butter. Cover with a cloth and place in a warm spot to rise until double in volume, about 45 minutes. • Beat egg whites with sugar until stiff but not dry. Fold whites into batter. Cook over medium heat in lightly greased 4-inch blini pans or make 4-inch pancakes on lightly greased griddle. Cook until golden on both sides. Serve warm with crème fraîche or sour cream and roe. Blini may be frozen and reheated in a microwave oven on high for 40 seconds.

Dinah Nargil
Marketing Director, Petrossian Caviar

PUKACAPAS   Makes 50 to 60

"The name 'Pukacapas' derives from the colored topping."

Dough:
4 cups flour   4 tablespoons shortening
1 tablespoon sugar   2 egg yolks
Dash of salt   ½ cup milk
1 teaspoon baking powder

Filling:
½ cup finely chopped onion   5 cups grated white cheese
1 tablespoon oil   (queso latino)
2 tablespoons ground red   1 small jar black olives
  peppers (ají panca)   3 hard-boiled eggs

Mix dry ingredients for dough. Add shortening and mix with wooden spoon. Add egg yolks and enough milk to make dough that is not very soft or dry. • Fry onions in oil until transparent, add red peppers and grated cheese. • Cut dough with biscuit cutter in 2-inch rounds. Place a teaspoon of onion, half a black olive and a small piece of egg on each round of dough. Top with another round. Seal well with a rope-like edge and brush dough edges with milk or egg. Mix a little shortening with some additional ground red peppers and brush tops. • Bake at 350° for 30 minutes. Serve hot.

Mrs. Ninett Delius
Embassy of Bolivia

CARPACCIO WITH ARUGULA, MUSTARD CAPER SAUCE AND PARMESAN

1 tablespoon Dijon mustard
1 tablespoon small capers
1 teaspoon balsamic vinegar
1 tablespoon olive oil
Freshly ground black pepper
½ pound eye of the round
   (partially frozen to facilitate slicing)

1 2-ounce piece Parmesan
  cheese
4 ounces arugula, washed,
  spun dry and cut into
  julienne strips

Make sauce by placing mustard, capers and vinegar in a small bowl. Add oil while whisking with a fork to emulsify sauce. Season to taste with pepper. • Cut eye of round into slices as thin as possible with sharp slicing knife or ask butcher to slice with an electric meat slicer to thickness of $\frac{1}{16}$ of an inch. • Spread a thin layer of mustard sauce on center of each salad plate. Cover with overlapping slices of beef. Use a vegetable peeler to shave thin curls of Parmesan onto plates. Garnish with arugula. Serve cold.

Nora Pouillon
Nora's Restaurant

STUFFED ENDIVE

3 tablespoons sour cream
3 tablespoons mayonnaise
6 tablespoons finely chopped
  scallions

½ teaspoon dill
2–3 heads of endive
Paprika
Fresh dill for garnish

Blend sour cream, mayonnaise, scallions and dill. • Separate endive leaves, wash and chill. • Fill each endive leaf halfway with mixture and garnish with paprika and fresh dill. • Chill for at least three hours before serving.

Mrs. Warwick M. Carter

1789 PORTOBELLO MUSHROOMS WITH ROASTED RED PEPPER SAUCE
Serves 12

3 marinated, grilled Portobello mushrooms (see recipe below)
24 garlic croutons (see recipe below)

Roasted red pepper sauce (see recipe below)
Parmesan cheese, grated
Fresh chives, chopped

Grilled portobello mushroom marinade:

1 cup balsamic vinegar
½ cup champagne vinegar
2 bunches fresh thyme, chopped
1 bunch sage, chopped

1 bunch oregano
2 tablespoons minced garlic
3 tablespoons minced shallots
2½ cups extra virgin olive oil
3 Portobello mushrooms

Place vinegars, herbs, garlic and shallots in a mixing bowl. Whisk in olive oil and pour over clean mushrooms. Marinate for 24 hours. • Remove mushrooms from marinade and place in a large pot. Pour marinade over mushrooms and simmer over low heat for 2 hours. • Remove mushrooms from pot and place in mixing bowl. Pour hot marinade over cooked mushrooms and let sit for 6 hours. • When ready to serve, grill mushrooms over high heat.

Garlic croutons:

1 French bread baguette
¼ cup extra virgin olive oil

2 cloves garlic, peeled

Slice the baguette thinly and diagonally into 24 slices. Brush each slice with olive oil and place on cookie sheet. Bake at 350° until golden brown and crisp. Remove from oven and rub each warm crouton with garlic. Cool before using.

Roasted red pepper sauce:

5 red peppers
2 cloves of garlic or shallots

Makes ½ cup
⅛ cup fresh lime juice
⅛ cup extra virgin olive oil

Coat peppers with oil and roast at 400° until skins start to brown. Let peppers cool and remove skins and seeds. Cut peppers into strips and put in an electric blender with garlic, lime juice, and olive oil. Mix well and adjust seasoning. Pass the sauce through a fine sieve. This may be kept for two days. • To assemble, slice grilled mushrooms into 24 small strips. Place one mushroom slice on each baked crouton. Drizzle small amount of roasted red pepper sauce on each mushroom. Garnish with Parmesan cheese and chives.

Chef Michael Patton
Assistant Chef Tom Blundell
1789 Restaurant

Soups

CLANDESTINE SOUP   Serves 4

2 3-ounce packages cream   3 tablespoons sherry (optional)
  cheese   Chopped parsley for garnish
1 can of consommé madrilène

Place cream cheese, consommé and sherry into blender and mix until all lumps are removed. Pour into soup bowls and refrigerate to set. Sprinkle with parsley before serving.

Cynthia R. Helms
Wife of Richard Helms, former Director of the CIA

COLD MELON SOUP   Serves 6

"This is a delicious soup for hot summer days. It was served at a luncheon with Mrs. Bush at the White House. I like it because it's so easy to prepare!"

1 large ripe cantaloupe   2 tablespoons fresh lime juice
½ teaspoon cinnamon   Fresh mint sprigs for garnish
2¼ cups orange juice

Remove rind and seeds from melon and cut into cubes. Place cantaloupe, cinnamon and ¼ cup orange juice in blender or food processor and purée. Combine remaining orange juice and lime juice and stir into purée. Chill thoroughly and serve in chilled soup bowls garnished with sprigs of mint.

Marcia Coats
Wife of Senator Daniel R. Coats (Indiana)

GAZPACHO I   Serves 4

"A favorite recipe of mine that is both 'Heart Smart' and fun."

3 11.5-ounce cans tomato juice   1 tablespoon white wine
1 cucumber, finely chopped   vinegar
1 green pepper, finely chopped   ¼ teaspoon Tabasco sauce
1 clove garlic, mashed   ½ cup ice water
2 tablespoons olive oil

Blend all of the above ingredients and keep refrigerated. Taste improves if prepared 24 hours before serving. Season to taste. • Serve with topping of croutons or chopped hard-boiled egg.

Senator Howard M. Metzenbaum
(Ohio)

GAZPACHO II   Serves 4 to 6

"In the summer I keep a pitcher full in the refrigerator.
It does not last long!"

3 pounds ripe, red tomatoes,   1 clove of garlic, minced
   peeled   2 tablespoons olive oil
1 Spanish onion, peeled   2 tablespoons wine vinegar
1 small green pepper, seeded   Salt to taste
1 hard roll, soaked in water
   to soften

For garnish:
1 tomato, seeded and chopped   1 green pepper, seeded and
1 cucumber, peeled, seeded   chopped
   and chopped   Salad croutons

Cut up tomatoes, onion, green pepper and soaked bread. Mix them in a large bowl with garlic, oil and vinegar. Blend mixture 3 tablespoons at a time in blender or food processor. Strain into a serving bowl. • When all of tomato mixture has been puréed and strained, add salt and 10–12 ice cubes. Refrigerate until ready to serve. Before serving, scatter garnish ingredients over top of soup.

Maria Gilbert

INDIAN CHICKEN SOUP   Serves 8

"An easy cold soup."

2 cans cream of chicken soup,   ½ teaspoon thyme
   undiluted   1 teaspoon curry powder, or to
1 soup can of half and half   taste
2 apples, peeled and cored or   2 teaspoons lemon juice
   1 cup applesauce   Salt and pepper to taste
½ cup sour cream   Chicken bouillon (optional)
⅛ teaspoon marjoram   Parsley, for garnish

Blend the above ingredients, except parsley and bouillon, in a food processor. If desired, thin soup with a little bouillon. Chill soup. • When ready to serve, garnish with parsley.

Sarah T. Minikes

JELLIED TOMATO BOUILLON   Serves 2 to 3

1 envelope unflavored gelatin   ⅓ cup dry sherry
1 cup beef consommé   1 tablespoon lemon juice
1 cup tomato juice

Sprinkle gelatin on ½ cup consommé in a saucepan. Place over low heat and stir until dissolved. Remove from heat and stir in remaining consommé and other ingredients. • Chill until firm. • Looks nice garnished with thin slices of lemon or freshly snipped chives.

Belinda McKenzie

PEANUT AND CARROT BISQUE   Serves 6 to 8

2½ cups chicken broth   1 leek, white and green parts,
1 pound carrots, scraped and   chopped coarsely
    sliced into ½-inch rounds   ¼ cup smooth peanut butter
1 onion, coarsely chopped   ¼ teaspoon cayenne pepper
                                   Salt and pepper to taste

Combine broth, carrots, onion and leek in a large saucepan. Bring to a boil, reduce heat and simmer, partially covered, for 30 minutes, until vegetables are tender. Remove from heat and cool slightly. Pour ⅓ soup into electric blender and purée. Pour into a bowl and mix well with peanut butter. Add cayenne and blend well. Purée remainder of vegetables and broth and return to clean saucepan. Add soup combined with peanut butter and mix well. If desired, mix in more chicken broth or water to attain thickness desired. Heat covered for about 5 minutes. Serve hot or cold.

Dorothy Singer

ROSEMONT FARM CHOWDER (PEA AND CORN CHOWDER)

Serves 6

"Enjoy hot or cold"

1 10-ounce bag frozen small
  peas
1 10-ounce bag frozen baby
  corn, preferably white

1½ cups chicken broth
1 tablespoon butter
Dash of Tabasco sauce
Pinch of onion salt

Defrost peas and corn. • Place peas and corn in a large saucepan with chicken broth and heat over medium heat almost to a boil. Remove from heat and cool. Place soup in a blender in small quantities and purée. Strain. Return puréed soup to saucepan, add butter and heat for approximately 5 minutes. Do not overcook. Add Tabasco sauce and onion salt. This soup may be served hot or cold.

Mrs. H. J. Heinz III

CHICKPEA SOUP WITH SWISS CHARD

Serves 8 to 12

*"This soup is even better the day after, when the flavors
have had a chance to meld."*

1 pound dried chickpeas
Salt
1 large onion, chopped
2 cloves garlic, minced
2 tablespoons olive oil

6 fresh sage leaves or 1
  teaspoon dried sage leaves,
  crumbled
1 bunch Swiss chard, washed,
  leaves cut into 2- to 3-inch
  pieces
Freshly ground pepper to taste

Soak chickpeas in lightly salted water according to package directions or bring to a boil, boil for 5 minutes and soak for 1 hour. • Sauté onion and garlic in olive oil in a large pot. Drain chickpeas and add to pot. Cover with lightly salted water. Bring to a boil, reduce heat and simmer until tender but firm, about 1 hour. Purée half of the soup in a blender with sage leaves and return to pot. Add Swiss chard. Season with salt and pepper and cook for 15 minutes more. • Serve with freshly ground pepper to taste.

NOTE: Try using different combinations of beans and greens, such as cannellini and spinach or lentils and kale. Place a slice of day-old country bread, toasted and rubbed with fresh garlic, at the bottom of each serving bowl for a satisfying one-dish meal.

*Phyllis Frucht, President
Washington Chapter, Les Dames d'Escoffier*

SENATE RESTAURANT BEAN SOUP   Serves 8

"Whatever uncertainties may exist in the Senate of the United States, one thing is sure: Bean Soup is on the menu of the Senate Restaurant every day. The origin of this culinary decree has been lost in antiquity, but there are several oft-repeated legends. One story has it that Senator Fred Thomas Dubois of Idaho, who served in the Senate from 1901 to 1907, when chairman of the committee that supervised the Senate Restaurant, gaveled through a resolution requiring that bean soup be on the menu every day. Another account attributes the bean soup mandate to Senator Knute Nelson of Minnesota, who expressed his fondness for it in 1903. In any case, Senators and their guests are always assured of a hearty, nourishing dish; they know they can rely upon its delightful flavor and epicurean qualities."

2 pounds navy beans	1 onion, chopped
4 quarts water	2 tablespoons butter
1½ pounds smoked ham hocks	Salt and pepper

Wash beans, then rinse with hot water. Bring 4 quarts water to a boil and add beans and ham hocks. Simmer, covered, for approximately 3 hours, until beans are tender. Sauté onion in butter and, when light brown, add to soup. Season with pepper to taste. Just before serving, season with salt to taste.

Senator Carl Levin
(Michigan)

SPANISH LENTIL SOUP   Serves 4 to 6

"A great winter meal."

2 cups lentils	2 bay leaves
1 small onion, chopped	1 tablespoon olive oil
2 cloves of garlic, peeled	1 teaspoon Spanish paprika
2 carrots, peeled and sliced	1 teaspoon salt
1 chorizo, sliced or	Boiling water
1 stick pepperoni, sliced	

Wash lentils well and remove stones and other foreign matter. Place lentils in a non-reactive saucepan with onion, garlic, carrots, chorizo or pepperoni slices, bay leaves, olive oil, paprika and salt. Cover with cold water, bring to a boil and simmer gently for 2 hours. Add water as needed to keep soup from becoming too thick. Serve hot with French bread.

Maria Gilbert

AUSTIN GRILL CORN SOUP   Serves 10

3 pounds corn kernels
1½ cups diced yellow onion
1½ cups finely diced Anaheim peppers (mild chili peppers)
1 tablespoon minced garlic
¼ pound butter
½ teaspoon cayenne pepper
½ teaspoon chopped oregano

½ teaspoon dried thyme
Salt to taste
2 cups chicken stock or water
4 cups cream
1 cup finely diced roasted poblano peppers (mild to hot chili peppers)

Purée half of the corn kernels in a blender and set aside. • Briefly sauté onions, Anaheim peppers and garlic in butter over medium heat. Add whole corn kernels, cayenne, oregano, thyme and salt. Add puréed corn, stock and cream. Simmer gently until corn is cooked through. Remove from heat, stir in poblanos and adjust seasonings.

Ann Cashion, Executive Chef
Austin Grill and Jaleo

Les Dames d'Escoffier

NEW ENGLAND CORN CHOWDER   Serves 6 to 8

8 ounces salt pork, diced
2 onions, chopped
2 tablespoons flour
6–8 medium potatoes, cubed
4 cups water
1 17-ounce can cream-style corn

1 13-ounce can evaporated milk
2 tablespoons butter
Salt and pepper to taste
Parsley, chopped
Paprika

In a large kettle, fry salt pork until browned and crisp. Add onions and fry until transparent. Remove salt pork, add flour and blend well. Add potatoes and water to cover and bring to a boil. Reduce heat and simmer, covered, for 15–20 minutes, until potatoes are cooked. Add corn, evaporated milk and butter. Season with salt and pepper and stir. Do not boil but heat well. Add pork if you wish to eat it. • Serve with parsley and paprika sprinkled on top.

Majority Leader George J. Mitchell
Senator from Maine

CABBAGE BORSCHT   Serves 6

6 cups beef broth
1 8-ounce can tomato sauce
3 cups chopped cabbage
  (about ⅓ medium cabbage)
1 cup diced beets (about 2
  small beets)
1 stalk celery, chopped
1 carrot, diced
1 small onion, chopped
2 cloves garlic, minced

1 bay leaf
4 tablespoons wine vinegar
1½ teaspoons Worcestershire
  sauce
3 tablespoons brown sugar
Juice of ½ lemon
Salt
Pepper
Sour cream (optional)

Simmer together all but the last 4 ingredients. When the vegetables are tender, add the lemon juice. Adjust the seasoning with salt and pepper. Serve with a dollop of sour cream on each portion, if desired.

NOTE: On a cold winter day, my mother occasionally made this borscht with a piece of beef and served it as the main course, along with dried French bread for dunking. If you want to make this heartier, main-course version, use beef neck bones or short ribs (about 1½ pounds meat with bones). Simmer the meat in water or beef broth until almost tender, about 1–1½ hours, skimming off any froth that forms during the cooking. Use the liquid from cooking the beef for the 6 cups broth called for and proceed as above.

Narsai M. David, Author
"Monday Night at Narsai's"

CARROT SOUP WITH CORIANDER   Serves 6

¼ pound butter
1½ cups chopped onion
½ cup dry white wine or
  sherry
6 cups (2 pounds) finely diced
  or coarsely grated carrots
2 teaspoons ground coriander

2 cups rich chicken broth
2 cups milk or cream
Salt and freshly ground pepper
1 cup toasted croutons
Chopped parsley, chopped fresh
  cilantro, or both

Melt butter in saucepan, add onion and cook, stirring, until golden brown. Add wine and carrots. Sprinkle with coriander and stir. Cover closely with round of wax paper and cook over very low heat for about 1 hour. Make sure carrots do not stick to bottom or burn. Remove wax paper and add chicken broth. Simmer for 20 minutes. Add milk, salt and pepper. Bring just to a boil and serve. Garnish with parsley.

Paula Jeffries

PEANUT SOUP   Serves 6

3 tablespoons butter
2 tablespoons finely chopped
  onion
2 tablespoons finely chopped
  celery
3 tablespoons flour

4 cups chicken broth (do not
  use chicken broth cubes
1 cup smooth peanut butter
½ cup heavy cream
Chopped peanuts
Parsley or chopped green of
  scallions

Melt butter in a saucepan over low heat. Add onions and celery and sauté until tender. Do not allow to brown. Add flour and stir. Stirring constantly, slowly add chicken broth. Continue stirring until smooth. Stirring constantly, add peanut butter. When thoroughly blended, cook for 5 minutes. Slowly add cream, stirring. Heat thoroughly for another 5 minutes. Serve in cups and garnish with 1 teaspoon peanuts and 1 teaspoon parsley or scallions.

Mrs. Charles W. Barker

TOMATO SOUP   Serves 8

4 tablespoons unsalted butter
4 medium stalks of celery,
  diced
1 onion, diced
2 sprigs parsley
2 sprigs thyme
10 large basil leaves and stems
1 sprig oregano

1 teaspoon pepper
½ teaspoon Tabasco
1 small lemon zest curl
12–14 medium tomatoes, very
  ripe, finely chopped
1 cup heavy cream, whipped
  and salted
2 teaspoons salt
8–10 basil leaves cut in strips

Melt butter in a heavy enamel pot. Add celery, onion, herbs, seasonings and the lemon zest. Simmer for 15–20 minutes until vegetables are very soft. Add tomatoes and cook until they are mushy. Put through a food mill or tight mesh sieve. • Heat again quickly and serve with the salted whipped cream and fresh basil leaves.

Mrs. Eugene B. Casey

PUMPKIN SOUP WITH PEPITAS   Serves 4

"...feast on what is seasonal and abundant."

1 2- to 2½-pound pumpkin
2 teaspoons canola oil
1 onion, chopped
1 celery rib, chopped
2 cups milk
2 cups water
2 tablespoons lemon juice
¼ teaspoon cumin

Pinch of allspice
2 tablespoons dry sherry or
  marsala
Sea salt and freshly ground
  pepper
2 tablespoons pepitas or
  pumpkin seeds for garnish
  (see note)

Preheat oven to 350°. • Cut the pumpkin in half and scrape out seeds. Place, cut side down, on a baking sheet and bake for 40 minutes, until tender and easily pierced with a fork. Remove from oven and allow pumpkin to cool for about 10 minutes. • While pumpkin is baking, heat oil in a small skillet and sauté onion and celery for about 3 minutes, until softened and clear. • Scoop out pumpkin pulp with a large spoon and place in a large bowl. Add onion, celery, milk and water. Stir to combine. Ladle some of this mixture into blender and purée in small batches, being careful not to overfill blender. Strain soup through a colander to remove any remaining fiber or seeds. Add lemon juice, cumin, allspice and sherry. Season to taste with salt and pepper. • Spread pepitas or pumpkin seeds on baking sheet and roast in oven for 10 minutes, until toasted. • To serve: reheat the soup, divide it among 4 warmed soup bowls and sprinkle with pepitas or pumpkin seeds.

NOTE: Pepitas are green pumpkin seeds which are a popular ingredient in Mexican cooking. They can be bought in specialty stores and are available salted, roasted and raw.

Nora Pouillon
Nora's Restaurant

HOLIDAY SOUP   Serves 8

1 butternut squash (about
   1 pound)
1 acorn squash (about 1
   pound)
4 teaspoons brown sugar
4 tablespoons unsalted butter
   or margarine

2 carrots, halved lengthwise
1 yellow onion, chopped
3–4 cups chicken broth
Ginger
Mace
Pepper
Parsley or chives, chopped

Preheat oven to 350°. • Cut both squash in half lengthwise and remove seeds. Place in a shallow roasting pan, skin side down. Divide brown sugar and butter evenly into the cavities of the squash. Place carrots and onion around the sides. Add 2 cups chicken broth to the pan. Bake, covered with foil, for about 1 hour, until tender. • Remove from oven and allow to cool. • Scoop out contents of squash and discard skins. In a large saucepan, place squash, carrots, onion and liquid. Add 1 cup chicken broth, ginger, mace and pepper to taste and simmer for 10 minutes. Add more chicken broth and seasonings if thinner soup is desired. • Pour all into food processor in small amounts and purée with steel blade until smooth. • Garnish with parsley or chives and serve hot. For a special presentation serve in a scooped-out pumpkin.

Mrs. Elizabeth Beach Rea

BLACK PEARL CHOWDER   Serves 6

4 tablespoons butter
1 cup finely chopped onion
¼ pound bacon, cut into small
   pieces
1 cup milk
3 cups canned clams with
   liquid
2–3 medium potatoes, cubed

½ teaspoon chopped parsley
½ teaspoon chopped fresh dill
½ teaspoon thyme
1 teaspoon salt, or to taste
Freshly ground pepper to taste
1 cup light cream
Sprig of dill

Melt 1 tablespoon butter over low heat in a skillet. Add onion and sauté until translucent. Remove onion to a large saucepan. • Fry bacon in skillet until crisp and add to saucepan. Add milk, clams with liquid, potatoes, parsley, dill, thyme, salt and pepper and simmer over medium heat until potatoes are tender, about 20 minutes. • Just before serving, add the cream and the remaining butter and simmer until thoroughly heated. Place in soup tureen or individual bowls, garnish with a sprig of dill and serve.

Linda Paris-Finkelstein

CLAM CHOWDER   Serves 6 to 8

1 quart shucked clams or   3 cups water
   quahogs   2 cups milk
⅓ cup diced salt pork   1 cup light cream
1 onion, diced   1 small can evaporated milk
4 cups finely diced potatoes

Remove hard necks of clams and discard. Chop clams coarsely. • Fry salt pork and remove pieces of pork. Add onion and cook until clear. Add water and potatoes. Cook 3–4 minutes. Add clams and cook until potatoes are done. Add milk, cream and evaporated milk. Season to taste with salt and pepper. Serve hot. This is better if made the day before.

Senator John H. Chafee
(Rhode Island)

CORN AND CRAB CHOWDER   Serves 4 to 6

5 tablespoons butter   3 ears of corn, cooked and
5 tablespoons flour   scraped to yield 1½ cups
2½ cups chicken broth   ½ teaspoon salt
2 cups milk   ¼ teaspoon pepper
1 medium onion, finely   ⅛ teaspoon cayenne pepper
   chopped   ½ cup heavy cream
1 cup crabmeat

Melt 4 tablespoons butter in a large saucepan. Stir in flour and cook for 2 minutes over low heat, stirring constantly. Add chicken broth and milk. Mix well and cook for 10 minutes, stirring occasionally. • In a skillet, melt remaining tablespoon butter. Add onion and cook 2–3 minutes. Do not allow onion to brown. Add crabmeat, corn, salt, pepper, and cayenne. Mix well and cook for 1 minute. Add skillet contents to chicken broth mixture and heat. Just before serving, add cream and simmer for 5 minutes.

Mrs. Rufus K. Griscom

FISH CHOWDER   Serves 4

1 medium onion, coarsely
   chopped
2 small cloves garlic, finely
   chopped
2 tablespoons olive oil
4 medium potatoes, peeled
   and cut into large cubes

3½ cups water
½ cup white wine
Salt and pepper to taste
1 pound fish fillets (any mild
   white fish: cod, halibut, etc.)
   cut into 2-inch pieces
½ cup chopped parsley

Sauté onion and garlic in olive oil on low heat until onion is limp. Add potatoes, water, wine, salt and pepper. Simmer until potatoes are tender, about 20 minutes. • Add fish fillets and simmer for 7 minutes, until fish is no longer opaque. Add salt and pepper to taste. Add parsley. Serve with crusty French bread. It's good for dunking!

Mrs. John K. Walker, Jr.

FOUR SEASONS SOUP   Serves 8

"If we eat this soup in the spring, it is 'Spring Soup,' etc."

2 cups peeled potatoes, sliced
   ¼ inch thick
1 cup peeled carrots, sliced
   ¼ inch thick
1 large onion, peeled and
   sliced ¼ inch thick
1 medium purple turnip,
   peeled and sliced ¼ inch thick

Olive oil
6 cups chicken stock
1 head Bibb lettuce, coarsely
   chopped
1 cup bay shrimp or shrimp
   meat, rinsed
Dash of salt and fresh pepper

Sauté vegetables in olive oil for about 10 minutes until onion has softened. Add chicken stock and bring to a boil. Lower heat, cover and simmer for 30–40 minutes, until vegetables are tender. • Remove from heat and mash until roughly puréed . (Do not use food processor as resulting texture will be too smooth.) • Return mixture to pot and bring to simmer. Add lettuce and cook, uncovered, until lettuce wilts. Add shrimp and heat thoroughly. Season to taste.

Mrs. Walter D. Knight

HOLLINGS SHE-CRAB SOUP   Serves 4 to 6

½ cup chopped celery, or
   ¼ teaspoon celery salt
2–3 tablespoons butter
2 teaspoons flour
2 cups milk
½ cup heavy cream
½ teaspoon mace

1 tablespoon Worcestershire
   sauce
Salt and pepper to taste
1 pound lump crabmeat,
   picked over to remove shells
Warm sherry, in a pitcher

Sauté celery in 1 tablespoon butter until soft. • In the top of a double boiler, melt 2 tablespoons butter. Add flour and stir until smooth. Slowly, add milk, cream, mace, celery or celery salt, Worcestershire sauce, salt and pepper. Mix well. Gently fold in crabmeat. • Serve hot with warm sherry.

Peatsy Hollings
Wife of Senator Ernest F. Hollings (South Carolina)

OYSTERS ROCKEFELLER SOUP   Serves 8

5 tablespoons butter or
   margarine
3–4 shallots, chopped
1 bunch of scallions, chopped
5 tablespoons flour
3 cups heavy cream, scalded
1½ cups chicken stock
2 10-ounce packages frozen
   chopped spinach, cooked
   and drained

3 cups oysters, drained and
   minced
Onion salt
Cayenne pepper
Tabasco sauce
Nutmeg
1 ounce Sambucca or Pernod
   (optional)

Melt butter in a large, heavy saucepan. Sauté shallots and scallions over low heat until tender. Add flour and continue cooking over low heat for 3 minutes, stirring constantly. Increase heat to medium and slowly add warm cream, whisking well to blend thoroughly. Add chicken stock, spinach and oysters. Stir and cook until oysters are almost firm—not rubbery. Remove from heat. • In a food processor or blender purée soup thoroughly, a little at a time. Return soup to saucepan and heat. Adjust seasoning and add Sambucca or Pernod if desired. • This soup may be made a day ahead.

Mrs. Robert H. Craft, Jr.

HUNGARIAN GOULASH SOUP   Serves 4 to 6

3 tablespoons cooking oil
1 medium onion, finely chopped
½ pound soup meat, cut into
   1-inch cubes (see note)
Salt
2 teaspoons Hungarian paprika
¼ teaspoon caraway seeds
4 cups beef stock or canned
   beef broth and water
   (approximately)

1 clove garlic, peeled and
   stuck on a toothpick
1 cubanella pepper or ½ bell
   pepper, cut into ½-inch strips
2 small fresh tomatoes, peeled
   and chopped, or 2 canned
   tomatoes, chopped
2 medium new potatoes

Heat oil in large heavy-bottomed pot. Sauté onion until it wilts. Push onion to the side and add meat, browning lightly on all sides. Sprinkle with 1 teaspoon salt, paprika and caraway seeds and cook for about 1 minute. Add 2 cups stock and scrape bits stuck to pan. Add garlic, pepper and tomatoes and bring to a simmer. Cover and simmer for 1 hour, adding more stock or broth and water as needed to keep meat covered. • Peel and dice potatoes into ½-inch pieces and add to soup. Add 1 teaspoon salt and enough stock to cover. Simmer until potatoes are done, about 20 minutes. Remove soup from heat and allow to stand. Discard garlic, skim off most of grease and correct seasonings (more salt may be needed). Bring soup back to a simmer and serve.

NOTE: A piece of shank is good for this. Put the bone into soup pot for added flavor.

Susan Derecskey, Author
"The Hungarian Cookbook"

The Smithsonian Castle

CHORBA HAMRA
(SPICY VEGETABLE SOUP)

Serves 4 to 6

¼ pound butter
½ pound lamb, cubed
1 large onion, minced
2 tablespoons minced fresh
  cilantro leaves
½ teaspoon cayenne pepper
Pinch of black pepper
Pinch of cinnamon
1 teaspoon salt

1 pound tomatoes, peeled
1 large potato
1 large carrot
1 medium zucchini
1 stalk celery
1 15-ounce can chickpeas,
  drained
¼ pound vermicelli (thin
  spaghetti)
1 lemon, thinly sliced

Melt butter in a large, deep saucepan. Add lamb, onion, cilantro, cayenne, black pepper, cinnamon and salt and stir well. Cook over medium heat until meat is well browned. Purée or mash the tomatoes and add to pot. Thinly slice potato, carrot, zucchini and celery. Add 6–8 cups of water to pot and bring to a boil. Add sliced vegetables and chickpeas. Cover and reduce heat to simmer until all of the ingredients are tender. Add water as needed. • Just before serving, bring mixture to a boil. Stir in pasta and cook until noodles are al dente, according to package instructions. • Serve in bowls with a slice of lemon floating on top.

Ali Rebatchi,
Embassy of Algeria

OXTAIL SOUP

Serves 10

"An excellent fall or winter soup. Can be prepared ahead and frozen"

4+ pounds oxtails
1 pound dried peas (optional)
Fresh dill
Fresh or dried thyme
Salt and pepper
Water

3–4 potatoes, washed and
  chopped
3–4 carrots, washed and
  chopped
1–2 cups dry vermouth
Fresh broccoli (optional)

Place oxtails, peas, dill, thyme, salt and pepper in a very large stock pot. Add cold water until just covered. Cover the pot and simmer for approximately 2 hours. • Add potatoes, carrots and vermouth. Continue simmering, uncovered, for 3–4 hours, until liquid has reduced to half of original amount. • Remove oxtails from pot and cut away all meat. Discard the bones and return the meat to the pot. Add broccoli, if desired, and simmer for 5–10 minutes. • Serve with fresh country bread.

Christie Weiss

SOLYÁNKA MYASNÁYA   Serves 6–8

*"A special feature of this slightly sour soup is the mixture of meats.
It has an interesting, different flavor—a nice change
from the usual vegetable beef soups."*

1 tablespoon olive oil
1 medium onion, finely
  chopped
2 tablespoons tomato paste
1 tablespoon butter
3 medium cucumbers or
  half-pickled cucumbers,
  peeled, halved and sliced
1 pound cooked beef, thinly
  sliced
½ pound cooked kielbasa
  sausage, thinly sliced

¼ pound cooked ham, salami
  or tongue, thinly sliced
1 tablespoon capers
1 quart beef stock or canned
  beef bouillon
Tomatoes, peeled and sliced
  (optional)
1 tablespoon pitted and sliced
  black olives
Sour cream
¼ lemon, peeled and cut into
  segments
Parsley or dill, chopped

Heat oil in a large skillet over medium heat. Add onion and cook until slightly browned. Stir in tomato paste and butter. If dry, add a little beef stock. Add cucumbers, meats and capers. Stir in beef stock and bring to a boil. Reduce heat and simmer for 5–10 minutes. Add tomato slices, if desired. Serve hot with sour cream, olives, lemon segments and parsley or dill.

*The Ambassador of the Russian
Federation and Mrs. Lukin*

HAM AND POTATO CHOWDER   Serves 6 to 8

2 teaspoons butter or
  margarine
1 cup chopped onion
1 cup diced celery
1 clove garlic, minced
2 cups diced cooked ham
2 cups (1 pound) cooked
  potatoes, peeled and diced

1 bay leaf
¾ teaspoon salt
½ teaspoon dried thyme
½ teaspoon hot pepper sauce
2 cups water
2 cups milk
1 1-pound can tomatoes,
  drained and chopped

Melt butter in a large pot. Add onion, celery, garlic and ham and cook until onion and celery are tender, but not browned. Stir in potatoes, bay leaf, salt, thyme, hot sauce and water. Add milk and tomatoes and heat. Do not boil.

Mary Doremus

YOGURT SOUP   Serves 6

6 cups chicken or other meat
   stock
⅔ cup hulled wheat or barley
3½ cups plain yogurt
3 tablespoons flour
2 egg yolks

2 cups water
Salt to taste
2–3 tablespoons unsalted
   butter
¼ cup dried mint leaves

Bring stock to a boil in a large pan, stir in wheat or barley, cover and simmer over medium heat for about 40 minutes, until grain is tender. • In a large bowl, mix yogurt with flour and egg yolks until smooth. Gradually add water. Pour yogurt mixture through sieve directly into stock. Season with salt. Cover and continue simmering gently for 10 minutes. • In a small saucepan, heat butter until frothy. Sprinkle in mint leaves, crushing them with back of spoon. Stir and allow mixture to sizzle for a second or two. Add to soup. • Serve hot. If soup is prepared ahead and reheated, thin soup with water as needed.

The Ambassador of Turkey and Mrs. Kandemir

MISSOURI APPLE SOUP   Serves 10 to 12

2 tablespoons butter
2 medium onions, thinly sliced
6 red Jonathan apples, peeled,
   cored and diced
4 cups chicken broth
2 tablespoons sugar

1 tablespoon curry powder, or
   to taste
Salt and white pepper to taste
1–2 cups light cream
Thin apple wedges
Sliced almonds

In a Dutch oven, melt butter and sauté onions until transparent. Add apples, broth, sugar and curry powder. Season with salt and pepper. Cook, covered, over low heat until apples are soft. • Strain apples and onions from broth and reserve. In batches, purée apples and onions in a food processor or blender, adding some broth each time. Put everything into a serving bowl, stir in cream according to taste and adjust seasoning. Garnish with thin apple wedges and a sprinkling of sliced almonds.

Mrs. Christopher Bond
Wife of the Senator from Missouri

Fish and Seafood

BANGUS RELLENO

Serves 2

1 piece bangus (milkfish), (see note)
Lime juice
2 cloves garlic, finely chopped
½ onion, finely chopped
1 tomato, finely chopped
Salt and pepper to taste
1 small potato, cooked and mashed
Raisins
Peas
2 eggs, well beaten
Oil for frying
6 tablespoons prepared pickle relish

Clean fish, taking care not to cut skin. Roll fish on a table, pressing on it to soften meat. Slit the back and remove backbone. Scrape meat with a knife. Soak skin in a mixture of lime juice, salt and pepper to cover. Place fish in a saucepan filled with salted water, bring to a boil and simmer until cooked. When thoroughly cooked, remove bangus from water and clean to remove all bones. • In a large skillet, sauté garlic, onion and tomato. Add flaked bangus and season with salt and pepper. Cook for 5 minutes and add potatoes, raisins and peas. Remove from heat and mix well with beaten eggs. • Stuff fish skin with sautéed mixture and sew opening. Rub the outside skin with flour and sauté in hot oil. Serve immediately with pickle relish.

NOTE: Bangus can be found in Asian food markets, but bluefish may be substituted.

Mrs. Buena R. Rabe
Embassy of the Philippines

BLUE DANUBE CARP

Serves 8

"A typical Austrian Christmas dish."

4 pounds carp
Salt to taste
⅔ cup flour
2 eggs, slightly beaten
1 cup bread crumbs
Juice from 4 lemons
½ cup oil (can also use butter)

Scrape and wash carp. Cut into slices 1 inch thick. Salt. Dip in flour, egg and bread crumbs. Sprinkle with lemon juice and salt. Allow to stand for 30 minutes before cooking. • Fry in hot oil until golden brown. Drain on paper towels.

Mrs. Helmut Tuerk
Wife of the Ambassador of Austria

COD À LA NANTAISE
(CABILLAUD À LA NANTAISE)

Serves 4

"A classic French recipe"

1½ pounds fresh cod
2 onions, chopped
1 cup Muscadet or other dry
   white wine
Salt and pepper to taste
½ teaspoon thyme
1 bay leaf
2 sprigs parsley
Juice of 1 lemon
6 ounces mushrooms, sliced

3 tablespoons butter
1 teaspoon softened butter
   mixed with 1 teaspoon flour
   and salt and pepper to taste
⅜ cup crème fraîche (do not
   substitute sour cream as it
   will separate during cooking)
1 egg yolk
Chopped chives and parsley
   for garnish

Preheat oven to 350°. • Wash, dry and season cod. Place cod on a bed of chopped onions in a greased ovenproof dish. • Combine wine, salt, pepper, thyme, bay leaf and parsley sprigs in a saucepan. Bring to boil and reduce by half. Add half of lemon juice. Allow to cool. • Pour wine mixture over fish and bake for 25 minutes. • While fish is cooking, sauté mushrooms in butter and remaining lemon juice. Set aside. • Remove fish from oven when done. Debone fish and remove skin. Remove to platter and keep warm. • Pour the cooking juices through a sieve into a saucepan. Slowly bring cooking juices and butter and flour mixture to boil over low-medium heat, stirring constantly. Add crème fraîche and let sauce thicken. Remove pan from heat and add egg yolk. Mix carefully. Add mushrooms. Pour sauce over fish. • Sprinkle with chopped chives and parsley and serve with rice or steamed potatoes.

Beverly Morisset
The Delegation of the Commission
of the European Communities

ELEGANT FISH DELIGHT   Serves 4

Fish:

1½ pounds fillet of sole or flounder

Seasoned salt and pepper

Juice of ½ lemon

Butter

Sauce:

2 tablespoons butter

10 small cooked onions

1 16-ounce can stewed tomatoes

Seasoned salt and pepper

1 teaspoon cornstarch

1 8-ounce can peas

Preheat oven to 425°. • Roll fish fillets and arrange in baking dish. Sprinkle with salt and pepper. Squeeze lemon juice over fish, dot with butter and bake for 10 minutes. • To make sauce, melt 2 tablespoons butter and add onions, stewed tomatoes, salt and pepper. Stir and simmer for 5 minutes. • Drain peas, reserving liquid. Mix cornstarch with ½ cup of liquid from peas and add to onion mixture. Stir in peas. • Spoon onion mixture over and around fish and return to oven for 10 minutes, or until fish flakes with a fork.

Mrs. Alvin A. Kraft

FISH AND LEEK CASSEROLE   Serves 6

4 tablespoons butter

3 leeks, trimmed and cut in julienne strips

2 pounds halibut or turbot, skinned and boned

1 cup white wine

1 cup water

1 bay leaf

Salt and pepper to taste

1 pint heavy cream

4 tablespoons chopped parsley

Heat 3 tablespoons of the butter and cook leeks until soft but not brown. • Cut fish into 2-inch cubes and place on top of leeks. Add wine, water, bay leaf, salt and pepper. Cover and poach slowly for 10 minutes. • When fish is no longer translucent, remove it and the leeks to a plate and keep warm. • Increase heat and reduce liquid by half. Add cream and cook, stirring, until it reaches the consistency of a sauce. • Remove from heat. Whisk in remaining butter until blended. Adjust seasoning. Pour off any liquid that has accumulated from fish and add to sauce. Pour sauce over fish. Garnish with parsley.

Christine van Mulders

FISH FILLETS KOWLOON   Serves 4

4 fish fillets, such as turbot,
  sole, flounder, baby halibut
  (about 5 ounces each)
Salt and pepper

3 tablespoons dry sherry or
  white wine
2–3 tablespoons oil
1½ tablespoons light soy sauce
3 scallions, thinly sliced

Place fillets on a dish, sprinkle with salt, pepper and sherry. Place dish on a trivet in a wok or other pot containing an inch or so of water (see note). Make certain dish is above the rim of pot to facilitate removal. • Cover and steam for about 2 minutes, until flesh is white and flakes easily. Precise timing depends on thickness of fillets. • While fish is steaming, pour oil and soy sauce into a small saucepan and heat almost to the boiling point. Remove fillet dish from steamer and strew scallions over top. Remove oil and soy sauce from heat, stir well to blend and pour over fillets. Serve at once.

NOTE: Lacking a wok or suitable pan, place each fillet on a piece of plastic wrap large enough to fold over fish. Season with salt, pepper and sherry and fold plastic wrap over fish to make a complete seal. Steam in steamer or simmer in boiling water in a large skillet. Timing will be similar to that in wok, about 2 minutes.

Carol Cutler, Author
"Catch of the Day"

NORWEGIAN FISH PUDDING   Serves 6

1½ pounds haddock or cod,
  skinned and boned
2 teaspoons salt
2 tablespoons potato starch or
  1½ tablespoons cornstarch

1 cup milk
1 cup heavy cream
¼ teaspoon nutmeg

Preheat oven to 350°. Cut fish into small pieces. Combine with salt, potato starch and 2 tablespoons of milk to form a smooth purée. Slowly, beat in remaining milk and then beat in cream until mixture is light and fluffy. Add nutmeg and pour into 1½-quart mold. Place mold inside a baking pan half filled with boiling water and bake in the middle of the oven for 1–1½ hours. The water in the baking pan should simmer. Usually served with a sauce béchamel, shrimp, lobster and cauliflower.

Mrs. Kjeld Vibe
Wife of the Ambassador of Norway

SIMPLE FISH MOLD   Serves 6 to 8

8 slices homemade-type
  bread, crusts trimmed
1 cup milk
2 pounds halibut or cod,
  chopped and sprinkled with
  fresh lemon juice
1 tablespoon chopped onion

2 eggs
1 cup heavy cream
2 teaspoons salt
White pepper to taste
2 tablespoons finely cut
  fresh dill

Soak bread slices in milk for at least 10 minutes. • In food processor, purée fish with onion until very smooth, scraping sides when needed. Add bread slices and all of milk and blend very well. Add eggs and blend well. Add cream and blend well. Add salt, pepper and dill and combine well. Pack mixture into a well-oiled 6-cup ring mold (or meatloaf pan or fish mold). Set it on a rack in an oven-proof pan; add hot water to come halfway up the sides of the mold. Cook in a preheated 375° oven for 35–40 minutes until it rises and shows faint lines of shrinkage from the sides of mold. • Allow mold to settle for 10 minutes before unmolding. Refrigerate for several hours or overnight. • Serve with sour cream cucumber sauce (recipe follows) or your favorite sauce.

Sour cream cucumber sauce:

2 cups thick sour cream
1 cup seeded and chopped
  cucumber
¼ cup finely chopped chives

¼ cup finely chopped fresh dill
1 teaspoon sugar
½ teaspoon fresh lemon juice
Salt and pepper to taste

Mix all ingredients together well. Refrigerate. Serve with unmolded fish.

Ariadna Miller

FILLETS OF SOLE SARI   Serves 6 to 8

Lemon juice
Salt and pepper to taste
8 fillets of sole
12 tablespoons butter,
  softened

½ cup mixture of chopped
  parsley, dill and tarragon
  (fresh, if possible)
1 cup mayonnaise
Chives
2 egg whites, beaten stiff

Preheat oven to 350°. • Sprinkle lemon juice, salt and pepper on sole. • In a small bowl, combine butter and herbs and spread on both sides of each piece of fish. Roll each fillet and place seam side down in a large baking dish or in individual ramekins. • Bake for 20 minutes, until flaky. Remove from oven and cool. (Can be done ahead to this point.) • Fifteen minutes before serving, preheat broiler. Combine mayonnaise, chives and egg whites and spread over fish fillet rolls. Broil at least 6 inches from heat source until golden brown (about 3 minutes).

Brooke Shearer

SHAD WITH ROE JEFFERSON   Serves 4 to 6

1 shad	Paprika
Salt	Butter
Flour	

Roe:

7 tablespoons butter	¼ cup white wine
1 small onion, chopped	¼ cup chopped parsley
3 shallots, chopped	Juice of half a lemon
1 set roe	2 eggs, separated
3 tablespoons flour	Paprika
¼ cup milk	Seasoned salt
¾ teaspoon salt	Lemon wedges

Place a thoroughly boned shad in a buttered ovenproof dish with 1- to 2-inch edge. Sprinkle fish with salt, a little flour and paprika and dot with butter. • Put 4 tablespoons butter in a large frying pan. When it foams, add onion and shallots. Sauté until onions are clear. Add roe. Work apart with a wooden fork or spatula. Sauté for 2 minutes until roe becomes gray and scoop to upper side of tilted pan. Add 2 tablespoons butter in lower part of pan. When butter melts, add flour, stirring. When smooth, add milk and stir into a stiff paste and remove from fire. Add salt, wine, parsley and lemon juice. Add egg yolks beaten until lemon-colored. Fold in stiffly beaten egg whites. Mix with roe and spoon mixture on top of boned shad, making sure edge of shad comes up on side of dish to keep mixture from flowing over. Sprinkle with paprika, seasoned salt and remaining butter. • Bake at 300° for 50 minutes. Serve with lemon wedges.

Paula Jeffries

SAUTÉED BROOK TROUT FILLETS WITH RASPBERRY SAUCE

Serves 4

2–3 heads of Belgian endive
1½ cups red wine
3 ounces soft raspberries
⅓ cup heavy cream
14 tablespoons unsalted
   butter, softened
Salt and pepper
8 boneless trout fillets

¼ cup flour, lightly seasoned
   with salt and pepper
4 ounces snow peas, cut
   lengthwise into ⅛-inch strips
2 tablespoons olive oil
Sliced or chopped almonds,
   toasted

Cut heads of Belgian endive in half lengthwise, remove hard root core and cut lengthwise into ⅛-inch strips. • To make raspberry sauce, place red wine and raspberries in a saucepan and simmer until liquid is reduced by ⅘. Add cream and again reduce by ⅘. Lower heat and gently simmer. Add 12 tablespoons butter, 1 teaspoon at a time, and whisk in. Add salt and pepper to taste. Pass sauce through a sieve and keep hot, but do not allow to boil. Sauce should be smooth, creamy and pink. • To prepare trout, place 1 tablespoon each of oil and butter in a large, non-stick frying pan. Lightly dip trout fillets into seasoned flour and sauté until golden brown on both sides. Remove trout from pan and keep hot. • Quickly wipe out pan and return to heat. Add remaining butter and oil. Stir in snow peas and sauté for 10–15 seconds. Add endive. Season to taste. Continue to sauté until snow peas start to wilt and turn golden brown. For each serving arrange snow peas and endive in a circle in the center of a hot plate, approximately 1 inch from edge. Place two trout fillets on snow pea mixture and sprinkle with toasted almonds. Pour a ribbon of sauce around the edge of snow pea mixture and serve immediately.

Willard Inter-Continental Hotel
Washington, D. C.

HALIBUT WITH CUCUMBER, TOMATOES, BABY SNAILS AND SAVORY HERBS

Serves 4

2 small cucumbers, peeled, cored and sliced into thin strips
1 4.5-ounce can small snails (see note)
2 large shallots, finely chopped
¾ cup white wine
2 cups fish stock
¾ cup cream
Salt
¼ teaspoon pepper
½ teaspoon lemon juice
2 pounds halibut fillets or steaks
1 cup peeled, seeded and chopped tomatoes
½ teaspoon summer savory

Cut cucumbers into fine strips and marinate in salted water for one hour. • In a large saucepan, boil snails and shallots in white wine and fish stock until ⅓ of juice has evaporated. Add cream and stir well. Continue cooking over medium low heat, stirring, until sauce is reduced to medium thickness. Add salt, pepper and lemon juice. • Steam halibut for about ten minutes (depending on thickness). • Remove cucumber from marinade and mix into wine sauce. Fold tomatoes into sauce. Sprinkle summer savory over sauce and pour over halibut. Serve with steamed potatoes. Any leftovers will make a wonderful chowder.

NOTE: Snails are available in cans. You do not need shells, which are often included. The 4.5-ounce can Helix Brand equals 2 dozen snails and is available in specialty food stores.

Chef Geert Piferoen
Embassy of Belgium
(Adapted by the Committee)

CEDAR PLANKED SALMON   Serves 2
WITH SOFT CORN PUDDING
AND PUMPKIN SEED VINAIGRETTE

Before starting, be sure you have on hand 2 pieces untreated cedar siding or shingle, about 4 x 6 inches, 4 finishing nails and picture wire.

Corn pudding:

2 cups milk
½ teaspoon minced garlic
½ cup corn kernels, fresh or
   frozen

8 or more tablespoons yellow
   cornmeal
1 tablespoon unsalted butter
Salt and pepper to taste

Pumpkin seed vinaigrette:

⅔ cup apple cider
3 tablespoons pumpkin purée
⅓ cup rice vinegar

4 tablespoons hulled raw pumpkin seeds, lightly toasted
¾ cup olive oil

Cedar planked salmon:

2 6-ounce salmon fillets,
   skinned and boned
1 teaspoon salt

¼ teaspoon dry mustard
1 tablespoon unsalted butter,
   softened

To cook the soft corn pudding, combine the milk, garlic, and corn kernels in a medium saucepan and bring to a boil. Lower the heat and simmer for 2 minutes. Slowly stir in the cornmeal and stir for 3 to 4 minutes, or until the pudding is the consistency of oatmeal. Add butter. Season to taste with salt and pepper. Keep warm until ready to serve. If pudding becomes too thick, add a bit of milk or water. • To make the pumpkin seed vinaigrette, purée the cider, pumpkin purée, vinegar, and 3 tablespoons of the seeds in a blender, slowly adding the oil until smooth. Blend in the last tablespoon of the seeds with a few short pulses of the blender so the mixture has a very slightly crunchy texture. Serve at room temperature. • To broil the salmon, start by soaking the cedar in cold water for 15 minutes. (A 9 x 11 inch cake pan filled with water with a weight on top of the cedar works well.) Preheat the broiler. Place the cedar under the broiler for 2 to 3 minutes, about 5 inches from the heat. This will give you a very hot surface to put the salmon on as it will not be turned during cooking. Or heat the cedar over a grill. Mix the salt and mustard together. Brush the tops of the salmon with butter and sprinkle both sides liberally with the mustard mix. Quickly wire the salmon to the hot plank, using 2 finishing nails put into the ends of the plank and wrapping the fish with picture wire around the cedar plank. When cooked on the grill, the salmon goes face down; under the broiler the salmon goes face up. Remove from the broiler and carefully remove fish from plank. Place a large spoonful of corn pudding in the center of each plate. Put the cooked salmon on top of the pudding. Spoon an ample amount of vinaigrette around the pudding and tilt the plate until the vinaigrette covers the entire plate.

NOTE: This recipe was adapted from one created by Larry Forgione.

Peggy Law, Co- Owner and Winemaker
Linden Vineyards

HEAVENLY SALMON Serves 8 to 10

1 side of salmon
Juice of ½ a lemon
Onion salt to taste
Pepper to taste
⅛–¼ cup white wine

1 bunch of scallions, finely
  chopped using all of the
  white and ⅓ of the green
Margarine or butter
Chopped parsley to garnish

Preheat oven to 375° unless planning to use microwave oven. • Rinse fish and pat dry. Place in a greased baking dish. Squeeze the lemon over all of the fish, add wine, and season with onion salt and pepper. Scatter scallions over the length of the fish and dot with margarine or butter. • Cover tightly with aluminum foil, or plastic wrap if using microwave oven. Bake for 20–30 minutes in oven or cook for 4–5 minutes in microwave, until fish is thoroughly cooked but moist. • Garnish with parsley. • To serve cold: after cooking, place upside down on a platter and peel off skin. Allow to cool and serve with watercress mayonnaise.

Watercress mayonnaise:

2 egg yolks at room
  temperature
1 teaspoon salt
½ teaspoon dry mustard

2 cups peanut or olive oil
Lemon juice
1 cup very finely chopped
  watercress

Beat egg yolks, salt and mustard in food processor or blender. Add oil very gradually and beat until thickened. Thin with lemon juice to taste. Blend in watercress and chill.

Committee

SALMON SOUFFLÉ
Serves 4

4 tablespoons butter
4 tablespoons finely chopped
  onion
4 tablespoons flour
1 cup milk
5 eggs, separated
1 tablespoon ketchup

1 15-ounce can salmon, well
  drained
1½ teaspoons crushed dill seed
1 teaspoon salt
1 tablespoon lemon juice
Dash cayenne pepper

Preheat oven to 400°. • Butter bottom and sides of a 2-quart soufflé dish with 1 tablespoon butter. Melt remaining butter in saucepan and add onion. Cook 3 minutes and remove from heat. Add flour all at once and stir to make a smooth paste. Add milk all at once and beat with a whisk. Return to medium heat, stirring constantly, until thick and smooth. Remove from heat. Beat in egg yolks, one at a time. Stir in remaining ingredients except egg whites. Set aside. • Beat egg whites until stiff. Add a heaping tablespoon of egg whites to salmon mixture. Fold in remaining whites gently and stir until no white streaks remain. Do not overfold. • Pour into prepared soufflé dish. Reduce oven temperature to 375° and cook for 35–40 minutes without opening oven door. Serve immediately.

JoAnne Nicholson

GRILLED SALMON WITH FENNEL CONFIT
AND OVEN DRIED TOMATOES
Serves 4

Salmon:
4 7-ounce salmon fillets
½ cup olive oil
2 sprigs thyme

2 sprigs rosemary
Cracked black pepper
Salt to taste

Tomatoes:
10–15 ripe, but not soft,
  Italian plum tomatoes
1–2 teaspoons sugar

Kosher salt, as needed
1 tablespoon minced fresh
  thyme

Fennel confit:
¼ cup chopped shallots
3 tablespoons olive oil
1 sprig rosemary
1 star anise pod

2 medium fennel, julienned
1¼ cups chicken stock
Basil, if desired

Read through the recipe before you begin to plan the timing of each step. • Marinate the salmon in olive oil, thyme, rosemary and pepper and salt for 2–4 hours. • Grill until just pink, about 3–4 minutes on each side. • Preheat oven to its lowest setting (175°-200°). • Remove the stem end of each tomato, then cut each lengthwise and carefully scrape out seeds. Place tomato halves on baking rack, cut-side up. Season with the sugar, salt and thyme. Place in oven for 4–5 hours until tomatoes look somewhat dry and shriveled but still retain a little moisture. Let cool on the rack. • To make fennel confit, sauté shallots in olive oil. Add rosemary, star anise and fennel. Pour in chicken stock and simmer until rosemary is softened and stock is reduced. • Serve salmon with tomatoes and fennel confit. Garnish with basil, if desired.

Patrick Clark, Executive Chef
The Hay-Adams Hotel

SALMON MOUSSE WITH SOUR CREAM DILL SAUCE

Serves 8

Salmon:
1 envelope unflavored gelatin
¼ cup cold water
½ cup boiling water
½ cup mayonnaise (see note)
1 tablespoon lemon juice
1 tablespoon grated onion
½ teaspoon Tabasco sauce

¼ teaspoon paprika
1 teaspoon salt
2 cups poached or canned
   (drained) salmon, finely
   chopped
1 tablespoon chopped capers
½ cup heavy cream
3 cups cottage cheese (see note)

Sour cream dill sauce:
1 egg
1 teaspoon salt
Pinch of freshly ground
   black pepper

Pinch of sugar
4 teaspoons lemon juice
1 teaspoon grated onion
2 tablespoons finely cut dill
1½ cups sour cream (see note)

Garnish:
Watercress

Lemon slices
Salmon roe (optional)

Soften gelatin in cold water, add boiling water and stir until gelatin is dissolved. Cool. • Add mayonnaise, lemon juice, onion, Tabasco, paprika and salt and mix well. Chill until the consistency of unbeaten egg whites. • Add salmon and capers and beat well. Whip cream, fold into salmon mixture and turn into a 2-quart oiled fish mold. Fill the remainder of the mold with cottage cheese. Chill until set. • To make dill sauce, beat egg until fluffy. Add remaining ingredients. Blend in sour cream last. Stir until blended and chill. • To serve, unmold on a platter and garnish with watercress and lemon slices and with salmon roe, if desired.

NOTE: To reduce fat, you may use light mayonnaise, low-fat cottage cheese, and light or no fat sour cream. They work well.

Bernice Feinstein

MARINATED GRILLED SALMON   Serves 25

Marinade:

1 cup maple syrup (from
   Vermont!)
1 cup dry white wine
1 cup soy sauce

3 cloves garlic, diced
1 sliced onion
1 9-pound salmon, butterflied,
   with the backbone removed

Combine all the marinade ingredients and pour over the salmon. Refrigerate at least 3 hours (overnight is too long). Turn occasionally. • Place the salmon on aluminum foil on a grill, skin side down, and grill over medium-hot charcoal until the salmon loses its translucence, about 20–30 minutes.

NOTE: Salmon steaks also work very well. Recipe can be reduced very easily for smaller amounts of salmon.

Marcelle Leahy
Wife of Senator Patrick J. Leahy (Vermont)

CRAB AND SHIITAKE CAKES   Serves 4 to 6
WITH TOMATO-GINGER SAUCE,
SAUTÉED TATSOI AND SNOW PEAS

4 tablespoons canola oil
2 tablespoons minced shallots
1 tablespoon minced garlic
3 ribs celery, washed and
   minced
1 small carrot, minced
1 small red or yellow pepper,
   seeded and minced

½ pound shiitake mushrooms,
   washed, stemmed and sliced
2 eggs, beaten or
   4 egg whites, beaten
4 tablespoons minced cilantro
1 pound jumbo lump crabmeat
Sea salt and freshly ground
   black pepper to taste

Heat oil in a medium saucepan. Add shallots and garlic and sauté, stirring, for about 1 minute. Add celery and carrot, lower heat and cook until softened, about 2 minutes. Add peppers and shiitakes, stir and sauté until mushrooms are soft and cooked through, about 3 minutes. Remove from heat and cool for about 10 minutes. • Preheat broiler. Combine sautéed vegetable mixture with eggs, cilantro and crabmeat, being careful not to break up large lumps of crab. Season with salt and pepper. Form 12 crab cakes. They will be very soft and delicate. • Place crab cakes on a sheet pan and broil on one side only for 3–4 minutes, until nicely browned. Do not turn. Remove from oven and serve immediately with tomato-ginger sauce.

Tomato-ginger sauce:

1 tablespoon canola oil
2 tablespoons chopped shallots
1 tablespoon minced garlic
1½ pounds tomatoes,
  coarsely chopped

1 2-inch piece of ginger, peeled
  and thinly sliced across the
  fibers
Sea salt and freshly ground
  black pepper

In a medium saucepan, heat oil. Add shallots and garlic and sauté until soft, stirring occasionally. Add tomatoes and ginger, stir and bring to a boil. Reduce heat and simmer for about 5 minutes. Remove from heat, cool slightly and purée in an electric blender until smooth. Season to taste with salt and pepper.

NOTE: Ginger and tomatoes are a great flavor combination. The sauce also goes well with Asian noodles or pasta. Adding tatsoi, carrots, bok choy, shrimp or chicken makes a wonderful simple meal.

Sautéed tatsoi and snow peas:

2 teaspoons canola oil
¼ pound snow peas
¼ pound tatsoi (see note)

Sea salt and freshly ground
  pepper to taste

Heat oil in a medium skillet. Add snow peas and sauté for 2 minutes. Add tatsoi and continue sautéing for another 2 minutes, until vegetables are bright green and slightly softened. Season with salt and pepper. Serve with crab and shiitake cakes.

NOTE: Tatsoi is a Chinese green that grows in small, loose bunches. Ward Sinclair, from Flickersville Farm, introduced it to me about two years ago. It's like a crunchy spinach.

Nora Pouillon
Nora's Restaurant

ROOF TERRACE CRAB CAKES   Serves 6

Vegetable oil
2 eggs
3 pounds crabmeat
3 tablespoons Dijon mustard
½ cup mayonnaise
1 tablespoon lemon juice
¼ bunch parsley, chopped
2 shallots, finely chopped

1½ tablespoons Old Bay
  seasoning
¼ tablespoon Worcestershire
  sauce
Salt and pepper to taste
½ cup finely crushed saltine
  crackers, plus some for
  crab cake coating

Pour oil ⅛ inch deep in a large frying pan and heat. • Beat eggs in a large bowl and add crabmeat, mustard, mayonnaise, lemon juice, parsley, shallots, Old Bay seasoning, Worcestershire sauce, salt and pepper. Mix thoroughly, but gently. Add crushed crackers and gently mix again. Form mixture into 6 large crab cakes or 12 smaller cakes and roll in reserved cracker crumbs. Fry until golden brown on both sides. • Good served with Pommery mustard sauce.

Chef Max-Philippe Knoepfel, Executive Chef
Restaurant Associates, Kennedy Center

SENATOR BARB'S SPICY BAY RECIPE (CRAB CAKES)

Serves 6

1 pound crabmeat
3 slices bread or 4 crackers
1 egg, beaten
1 tablespoon Dijon mustard
2 teaspoons Old Bay or Wye
   River seasoning

1 tablespoon snipped fresh
   parsley
1 tablespoon mayonnaise
Fat, for frying

Pick over crabmeat. Remove crusts from bread and break into small pieces. Mix bread with beaten egg. Add mustard, seasoning, parsley, mayonnaise and crabmeat. Form into cakes and sauté quickly in a small amount of fat. Cakes may also be broiled.

Senator Barbara A. Mikulski
(Maryland)

BARBEQUED SOFT-SHELL CRABS

Serves 6

12 medium-large soft-shell
   crabs
1/3 cup vinegar
4–6 tablespoons lemon juice
Chopped parsley to taste

2 tablespoons thyme
1 tablespoon Creole seasoning
2 tablespoons garlic, finely
   chopped
Lemon pepper to taste

Clean crabs. • Mix all other ingredients to make marinade. Immerse crabs in marinade for 3–4 hours. • Grill over medium coals for 5–10 minutes, turning once, until crisp and browned.

Lynn Meier Novelli

GRILLED SOFT-SHELL CRAB

Serves 4

Marinade:
1 cup canola or olive oil
1/3 cup vinegar
Juice of 1 lemon
1/4 cup chopped parsley
1/2 tablespoon thyme

1 tablespoon Old Bay seasoning
   or Paul Prudhomme's
   Seafood seasoning
2 tablespoons minced garlic
Generous sprinkling lemon
   pepper
8–12 soft-shell crabs

Mix all marinade ingredients in a large bowl. Add crabs and marinate in refrigerator for 2–4 hours. • Remove crabs from marinade and grill over hot fire 3–4 minutes per side.

Lynn Meier Novelli

SAUTÉED SOFT-SHELL CRAB WITH HAZELNUTS

Serves 4

Sauce:

¼ cup mayonnaise
Juice of 1 lemon
1 tablespoon Dijon mustard

1½ teaspoons dry mustard
Salt and pepper to taste

Crabs:

4 soft-shell crabs, dressed
Flour seasoned with salt and
    pepper, for dredging
½ cup clarified butter
2 tablespoons brown butter

1 tomato, peeled, seeded and
    diced
⅓ cup toasted hazelnut slivers
1 tablespoon chopped coriander
    (cilantro)
Juice of 1 lime

Garnish:

1 cup green beans, blanched
1 tablespoon vinaigrette
    (make your own)

Lime segments
Cilantro leaves
1 tablespoon snipped chives

Preheat oven to 400°. • Make sauce by mixing all ingredients into a smooth paste. Season to taste with salt and pepper and set aside. • Dredge the crabs in the seasoned flour, shaking off the excess. Sauté them in the clarified butter. Turn the crabs over, drain the liquid and add the brown butter, tomato, hazelnuts and coriander. Place in oven and cook for 2 minutes. Remove the crabs from oven and drizzle with lime juice. • To serve, dress the green beans with the vinaigrette, then arrange them on four plates. Place the crabs on top of the beans and garnish with the diced tomato and hazelnuts from the pan, and the lime segments and cilantro leaves. Drizzle the sauce over all and sprinkle with chives.

Patrick O'Connell, Executive Chef
The Inn at Little Washington

CRABMEAT AND SHRIMP CASSEROLE

Serves 6 to 8

*"This is an elegant casserole which works beautifully
at large buffet dinners."*

1½ pounds crabmeat
½ pound small shrimp
½ green pepper, chopped
⅓ cup chopped parsley
2 cups cooked rice
1 cup mayonnaise

1 10-ounce package frozen
    small peas
Salt and pepper to taste
2 tablespoons lemon juice
Dash of red pepper

Preheat oven to 375°. • Pick over crabmeat, removing shells. Clean and peel shrimp. Combine crabmeat and shrimp with all of the ingredients, tossing gently. Place in greased casserole. Bake covered for 45–50 minutes (or until heated through).

NOTE: This may be assembled the day before and refrigerated. Let it sit at room temperature for 1 hour, then bake as described above.

Katie Hunnicutt

CRABMEAT REMICK   Serves 6 to 8

1 scant teaspoon dry mustard
½ teaspoon paprika
½ teaspoon celery seed
¼–½ teaspoon dried tarragon
A few drops of Tabasco sauce
½ cup chili sauce

1¾ cups mayonnaise
1 teaspoon white wine vinegar
2 pounds lump crabmeat, shells
   removed
3 strips crisp bacon, crumbled
Parsley or watercress sprigs

Combine mustard, paprika, celery seed, tarragon, Tabasco, chili sauce, mayonnaise and white wine vinegar. (This may be prepared ahead of time.) • Pile crabmeat into 6–8 coquille shells or ramekins. Heat in a moderate oven (350°) until warmed through, about 10 minutes. Top with bacon. Pour sauce over crabmeat, coating completely. Glaze under broiler, watching very closely. • Serve garnished with parsley or watercress sprigs.

Mrs. John C. Gore

CRABMEAT SUPREME   Serves 4

1 cup diced celery
8 slices cubed white bread
2 cups crabmeat (fresh claw)
1 yellow onion, finely
   chopped
½ cup mayonnaise

½ cup chopped green peppers
4 eggs, slightly beaten
3 cups milk
1 cup canned mushroom soup
Dash of paprika

Cook celery in boiling water for 10 minutes. • Place half of cubed bread in the bottom of an ovenproof pan. • In a bowl, mix crabmeat, onion, mayonnaise, green pepper and celery and spread over bread cubes. Place remaining bread cubes over crab mixture. Mix eggs and milk and pour over all. Cover and refrigerate for at least 1 hour. • Remove casserole from refrigerator and bake in a 325° oven for 15 minutes. Spoon undiluted soup over casserole and sprinkle with paprika. Bake for 1 hour.

Senator and Mrs. Connie Mack
(Florida)

HOT WEATHER COQUILLES   Serves 4

"Guests like this light form of coquilles St. Jacques for summer."

2 medium-sized cucumbers
1½ cups well-seasoned white
    sauce

6½ ounces crabmeat or
    1 cup shrimp, salmon, tuna
    or flaked cooked fish
½ cup potato chips

Preheat oven to 350°. • Dice cucumbers and simmer in salted water until transparent, about 10 minutes. Drain well. • Combine with white sauce and crabmeat. Turn into 4 shells (or ramekins) and top with crushed potato chips. Bake for 15 minutes.

Nancy Ford

SEAFOOD BAKE   Serves 4 to 6

1 green pepper, diced
1 cup thinly sliced celery
8 ounces king crab or other
    crabmeat
1 cup shrimp

½ cup scallops, slightly cooked
1 cup mayonnaise
1 cup buttered breadcrumbs
Salt and pepper to taste

Preheat oven to 350°. • Mix pepper, celery, all of the seafood and mayonnaise and pour into a casserole or individual serving dishes. Cover with bread crumbs and bake for 30–45 minutes.

Mrs. John N. Parker

OYSTER CASSEROLE   Serves 4

24–28 medium oysters,
    shelled
3½ tablespoons butter
1½ cups water
1 chicken bouillon cube
3 tablespoons flour
2½ cups hot milk
1 cup crumbled saltine
    crackers, lightly mixed with
    2 tablespoons melted butter

Preheat oven to 350°. • Place oysters in a saucepan with 1½ tablespoons butter, water and bouillon cube. Bring to boil and simmer for 8 minutes. • In a separate saucepan, melt remaining 2 tablespoons butter and add flour. Stir to make a roux. Slowly add ½ cup hot milk, stirring. Set white sauce aside. • Drain oysters, reserving liquid. Add liquid to remaining 2 cups hot milk and bring to a boil. Add white sauce and stir until smooth. Simmer until sauce is medium thick. (If sauce does not thicken, mix a little sauce with 2–3 teaspoons flour in a cup and return to sauce.) • Spread a little sauce on the bottom of a small casserole. Sprinkle with half of the buttered cracker crumbs. Place oysters on crumbs and cover with remaining sauce. Sprinkle remaining cracker crumbs over sauce and bake for 20 minutes.

Senator Lauch Faircloth
(North Carolina)

BAKED SCALLOPS AND MUSHROOMS   Serves 4

1 pound scallops, either fresh
  or frozen
½ cup butter

½ cup fresh mushrooms, or
  4-ounce can mushrooms,
  drained

White sauce:
3 tablespoons butter
3 tablespoons flour

1 cup scalded milk
Salt and pepper to taste

Topping:
Buttered breadcrumbs

Preheat oven to 350°. • If scallops are very large, cut into bite-sized pieces. Over a low flame, sauté scallops in butter until tender. Remove from pan. If using fresh mushrooms, sauté in same pan until tender. Place scallops and mushrooms in a greased casserole. • For the sauce, melt butter in a double boiler. Add flour and stir until blended. Add hot milk gradually, stirring constantly. Continue cooking until thickened. Season with salt and pepper. • Cover scallops with white sauce and top with buttered breadcrumbs. Bake until breadcrumbs are brown and flavors are developed, about 30 minutes.

NOTE: For a buffet (to serve 12–15) use 4 pounds scallops, 2 cups fresh mushrooms or 4 4-ounce cans, and for sauce, ½ cup each butter and flour, and 1 quart milk. This amount will fit into a 13 x 9 x 2 inch pan or several small casseroles.

Mrs. Charles Carpenter

SALMON-WRAPPED SCALLOPS   Serves 6 to 10
WITH JADE SAUCE

"This recipe can be prepared with large scallops and served as a first course or with smaller scallops and served as an appetizer or hors d'oeuvre."

Salmon-wrapped scallops:

1 pound fresh scallops
2 tablespoons soy sauce
1 clove garlic, minced
Juice of ½ lime
1 tablespoon finely chopped dill (or basil, tarragon or cilantro)

1¼ pounds fresh salmon fillet
Freshly ground black pepper
Salt
4 tablespoons butter

Jade sauce:

¾ pound fresh spinach, washed and stemmed
2 scallions
½ bunch cilantro
10–12 fresh basil leaves
1 piece fresh ginger, peeled (about 1–1½ inches long)

2 tablespoons oyster sauce (available in Asian markets)
½ teaspoon crushed red pepper
½ teaspoon salt
1 cup heavy cream
1 tablespoon cornstarch mixed with 1 tablespoon water

Clean scallops and remove muscle, making sure they are free of sand and grit. Marinate for 1 hour in mixture of soy sauce, garlic, lime juice and dill. • Cut salmon into thin strips. Strips should be about ¼ inch wide and long enough to encircle scallop — about 4 inches for large scallops. (Salmon will slice more easily if partially frozen.) Season strips with a little salt and pepper. Wrap each scallop with a salmon strip and secure with toothpick. • Sauté gently over medium heat in butter, turning once (approximately 2 minutes per side). • To make jade sauce, finely mince spinach, scallions, herbs and ginger in a food processor fitted with steel blade. Add oyster sauce, crushed red pepper, salt and cream to greens and process 15 seconds longer. • Transfer sauce to pan and bring to simmer. Gradually add cornstarch mixture to sauce to bring to desired consistency and simmer 3 minutes longer. Taste for seasoning.

NOTE: Sauce may be made in advance, except for cooking, and refrigerated It should be cooked at the last minute.

Jon Jividen, Executive Chef
Ridgewell's

MOUSSELINE DE COQUILLES ST. JACQUES   Serves 4 to 6

14 ounces scallops
4 egg whites
½ cup heavy cream
Salt, pepper and nutmeg to
   taste

1 tablespoon very finely
   chopped parsley
4–6 shrimp
2 tomatoes, puréed and
   seasoned

Preheat oven to 350°. • In an electric blender, purée scallops until very fine.
Add egg whites, cream, salt, pepper, nutmeg and parsley. • Butter individual
molds and fill with scallop mixture. Cover with aluminum foil. Place in a pan
with enough water to reach ¾ the height of the molds. Bake for 15–20 minutes. Cool slightly. Unmold and decorate with a large shrimp on each. Serve
with well seasoned tomato coulis or sauce.

Mrs. Raoul Calvignac

SCALLOPS PAR EXCELLENCE   Serves 4

Scallops:
2 pounds sea scallops,
   well rinsed and halved
½ cup fresh lemon juice

White pepper to taste
¼ teaspoon salt

Dressing:
2 cloves garlic
1 small onion
¼ cup red wine vinegar
½ cup olive oil
1 heaping tablespoon
   Dijon mustard

⅓ teaspoon salt
White pepper to taste
Fresh dill (reserve some
   for garnish)

Garnish:
Shredded romaine lettuce
½ cup blanched snow peas
1 tablespoon pine nuts

Marinate scallops in lemon juice, white pepper and salt for 2 hours at room
temperature, or in refrigerator for one day. • For dressing, in a blender or food
processor, blend together garlic, onion, vinegar, olive oil, mustard, salt, white
pepper and dill. • Line individual ramekins with lettuce and snow peas.
Remove scallops from marinade and arrange on top. Add dressing. Sprinkle
with pine nuts and reserved dill.

NOTE: Serves 8 as an appetizer. If dressing is too thick, dilute with a little
of the marinade.

Anastasia Shaw

JEAN-LOUIS MAINE LOBSTER
AND LOBSTER CORN CAKES

Serves 4

4 live Maine lobsters, 1–1½ pounds each

Corn cakes:

Salt water (2 teaspoons coarse salt mixed with 2½ quarts water) for cooking corn

2 7-inch ears yellow corn, shucked

Ice water for cooling cooked corn

1¼ teaspoons unflavored gelatin

2 tablespoons cold lobster consommé or other consommé

5 1-inch long snippets of dill sprigs

½ cup heavy cream

½ teaspoon chives, sliced very finely

Fine sea salt and freshly ground pepper

Balsamic vinaigrette:

⅔ cup vegetable oil

2 teaspoons extra virgin olive oil

2 tablespoons balsamic vinegar

Fine sea salt and freshly ground black pepper

For serving:

4 cups mixture of small tender salad greens loosely packed (mâche, lamb's lettuce, radicchio, and frisée)

Sprigs of fresh dill for garnish

Special utensils:

Steamer or stockpot fitted with a deep basket

4 metal or wooden skewers longer than lobster tails but short enough to fit into steamer with basket and lid in place

Fine mesh strainer

5 flan molds, ¼-cup capacity, 2¼ inches in diameter at outside base

To prepare lobsters, bring to boil a large pot of water. Ease lobsters into boiling water head first. Cover and cook for precisely 1 minute. Drain on paper towels and cool. Protecting your hands with thick dish towels, break off big claws and reserve. Break off tails. Soft sides up, insert a metal or wooden skewer that is longer than lobster tail through the anal opening and push through the length of meat to keep tail flat when steaming. (Rest of body can be frozen for future use.) • Fill a steamer fitted with a deep basket with water and bring to a boil over high heat. Uncover and quickly add claws, then tails. Cover and steam until tail meat is cooked, about 4 minutes. Immediately, transfer tails to a dishtowel to drain. Cover steamer and continue cooking claws for another 3 minutes. Drain claws on towels. • With skewers still inserted, remove all shells from around tail meat, keeping meat intact. Remove shells from claw meat. Refrigerate tail and claw meat until ready to continue. • Remove from refrigerator and withdraw skewers from lobster tails. At thicker end of each tail, cut 6 diagonal ¼-inch thick slices, leaving about 2½ inches of tail in one piece. If meat is not completely cooked through, return to steamer but do not overcook. Set aside 14 slices of lobster, cover and refrigerate. Arrange remaining slices, uncut portions of tails and claw meat on 4 serving plates, leaving place for salad and corn cakes. Cover plates and refrigerate until serving time. This may be done several hours before serving. • To make corn cakes, bring 2½ quarts water with 2 teaspoons coarse salt to rolling boil in a large pot. Add corn and cook until tender, about 3 minutes. Drain and cool corn in ice water; drain again. Cut kernels off cobs and purée in a food processor. Strain corn purée, forcing corn through strainer with a sturdy ladle, to make about ½ cup. Set aside. • Soften ¼ teaspoon gelatin in consommé in a small saucepan for about 2 minutes. Cook over low heat until gelatin completely dissolves, 1–2 minutes, stirring constantly, and immediately pour into 5 small ungreased flan molds. Arrange a snippet of dill on each portion. Place molds on a cookie sheet and refrigerate until jelled, at least 10 minutes. • Whip 6 tablespoons of cream in a chilled medium-sized bowl just until soft peaks form. Refrigerate. • Heat remaining 2 tablespoons cream and 1 teaspoon gelatin over low heat until cream is hot and gelatin dissolves, about 3 minutes, stirring constantly. Remove from heat and continue stirring until cool, about 2 minutes. Working as quickly as possible, gradually add gelatin and cream mixture to reserved whipped cream, folding in with a rubber spatula. Fold in corn purée and chives to blend. Do not overmix. Season generously with salt and pepper. Spoon 1 scant tablespoon batter into each chilled flan mold and smooth surface. Top with 1 slice of reserved lobster tail meat, another scant tablespoon batter, another slice of lobster meat and fill mold to the top with batter. Expel air bubbles by gently tapping molds on a flat surface. Refrigerate until firm, at least 30 minutes. If made several hours before use, keep refrigerated. • To make vinaigrette, combine all ingredients in a medium-sized bowl and whisk together until thoroughly blended. • To serve, remove chilled plates from refrigerator and unwrap. Unmold lobster corn cakes by placing one of molds in a small pan filled with 1¼ inches of very hot water for exactly 45 seconds. Remove mold from hot water, insert a thin flexible-blade knife between cake and mold to create an air pocket, and invert onto serving plate. Repeat with 3 additional molds. Brush lobster meat with vinaigrette and toss salad greens with enough remaining vinaigrette to lightly coat leaves. • Arrange greens on each plate to resemble a flower and garnish centers with lobster slices. Garnish lobster slices with dill sprigs and serve immediately.

Jean-Louis
Jean-Louis Restaurant

THE 60-HOUR GOURMET

RECIPES FOR PEOPLE WHO HAVE TIME TO SPARE, AND THEN SOME

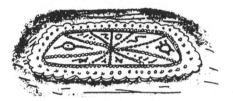

Painstakin' Peas

Before cooking, peel six hundred peas. Boil. Then arrange in a festive manner on a serving platter.

Never-Ending Bread

Mix bread dough as usual. Let rise until double. Punch down. Let rise again. Punch down. Let rise. Punch down. Let rise. Punch down. Rise. Punch. Rise, punch, rise, punch, rise. Bake and serve.

Slow 'n' Steady Chicken

Wash chicken in a lukewarm bubble bath for ± one hour. Then rinse for thirty minutes. Stuff with Difficult Stuffing*, using a doll spoon, and truss with an itsy-bitsy needle and the teensy-weensiest stitch you can. Cook at 125°F. for 32 hours. Just prior to serving, carve into the shape of a rose.

   * see page 883

Handmade Carrot Juice

Begin by mincing raw carrots with a butter knife. Then keep going until the whole thing reaches a liquid consistency.

R. Chast

Drawing by R. Chast; ©1994
The New Yorker Magazine, Inc.

CHINGRI CUTLETS
(PRAWN CUTLET CURRY)

Serves 4

"I am happy to enclose a favorite recipe of ours. As a point of interest this is a family recipe from the vast collection of the Ambassador's maternal grandmother."

Cutlets:

8 large prawns
1 small onion, ground or
   grated
1 small piece of ginger,
   ground to a fine paste
2 cloves garlic, minced

Juice of ½ lime
Salt to taste
1 egg
1 tablespoon flour
1 cup toasted breadcrumbs
Oil for frying

Sauce (optional):

2 cups fresh coconut milk
   (obtained by grating the
   meat of 1 coconut into 2¼
   cups water)
1 teaspoon salt

Sugar to taste
6–8 green chilies, chopped fine
Juice from 2 limes
1 tablespoon cumin seed, fried
   and ground to a powder

Chop off heads of prawns, peel, devein and keep tails intact. With a sharp knife, cut prawns almost in half down the back. Flatten the two halves with a mallet or flat end of a bread knife. Beat prawns to ⅛-inch thickness. Shape by rounding the upper portion of prawns, i.e., the portion away from the tail, and taper it down toward the tail to look something like an elongated balloon. • Place prawns in a flat dish and coat with onion, ginger paste, garlic and lime juice. Sprinkle with a little salt and marinate for several hours, turning once or twice. • Beat together egg and flour with a little salt. One at a time, dip prawns in egg mixture, then into breadcrumbs. Heat oil in a frying pan until just smoking and fry prawns to a golden brown color. • To make coconut milk, combine grated coconut and water. Simmer until foamy and drain through cheese cloth. Set aside. • To make sauce, bring coconut milk to a boil. Reduce heat. Add salt, sugar and chilies and simmer until milk is thickened and creamy. Add prawn cutlets and simmer for another 10 minutes. • Remove from heat and sprinkle lime juice over cutlets. Carefully remove cutlets to a serving dish and cover with sauce. Sprinkle with cumin and serve.

Maya Ray
Wife of the Ambassador of India

CURRIED SHRIMP IN RICE RING   Serves 8

"Excellent to serve cold as a main dish with salad or on a buffet."

1 small onion
2 bay leaves
Juice of ½ lemon
5 peppercorns
½ teaspoon dried thyme
½ teaspoon dried dill
Salt to taste
1 quart water
1½ cups long-grain rice

½ teaspoon saffron
1 pound medium-sized shrimp
    cut into ½-inch pieces
1 cup mayonnaise
1 medium onion, grated
1 tablespoon curry powder
1 tablespoon chopped fresh dill
Parsley sprigs

Place onion, bay leaves, lemon juice, peppercorns, thyme, dried dill and salt in water and bring to a rolling boil. Boil for 15 minutes. Add the shrimp, boil for 1 minute, drain and allow to cool. • When cool, mix shrimp with mayonnaise, grated onion, curry powder and dill. Refrigerate. • Boil rice according to package directions. Add saffron. • Wipe a ring mold with a wet cloth and fill with rice. Pack full and let sit for 1 hour. Invert onto a platter. • Fill the inside of the rice ring with shrimp mixture and decorate with parsley sprigs.

Mrs. Albert deP. d'Amecourt

PENANG SHRIMP CURRY   Serves 6 to 8

4 ounces butter
1 clove garlic, crushed
1 large onion, peeled and
    finely chopped
3 stalks celery, chopped
1 green pepper, seeded and
    chopped
1 tart apple, peeled, cored
    and chopped
1 carrot, peeled and sliced
2 tomatoes, peeled, seeded
    and chopped
1 tablespoon chopped parsley
1 bay leaf, crumbled
Pinch of thyme
Pinch of marjoram

Pinch of dried mint
2 whole cloves
¼ teaspoon basil
2½ tablespoons flour
1 tablespoon curry powder
½ teaspoon salt
½ teaspoon pepper
¼ teaspoon cayenne pepper
¼ teaspoon nutmeg
1½ cups beef consommé
1 cup dry white wine
2 pounds freshly boiled shrimp,
    shelled and cleaned
1 cup rice
Fresh parsley, finely chopped

Melt butter in a large saucepan and add garlic, onion, celery, green pepper, apple, carrot, tomatoes, parsley, bay leaf, thyme, marjoram, mint, cloves and basil. When vegetables are soft, sprinkle with a mixture of flour, curry pow-

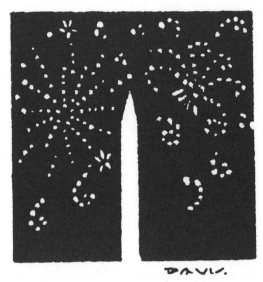

der, salt, pepper, cayenne pepper and nutmeg and mix well. Continue stirring and cooking for about 5 minutes. Slowly add consommé, stirring. When mixture thickens, add wine. Cook over low heat for about 30 minutes, uncovered. • Decide if you want a thick or thin sauce. If you prefer a thick sauce, add shrimp to sauce at this point and cook for 10 minutes. If you prefer a thin sauce, strain the sauce and add shrimp. Simmer for 10 minutes. • Cook rice and mold into a ring. To serve, pour shrimp curry into center of ring and sprinkle with parsley. Serve with an assortment of condiments, such as chutney, chopped peanuts, finely chopped crisp bacon, finely chopped lemon rind, chopped hard-boiled egg white, chopped hard-boiled egg yolk, flaked coconut, chopped chives, seedless raisins , finely chopped scallions, or lemon wedges.

NOTE: Cooked roast lamb may be substituted.

Karin G. Weber

PRAWN MALAI CURRY   Serves 4

1 pound large prawns or shrimp, shelled and deveined
½ coconut, finely grated
1 teaspoon salt
½ teaspoon turmeric

1 teaspoon cumin seed
4 tablespoons oil
½–¾ cup water
1 green or red pepper, cut into fine strips

Mix prawns with grated coconut, salt, tumeric and cumin. Marinate for 30 minutes. • Heat oil in pan and add prawns. Sauté for 5 minutes and add water. Cook until tender and gravy has thickened. Add pepper strips and stir well. Remove from heat and serve with rice.

Usha Kaul

BAKED SHRIMP WITH PEPPERS AND ONIONS

Serves 6 to 8

¾ cup olive oil
½ cup butter
3 white onions, sliced on diagonal
5 red bell peppers, roasted, seeded and sliced in strips
5 green bell peppers, roasted, seeded and sliced in strips
½ teaspoon salt

¼ teaspoon ground black pepper
2 pounds medium shrimp, shelled and deveined
8 ounces Oaxaca, Manchego or Muenster cheese, grated
8 ounces Monterey Jack cheese, shredded or grated

Preheat oven to 325°. • Heat oil and butter in a large skillet over medium heat and brown onions. Add peppers and cook over low heat for 15 minutes. Season with salt and pepper. Stir in shrimp and cook for 5 minutes. Correct seasoning. • Spoon mixture into a casserole and cover with cheeses. Bake for 20 minutes, or until cheeses have melted.

Mrs. Lloyd Bentsen
Wife of the Secretary of the Treasury

SHRIMP AND CHICKEN JAMBALAYA

Serves 6

6 ounces shrimp
6 ounces boned chicken breast
1 tablespoon crushed garlic
Pinch of red pepper
Pinch of thyme
Pinch of oregano
1 teaspoon butter
Salt and black pepper to taste
6 ounces cooked ham

6 ounces Tasso ham
6 ounces Andouille sausage
1 cup diced bell pepper
1 cup chopped celery
1 cup diced onion
1 cup diced tomato
3 ounces spaghetti sauce
1 bay leaf
2 tablespoons roux

Preheat oven to 350°. • Peel shrimp and set aside. • Dice chicken and put in pan with garlic, red pepper, thyme, oregano, butter, salt and black pepper. Bake this mixture for 25–30 minutes. • Dice hams and sausage and place in a saucepan with bell pepper, celery, onion, tomato, spaghetti sauce and bay leaf. Over low heat, bring to a boil. Add cooked chicken pieces and juices. Thicken with roux. Add shrimp. Jambalaya is done when the shrimp turns opaque. Serve immediately.

The Comus Inn
Clarksburg, Maryland

EGGPLANT STUFFED WITH SHRIMP AND CRABMEAT

Serves 6

3 medium eggplants
1 medium white onion, finely chopped
1 small bunch scallions with tops, chopped
½ red bell pepper, chopped
½ green bell pepper, chopped
2 stalks celery, finely chopped
3 tablespoons olive oil
6 large cloves garlic, minced
½ teaspoon dried thyme
1 teaspoon dried oregano

1 large tomato, peeled and chopped
1 pound fresh small shrimp, peeled and deveined
1 pound crabmeat
1½ cups seasoned breadcrumbs
2 eggs, well beaten
6 tablespoons chopped parsley
Salt and freshly ground pepper to taste
3 dashes Tabasco sauce
1 tablespoon butter or margarine, melted

Preheat oven to 350°. • Slice eggplants in half lengthwise and parboil for about 10 minutes or cook in microwave for 5 minutes, until soft. Cool and scoop out pulp, saving shells for stuffing. Place eggplant pulp in a large bowl and set aside. • In a large skillet, sauté onion, scallions, peppers and celery in olive oil for about 5 minutes, until soft. Add garlic, thyme, oregano and tomato. Stir well and cook for 2 minutes. Add shrimp, crabmeat, 1 cup breadcrumbs, eggs, parsley, salt, pepper, Tabasco sauce and reserved eggplant pulp. Mix well. Fill eggplant shells with mixture. Arrange shells in a shallow baking dish containing ¼ cup water. Top each shell with remaining breadcrumbs and melted butter or margarine. • Bake for 35–40 minutes, until top is brown. These may be frozen and reheated.

Mrs. J. Bennett Johnston
Wife of the Senator from Louisiana

LOUISIANA SHRIMP RÉMOULADE   Serves 8

Shrimp:

1 medium onion, chopped
½ lemon, sliced
1 teaspoon Tabasco sauce
1 teaspoon red pepper
2 tablespoons salt

Celery tops
1 package Shrimp Boil Mix
4 pounds medium or large
   shrimp, fresh or frozen,
   with or without shells

Fill a large pot ¾ full of water. Bring to boil and add all above ingredients except shrimp. Boil for 20–30 minutes. Add fresh or defrosted shrimp. Cook medium shrimp with shells for 6 minutes; large shrimp with shells for 8 minutes; peeled shrimp for 3–4 minutes. Do not overcook; shrimp will get tough and mealy. • Remove shrimp and rinse in cold water. If necessary, shell and devein. Cool. While cooling, make marinade.

Marinade:

1½ cups Creole or Dijon
   mustard
½ cup tarragon vinegar
1½ cups vegetable oil
¼ teaspoon sugar
4 teaspoons salt
4 teaspoons paprika

1½ teaspoons cayenne pepper
3 medium garlic cloves, pressed
1 cup chopped scallions
1 cup chopped onions
½ cup chopped celery
2 tablespoons ketchup

Place all above ingredients in blender and process until chopped, but not puréed. Pour over cooled shrimp and refrigerate for several hours.

Assembly and garnish:

Lettuce
Sliced tomatoes

Cucumber slices
Chopped parsley

Arrange lettuce leaves and tomato slices on each plate. Top with marinated shrimp. Garnish with cucumber slices and chopped parsley.

NOTE: This dish can be served as an appetizer or as a main course.

Mrs. Russell Long

SHRIMP LINGUINI MARINARA   Serves 4

1 medium onion, chopped
1 clove garlic, chopped
1 teaspoon dried basil
1 teaspoon salt
1 teaspoon parsley, chopped
5 tablespoons olive oil
1 14- to 16-ounce can Italian
   tomatoes

1 tablespoon butter
1 pound medium shrimp,
   shelled and deveined
¼ teaspoon garlic powder
¼ teaspoon pepper
1 pound linguini

Sauté first five ingredients in 1 tablespoon olive oil until onions are transparent. Stir in tomatoes and add butter. • Sauté shrimp in remaining 4 tablespoons olive oil. Add shrimp, garlic powder and pepper to onions and tomatoes. Set aside and keep warm. • Cook linguini al dente and drain. Pour shrimp sauce over linguini and serve.

Anna Maria Via

TAGIN OF GAMBARY   Serves 4 to 6
(SPECIAL SHRIMP DISH)

1 medium onion, chopped
4 tablespoons corn oil
2 cloves garlic, finely chopped
2 stalks celery, chopped
1 teaspoon chopped parsley

3 medium-sized tomatoes
Juice of 3 limes
1 cup tomato juice
30–36 shrimp, cleaned and
   deveined

Preheat oven to 350°. • Heat oil in a 12-inch skillet. Sauté onion in oil until golden. Add garlic, celery, parsley, 2 diced tomatoes, juice of 2 limes and tomato juice. Let the mixture boil for 2 minutes. • Arrange shrimp in one layer in a baking dish. Pour the mixture over shrimp and top with slices of remaining tomato and lime juice. Bake for 30 minutes, or until top is golden and crisp. • Serve with white rice.

Mrs. Ahmed Maher el Sayed
Wife of Ambassador of Egypt

SHRIMP AND CRAB "POULETTE"   Serves 12

"A marvelous buffet dinner dish."

1 cup butter	2 cups milk
1 small onion, chopped	2 cups heavy cream
32 large shrimp, peeled	1 teaspoon lemon juice
and deveined	Salt and pepper to taste
½ cup dry white wine	3 egg yolks
½ cup sherry	2 cups lump crabmeat
¾ cup flour	

Melt ¼ cup butter in saucepan. Sauté onion until soft and push to side of pan. Add shrimp and cook over medium heat 5 minutes. Add white wine and sherry and bring mixture to a boil. Remove from heat. • In a separate large saucepan, melt remaining butter, add flour and stir with wire whisk until blended. Add milk and cream, stirring constantly until sauce is thickened and smooth. Season sauce with lemon juice, salt and pepper. • Lightly beat egg yolks with a little of the sauce and add to the rest of the sauce, stirring constantly. Combine sauce with the shrimp mixture. Stir thoroughly. Add crabmeat. • "Poulette" may be simmered for 5 minutes and served immediately, or it may be made several hours ahead. In this case, keep in refrigerator until ready to cook. Heat in chafing dish or casserole in preheated 350° oven about 20 minutes.

Mrs. Lewis R. Townsend

TEMPURA

Your favorite seafood, such	1 egg yolk
as shrimp, scallops, squid,	1 cup flour, sifted, plus
white meat fish or soft-shell	additional flour for dusting
crab	Vegetable oil
Your favorite vegetables, such	3 tablespoons sesame oil
as onion, sweet potato,	
pumpkin, shiitake	
mushrooms, asparagus,	
eggplant or green squash	

Cut seafood into 1½ -inch squares. If using shrimp, shell and devein, leaving tail on. Then cut edge of the tail and squeeze out water by pressing with the side of knife. • Cut vegetables into pieces ½–⅓ inch thick. • Prepare batter by mixing egg yolk with very cold water to make 1 cup. All at once add flour and mix with chopsticks until ingredients are loosely combined. Do not stir too much, as batter will become sticky. • Place vegetable oil in deep fryer to fill half the pan. Add sesame oil and heat to 320°-350°. To test, drop a bit of

batter into oil. It should sink halfway and then return to surface. If it sinks to the bottom, oil is not hot enough. • Dust seafood with a thin coating of flour and dip into batter. Dip vegetables into batter. Fry small amounts of seafood and vegetables until golden and well cooked. (To prevent oil temperature from dropping, fry small amounts at a time so as not to cover more than 60% of the total oil surface.) Lift cooked pieces from oil and drain. Arrange tempura on paper to keep crispy.

Tempura sauce:

2 cups water
½ cup soy sauce
½ cup mirin (Japanese sweet rice wine)
½ cup katsuo-bushi (dried bonito flakes)

Daikon (white radish), if desired
Slices of lemon for flavor, if desired

Place water, soy sauce, mirin and katsuo-bushi in a saucepan and bring to a boil. Remove from heat and strain to remove katsuo-bushi flakes. Grate daikon and drain excess water. Add a small amount of daikon to sauce, if desired. • To serve, put sauce in bowl and surround with tempura. Garnish with lemon slices, if desired.

Mrs. Takakazu Kuriyama
Wife of the Ambassador of Japan

VATAPA   Serves 20 to 25

2 coconuts
½ loaf French bread
2½ pounds dried, peeled
   shrimp (available at
   oriental markets)
5 pounds fish steaks which
   have been fried with
   2 tablespoons oil, 2 grated
   onions and 2 chopped
   tomatoes

2 green peppers
2 onions
1 pound fresh tomatoes
3 coriander seeds
Salt and pepper to taste
3 cloves garlic, minced
2 cups dendê oil
2½ pounds fresh shrimp,
   peeled and cleaned

Remove the thick milk from coconuts and set aside. Grate coconut meat, add 4 quarts of water to the grated coconut meat, and squeeze out thin coconut milk. Remove crust from bread and soak in thin coconut milk. • Place dried shrimp in blender and grind. • Cut fish steaks into strips and place in very large pan. Add ground shrimp, bread and thin coconut milk. • Chop green peppers, onions, tomatoes and coriander and add to fish mixture. Season with salt, pepper and garlic. Add the dendê oil and raw shrimp and cook over low heat until shrimp is cooked and some of the liquid has evaporated. • When cooked, remove from heat and add thick coconut milk. Serve with rice and hot sauce.

Mrs. María Luiza Penna Moreira
Embassy of Brazil

Poultry and Game

CHICKEN AND SWEETBREAD CASSEROLE   Serves 6 to 8

Sweetbreads:

1–1½ pounds sweetbreads   1 teaspoon salt
1 tablespoon vinegar

Chicken:

3 chicken breasts, split   2 stalks celery
1 whole onion   2 teaspoons salt

Sauce:

½ pound fresh mushrooms,   1 cup light cream
  thinly sliced   Juice of 1 lemon
1 onion, finely chopped   3 tablespoons white vermouth
6 tablespoons butter   1 teaspoon seasoned salt
4 tablespoons flour   Grated Parmesan cheese
1½ cups chicken stock   Breadcrumbs

Drop sweetbreads into enough boiling water to cover. Add vinegar and salt and simmer for 25 minutes. Remove and place sweetbreads in cold water. Remove as much membrane as possible and cube sweetbreads. • Poach chicken in 6 cups water, to which onion, celery and salt have been added. Drain and cube chicken and discard onion and celery. • To make sauce, sauté mushrooms and chopped onion in 2 tablespoons butter. Set aside. • Melt remaining 4 tablespoons butter. Add flour, chicken stock, cream and lemon juice, stirring. Cook until it thickens. Add vermouth and salt. Add sautéed mushrooms, onion, seasoned salt and mix. • Place chicken and sweetbread cubes in a casserole and cover with sauce. Refrigerate over-night. • To serve, bring to room temperature and sprinkle cheese and breadcrumbs over casserole. Bake at 375° for 20 minutes.

Paula Jeffries

CHICKEN BREASTS AND VEGETABLE FRICASSEE

Serves 4

½ cup dry white wine
½ cup chicken broth
½ teaspoon salt
½ teaspoon thyme
¼ teaspoon tarragon
Pepper to taste
1 pound chicken breasts, boned and skinned

¼ cup flour
¼ cup butter or margarine
½ pound snow peas
2 small yellow squash, cleaned, quartered and cut into 2-inch strips

Mix together wine, broth, salt, thyme, tarragon and pepper. Set aside. • Dip chicken breasts into flour and gently shake off excess. Set aside. • In a large skillet, melt butter or margarine over medium heat. Brown chicken on both sides, about five minutes. Remove chicken from skillet and set aside. • Add broth/wine mixture to butter in skillet and bring to a boil, stirring constantly. Reduce heat to medium and add snow peas. Cook for 2 minutes. Add squash and return chicken to skillet. Cook, uncovered, for 3 minutes, or until chicken is cooked, stirring occasionally.

Senator Dale Bumpers
(Arkansas)

BINNIE BUNS

Serves 4

2 whole chicken breasts, skinned and boned
1 large loaf of French bread
8 tablespoons butter, melted

6 small bell peppers or roasted peppers in a jar
6 slices prosciutto or other ham
Sweet or hot paprika

Pound chicken breasts thin. • Cut bread in half crosswise, then split each half horizontally to make sandwiches. To make buns, cut split halves into thirds or quarters. Melt butter in a baking pan with low sides. Dip soft parts of buns into butter and arrange bottom halves in a single layer. • Preheat oven to 400°. • Cut chicken, peppers and prosciutto to fit buns and layer bottom parts of buns in that order. Sprinkle with paprika and sandwich with top bun. If necessary, secure with toothpicks. • Bake for 15 minutes, until bread is crisply browned. At this point, chicken will be done.

NOTE: Turkey breast, veal scaloppine, tomato slices and/or cheese, may be substituted for chicken, ham and peppers.

Helen Worth
Cookbook Author and Teacher

BRAVO! CHICKEN   Serves 4 to 6

"Good for a buffet."

3 whole boneless chicken
   breasts, cut in half
1 tablespoon chopped
   scallions
1 clove of garlic, minced
2 tablespoons olive or
   peanut oil
¼ cup Marsala wine

½ teaspoon curry powder
⅓–½ cup fresh orange juice
Salt and pepper to taste
4 tablespoons unsalted butter,
   cold and cut into small pieces
6 slices of orange or
   18 sections of mandarin
   oranges

In a large skillet, brown chicken breasts, scallions and garlic in oil over medium heat. Turn once. • Add Marsala and cover. Reduce heat and cook for 5 minutes. • Remove chicken to a platter and keep warm. • Add curry powder and orange juice to skillet with cooking juices, scallions and garlic. Increase heat and reduce liquid. Add salt and pepper. Add butter pieces and remove sauce from heat. • Place orange slices or mandarin orange sections over chicken pieces and top with sauce. • Can be made in advance to this point and refrigerated. When ready to serve, heat through in 300° oven for 30 minutes. • Serve with rice and a salad.

Mrs. Porter K. Wheeler

CHICKEN BREAST DINNER   Serves 12 to 16

8 whole chicken breasts,
   skinned, boned and halved
16 slices bacon
1 can cream of mushroom soup

1½ cups sour cream
¾ cup milk
1 8-ounce package dried beef

Preheat oven to 350°. • Butter a large baking dish. Roll one slice of bacon around each chicken piece and arrange in prepared dish. • In a saucepan, combine soup, sour cream and milk over low heat. • Cut dried beef into small squares and add ¾ of beef to soup mixture. Heat. Pour warm soup mixture over chicken and bake for about 1 hour, or until almost done. Sprinkle remaining beef over chicken and continue baking for 10 minutes.

Senator Paul D. Coverdell
(Georgia)

COUNTRY CHICKEN WITH MOREL MUSHROOMS

Serves 4

7 ounces morel mushrooms,
  carefully washed
4 tablespoons oil
7 tablespoons butter
2 tablespoons finely chopped
  shallots

1 2–3 pound chicken, cut
  into pieces
Salt and pepper to taste
2.5 ounces Calvados
3 cups fresh cream

In a frying pan, cook mushrooms in 2 tablespoons oil and 3 tablespoons butter. Add the shallots. Cook approximately 10 minutes and put aside. • In a shallow casserole, heat remaining butter and oil. Cook chicken pieces slowly on moderate heat turning often for about 6–8 minutes. Add salt and pepper to taste. Add the Calvados and light flame to singe while stirring. Add the fresh cream, cover and cook for 25–30 minutes. Add the mushrooms before end of cooking. • Serve the chicken with mushrooms accompanied by rice.

Pamela Harr iman
U.S. Ambassador to France

BROCCOLI-CHICKEN CASSEROLE

Serves 4

2 10-ounce packages frozen
  broccoli
4 chicken breast halves
3 tablespoons butter

1 package Hollandaise sauce
1 can cream of chicken soup
⅔ cup milk
2 tablespoons white wine

Preheat oven to 350°. • Cook broccoli according to package directions. • In a skillet, sauté chicken breasts in butter. Combine broccoli and chicken in a large casserole. • In a small bowl, combine Hollandaise sauce, soup, milk and white wine and pour over chicken and broccoli. • Cover and bake for 20 minutes.

Senator and Mrs. Connie Mack
(Florida)

CONCUBINE DELIGHT   Serves 6 to 8

2 pounds chicken breasts,
    skinned, boned and sliced
3 egg whites, lightly beaten
Dash of salt
Dash of pepper
2 tablespoons Cointreau
1 tablespoon honey
½ pound snow peas or
    ½ pound green peppers,
    sliced
12 dried mushrooms, sliced
    and soaked overnight

2 or 3 slices ham, minced
A few scallion stalks
Peanut or salad oil
1 tablespoon minced fresh
    ginger or 1 tablespoon
    chopped preserved ginger
1 tablespoon cornstarch
¼ cup chicken broth
¼ cup soy sauce
Lemon juice to taste

Mix chicken slices with egg whites, salt, pepper, 1 tablespoon Cointreau and
½ tablespoon honey. • In a large skillet, sauté snow peas or green peppers,
dried mushrooms, ham and scallions in oil. • In medium skillet, sauté chick-
en. Add ginger. • In a small saucepan, blend cornstarch with chicken broth,
soy sauce, lemon juice, remaining Cointreau and honey. Bring to a boil, stirring constantly. Boil for 1 minute, until slightly thickened. Remove from heat.
• In the large skillet, add chicken to snow peas. Lightly sauté again. Pour in
hot chicken broth sauce. • Serve with rice cooked in tomato juice or noodles.

NOTE: This may be prepared the day before and reheated before serving.

Anna Chenault

COUSCOUS CHICKEN FROM ALGERIA   Serves 4 to 6

1 chicken, cut into pieces
¼ cup olive oil
2 tablespoons clarified butter
1 onion, sliced into rounds
1 large ripe tomato
½ teaspoon freshly ground
    pepper
1 cinnamon stick

½ teaspoon salt
1½ cup water, plus more as
    needed
¼ cup dried chickpeas, soaked
    overnight
12 ounces couscous or use
    packaged 5-minute couscous

In a large pot, combine chicken, oil, butter, onion, tomato, pepper, cinnamon
and salt. Stir over medium heat to brown chicken for about 5 minutes. Add
1½ cups water to cover and bring to a boil. Add chickpeas and simmer, covered, for 30–40 minutes, until chicken is tender. Remove chicken pieces and
set aside. • Continue simmering the mixture in the pot for 1½ hours or until
chickpeas are tender, adding more water if necessary to retain roughly the
same level. When chickpeas are done, return chicken to the pot to heat thor-

oughly. • To prepare couscous the traditional North African way, cover with cold water and allow to sit for 10 minutes. Drain off excess water and scrape damp grain onto a clean linen towel or absorbent cloth. Allow grain to swell for 15 minutes. Line a colander with cheesecloth (so that grains will not fall through colander holes), place grains inside and place over boiling water. Steam, uncovered for 20 minutes. • Return couscous to bowl or onto a towel. Sprinkle with about ½ cup of cold water and rub grains between your fingers to break up any lumps. Allow to sit for 10 minutes. Grease your fingers with oil and rub grains once again. Finally, steam the couscous again for 25 additional minutes. • To serve, place couscous in a large bowl and pour over it as much liquid from the stew as couscous can absorb. Place chicken in the center of couscous and spoon chickpeas and remaining liquid over all. • The sauce may be frozen. The steamed couscous may be refrigerated and then warmed before serving.

Ali Rebatchi

PAKISTANI CHICKEN CURRY   Serves 4

1 chicken	Crushed red pepper flakes
3 tablespoons vegetable oil	to taste
3 medium onions	1 stick cinnamon
3–4 cloves garlic	3–4 whole cloves
1 teaspoon grated fresh ginger	3–4 cardamom seeds
1 tablespoon coriander	Salt to taste
1 teaspoon cumin	½ cup yogurt
1 teaspoon ground red pepper	10 sprigs fresh cilantro leaves

Skin chicken and cut into 8 pieces. Fry in oil until golden and remove from pan. • Chop onions and brown. Crush garlic and ginger, mix together and add to onions. Fry for a few minutes, stirring. • Mix ground spices with water to make a paste and add remaining seasonings except cilantro leaves to onion mixture. Cook for a few minutes. Add yogurt and return chicken to pan. Stir to coat chicken evenly with sauce. Add water if necessary. Cover and cook for 20 minutes. Uncover and continue cooking to evaporate most of liquid, stirring frequently. Chop cilantro leaves and add to curry a few minutes before serving.

Cecille Burney

DYNAMITE CHICKEN AND
NO-BRAIN COUSCOUS

Serves 4 to 6

"The combination of spicy chicken and onion-sweet couscous is enough to make you swear off expensive restaurants for at least a week...But this recipe doesn't work with your garden variety chicken."

1 2½–3 pound free-range
   frying chicken of the best
   quality
Red pepper flakes
Kosher salt
Extra virgin olive oil
1 large onion, coarsely
   chopped

2 tablespoons butter
1 cup water
1½ teaspoons salt
1 cup tipiak couscous
   (medium grain, does not
   need precooking)
Lemon wedges

With a very sharp knife, cut through to breast bone of the chicken. Using your knife to scrape meat from bone, remove breast and wishbone. Turn butterflied chicken over and press on back to break ribs. This will give you a whole chicken of uniform thickness, ready to broil. Rub chicken liberally with red pepper, kosher salt and olive oil in that order. Allow to stand for 1 hour. • Cover a broiling pan with aluminum foil and place in oven while you heat broiler. Place chicken on hot broiler pan and broil on each side for 15 minutes. It should be brown on the outside but firm and moist on the inside. • While chicken is broiling, soften onion in butter in a heavy saucepan with lid. Add water and salt and bring to a boil. Add couscous and remove saucepan from heat. Stir well. Cover and let stand for 5 minutes. Fluff with fork. • Pour a few drops of olive oil over chicken just before serving and garnish with lemon wedges. Serve with couscous. All you need to complete this meal is watercress salad and a fresh ripe peach.

Sidney Moore, Author
"Sidney Moore's Favorite Recipes"
(Sutton Place Gourmet)

ROSEMARY CHICKEN

Serves 6 to 8

10–12 chicken pieces
1 cup soy sauce

2 tablespoons minced rosemary
Juice of 2 lemons

Place chicken pieces in ovenproof casserole, skin side up. Pour soy sauce over chicken and sprinkle with rosemary. Pour lemon juice over all and bake at 350° for 45 minutes. This may be served hot or cold.

Sydney Ferguson

SKEWERED BABY CHICKEN EN CRAPAUDINE   Serves 2

2 small chickens (about 1 pound each) or 1 Cornish hen
Vegetable oil for broiler rack

Cilantro sprigs for garnish

Marinade:

1 small onion, peeled and quartered
2 garlic cloves, peeled and halved
½ cup plain yogurt
1 tablespoon coriander

1 teaspoon paprika
1 teaspoon ginger
Pinch of cayenne
2 tablespoons lime juice
Salt and pepper to taste

Set chicken, breast side down, on a board. Cut along each side of backbone with poultry shears and discard backbone. Trim flaps of skin and cut off wing tips. Force bird open and snip wishbone. Wipe inside with paper towels. With breast side up and legs turned in, push down sharply on breast of chicken with the heel of your hand to break breastbone and flatten bird. Make a small cut in skin between leg and breast bone and tuck in leg knuckles. Thread a skewer through the wings to hold bird flat. Thread a second skewer through legs. Repeat for second bird. • To make marinade, combine marinade ingredients and purée in a food processor. Transfer to a shallow baking dish. Add skewered chickens and coat with marinade. Cover and refrigerate for at least 3 hours. • Heat broiler and brush broiler rack with oil. Scrape marinade from birds, dry with paper towels and set them on oiled broiling rack, skin side up. Broil birds 5 inches from heat, basting once with marinade, for about 15 minutes. Turn, baste again and broil for another 10 minutes. Turn again, breast side up, brush with marinade and continue broiling until well done, about 10 to 15 minutes longer. To test, pierce thigh with a knife—the juice should run clear, not pink. Remove skewers and garnish with cilantro sprigs and serve.

Anne Willan, President
École de Cuisine, La Varenne

CHICKEN EN GELÉE WITH GREEN SAUCE   Serves 12

"This dish should be prepared one day in advance."

3 medium-sized chickens	2 tablespoons chopped
2 carrots	fresh tarragon or
2 stalks celery	2 teaspoons dried
1 leek	Juice of 1 lemon
1 large onion	½ cup Madeira wine
	2 envelopes unflavored gelatin
	Salt and pepper to taste

In a large pot cover chickens, carrots, celery, leek and onion with water and boil until tender. • Allow to cool and skim off the grease. Remove chicken and vegetables and strain cooking juices through cheesecloth. To the strained juices, add tarragon, lemon juice and wine. Mix well. • Soften gelatin in water and add to soup. • Remove skin from chicken, discard bones and cut chicken meat into bite-sized pieces. Arrange in a large glass dish or casserole. • Pour soup over chicken pieces to cover. Refrigerate overnight. • When jellied, garnish with parsley and serve with sauce verte.

Sauce verte:
1 bunch fresh dill
1½ cups mayonnaise

Place dill in food processor and grind, or chop finely by hand. Combine dill with mayonnaise, season to taste, and serve in a sauce boat.

Mrs. Albert deP. d'Amecourt

GROUND CHICKEN CUTLETS   Serves 4 to 6

2 whole chicken breasts	2¼ cups white breadcrumbs
(about 2 pounds), skinned,	13 tablespoons unsalted butter,
boned and cut into small	softened
pieces (see note)	¾ teaspoon salt
1 tablespoon chopped onion	¼ teaspoon white pepper
¼ cup milk	5 tablespoons oil

Grind chicken and onion twice through the finest blade of a meat grinder. Combine ground chicken with milk. Add ¼ cup breadcrumbs and mix well. Add 8 tablespoons softened butter, salt and pepper. Beat until mixture is smooth, cover and refrigerate for at least 2 hours. • Dip your fingers in cold water and shape the chicken mixture into oval patties, each about 1½ inches thick. Roll patties in remaining breadcrumbs to coat thoroughly. • Fry patties in remaining butter and oil over moderate heat, about 5 minutes on each side. • Serve at once. • Alternatively, place cooked chicken patties in a casserole and cover with your favorite white sauce. Cover and refrigerate. Bake at 350° for 35–45 minutes and serve with rice or noodles.

NOTE: This recipe may be made with fish (adding lemon juice), veal or pork.

Mrs. G. William Miller

BAKED IMPERIAL CHICKEN WITH CUMBERLAND SAUCE

Serves 8

*"Do encourage the guests to use the sauce
as it is delicious and moistens the chicken."*

½ cup Parmesan cheese
2 cups seasoned breadcrumbs
3 tablespoons sesame seeds
5–6 pounds chicken pieces
   (from broilers or fryers) or
   chicken breasts, if preferred

½ cup melted butter or
   margarine
Additional butter or margarine

Combine Parmesan cheese, breadcrumbs and sesame seeds. Dip each piece of chicken into melted butter and roll in breadcrumb mixture. Freeze or refrigerate, as desired. • When ready to bake, bring to room temperature, preheat oven to 350°, place chicken in a shallow pan and dot with butter or margarine. Bake for 1 hour.

Cumberland sauce:
1 cup red currant jelly
1 6-ounce can frozen orange
   juice concentrate, defrosted
4 tablespoons dry sherry

1 teaspoon dry mustard
⅛ teaspoon ginger
¼ teaspoon hot pepper sauce

In a saucepan, combine all ingredients. Simmer, stirring, until smooth. Serve with chicken in a gravy boat or pour over chicken before serving.

*Mrs. Norman D. Dicks
Wife of the Representative from
Washington*

GRILLED CHICKEN IN VINEGAR   Serves 4

1 2½-pound chicken, cut into
   pieces, with skin
¼ cup chicken broth
½ cup balsamic vinegar
½ cup chopped scallions
2 tablespoons Dijon mustard
1 teaspoon dry mustard

2 cloves garlic, minced
1 tablespoon sugar
2 teaspoons Worcestershire
   sauce
1 teaspoon pepper
Salt to taste

Rinse chicken and dry. Place in a shallow baking dish. • Combine all other ingredients and whisk briskly to blend. Pour mixture over chicken, cover and refrigerate for 24 hours. Turn chicken occasionally. • When ready to cook, bring chicken and vinegar mixture to room temperature. Bake for 30 minutes at 325°. Remove chicken from marinade and broil for several minutes on each side. Serve immediately.

Elena Schupp Darden

CHICKEN BREASTS   Serves 6 to 8
À LA "LITTLE MERMAID"

8 chicken breast halves,
   skinned and boned
½ pound jumbo crabmeat
1 stalk celery, diced
½ onion, finely chopped
½ red bell pepper, diced
4 tablespoons mayonnaise

Salt and pepper to taste
4 thin slices Creamy Danish
   Havarti cheese with mustard
   seeds, halved
2 tablespoons butter
3 cups heavy cream
Toothpicks

Preheat oven to 350°. • Rinse chicken and pat dry. Pound chicken to flatten. • In a large bowl, mix crabmeat, celery, onion, red pepper and mayonnaise. Season with salt and pepper. • Place a scoop of crabmeat mixture in the center of each chicken breast. Top with half a slice of cheese. Roll chicken breasts and fasten with a toothpick. • In a large skillet, brown butter. Add chicken rolls and brown on all sides. Transfer chicken to a large baking dish. Boil cream and pour over chicken. Bake for 25 minutes. • Remove chicken from liquid and arrange on a warm platter. Pour liquid into a saucepan and boil until thickened. Pour over chicken. • Serve with rice pilaf and warm, crisp French bread.

Karen Dyvig
Wife of the Ambassador of Denmark

JOAN'S CHINESE CHICKEN   Serves 8

*"This can be made for the masses and is popular
with adults and children alike."*

20 pieces of chicken
  (wings, thighs, legs)
1½ cups plum sauce
⅓ cup black bean sauce
2 tablespoons soy sauce

3 tablespoons chopped fresh
  ginger
Peel from 3 oranges, julienned
¼ cup fresh orange juice

Marinate chicken overnight in all of the ingredients listed above (reserving
some orange peel for baking). • Before cooking, drain, reserving marinade.
Place chicken in a covered casserole, add some fresh orange peel and some of
marinade. Bake at 350° for 45 minutes to 1 hour.

Mrs. Arthur Wexler

CHICKEN MARENGO   Serves 8

*"This is a great buffet casserole which profits
by a day's aging in the refrigerator"*

8–12 assorted chicken pieces
¼ cup olive oil
Onion salt
½ cup dry white wine
2 garlic cloves, crushed
½ teaspoon thyme
1 bay leaf
Sprigs of parsley
1 cup chicken stock

2 cups tomatoes
16–20 frozen pearl white
  onions
1 pound mushrooms, sliced
¼ cup butter
Juice of 1 lemon
1 cup pitted black olives
1 jigger brandy or cognac
Chopped parsley

Sauté chicken pieces in olive oil. Sprinkle with onion salt. Add wine, garlic,
thyme, bay leaf, parsley, chicken stock and tomatoes. Simmer for 30 minutes,
until chicken is tender. • Sauté onions and mushrooms in butter and lemon
juice. • Arrange chicken mixture in a deep earthenware casserole. Add mushrooms, onions and olives. Sprinkle with cognac and bake for 30 minutes at
350°. • Garnish with parsley and serve with rice and a salad.

Mrs. Philip W. Pillsbury, Jr.

CHICKEN MARINARA   Serves 6

¾ cup fine breadcrumbs
½ teaspoon salt
¼ teaspoon pepper
6 chicken breast halves,
   skinned and boned
2 eggs, beaten
¼ cup butter or margarine
1 15.5-ounce jar marinara
   sauce with mushrooms

½ cup half and half
3 1-ounce slices mozzarella
   cheese, cut in half
6 1-ounce slices Swiss cheese
1 tablespoon Parmesan cheese,
   freshly grated

Preheat oven to 350°. • Combine breadcrumbs, salt and pepper. Dip each chicken breast in eggs and coat with breadcrumb mixture. • Melt butter in a large skillet over medium heat. Sauté chicken for about 2 minutes on each side, until light golden brown. Remove chicken and drain. Set aside. • Combine marinara sauce and half and half, mixing well. Reserve ¼ cup plus 2 tablespoons of the marinara mixture and set aside. • Pour remaining sauce into a lightly greased 13 x 9 x 2 inch baking dish and top with chicken. Cover and bake for 25 minutes. • Place one slice each of mozzarella and Swiss cheese on each chicken breast. Top with a tablespoon of the reserved sauce and sprinkle with Parmesan cheese. Cover and bake an additional 5 minutes. • Serve with noodles.

Roy Rafey

MEDITERRANEAN CHICKEN   Serves 4

2 whole chicken breasts
   (about 2 pounds), halved
   and skinned
Non-stick cooking spray
1 tablespoon olive oil
1 large yellow onion, chopped
4 cloves garlic, thinly sliced
1 sweet red pepper, cored,
   seeded and cut into 1-inch
   squares
1 medium zucchini (about
   ½ pound), halved lengthwise
   and sliced ¼ inch thick

1 small eggplant, sliced ¼ inch
   thick and cut into wedges
1 28-ounce can tomatoes,
   drained and chopped
¼ teaspoon basil
¼ teaspoon thyme
¼ teaspoon oregano
12 jumbo pitted ripe olives,
   halved
2 tablespoons minced parsley

Brown chicken over medium heat in a large, heavy skillet or wok coated with cooking spray, for about 5 minutes on each side. Transfer to a large bowl and set aside. • Add olive oil, onion and garlic to skillet and cook, uncovered, for 5 minutes, stirring occasionally. Add red pepper and cook for 5 minutes. Add zucchini and continue cooking for an additional 5 minutes. Transfer vegetables to bowl containing chicken. • Raise heat to medium high and cook eggplant for 5–7 minutes, stirring occasionally. Return chicken and vegetables to skillet. Add tomatoes, basil, thyme, oregano and olives. Lower heat to medium, cover and simmer for an additional 15 minutes. Arrange on a serving platter and sprinkle with parsley.

Sarah T. Minikes

OLD BAY CHICKEN WITH COOL CUCUMBER SAUCE

Serves 4

Sauce:

1 cucumber, peeled, seeded and coarsely shredded
½ cup nonfat yogurt
¼ cup sour cream
¼ cup minced fresh chives or dill

½ teaspoon black pepper
¼ teaspoon kosher salt
Pinch of cayenne

Chicken:

4 chicken breast halves, skinned and boned
¼ cup cornmeal
2 tablespoons Old Bay seasoning

1½ teaspoons dry mustard
½ teaspoon mace or freshly ground nutmeg
⅛–¼ teaspoon cayenne
2–3 tablespoons corn oil

To make cucumber sauce, squeeze shredded cucumber to remove liquid. You should have about ⅔ cup cucumber. Stir cucumber, yogurt, sour cream, chives, pepper, salt and cayenne together. Taste and adjust seasoning. Refrigerate. • Halve each chicken breast lengthwise. Mix cornmeal, Old Bay, dry mustard, mace and cayenne. The coating will taste milder after cooking. Sprinkle cornmeal mixture onto a dinner plate and coat both sides of chicken. Heat 1½ tablespoons oil in a 10-inch heavy skillet on medium heat and sauté half the chicken for 3 minutes, shaking pan occasionally to keep chicken from sticking. Add ½ tablespoon oil, turn chicken and sauté for 2 or 3 minutes, until firm but slightly springy, removing fillets as soon as cooked. Set chicken on paper towels and keep warm. Sauté remaining chicken, adding 1 tablespoon oil, if necessary. • Serve chicken with cucumber sauce.

Leslie Beal Bloom, Author
"Chicken on the Run"

CHICKEN OREGANO   Serves 6

3 skinless, boned chicken
   breasts, halved
Salt and white pepper to taste
2 cloves garlic, minced

1 tablespoon oregano
Juice of 2 large limes, plus
   lime shells
Olive oil

Preheat oven to 325°. • Rinse chicken and pat dry. Place in an oblong baking dish. Sprinkle chicken with salt, pepper, garlic and oregano. Pour lime juice evenly over chicken. Put lime shells in corners of baking dish. Drizzle with olive oil and refrigerate, if prepared ahead. When ready to serve, bake, covered, for 45 minutes. Uncover and baste with pan juices. Return to oven uncovered for 10 to 15 minutes, until chicken is lightly browned. • Discard lime shells before serving.

Mrs. John K. Walker, Jr.

CHICKEN WITH PICKLED LEMONS   Serves 8 to 10
AND OLIVES
(DJAJ M'KALLI)

2 or 3 whole chickens, halved
3 teaspoons salt
8 cloves garlic, crushed
¾ cup vegetable oil
2 teaspoons ginger
1 teaspoon turmeric

1 teaspoon black pepper
1 pinch saffron
2 medium onions, grated
¼ pound unsalted butter
6-ounces Kalamata olives
2 pickled lemons

To allow time for marinating, start the night before or early in the day. Clean chicken and remove all fat. Rub with a mixture of 2 teaspoons salt and 6 crushed cloves of garlic. Place in a large pot, cover with water and let stand for 1 hour. • Remove chicken and rub with a mixture of oil, ginger, turmeric, black pepper, saffron and remaining teaspoon salt. Marinate in the refrigerator overnight or for several hours. • To cook, cut chicken halves into individual portions and place in a large pot. Add onion, butter, remaining garlic and 1 quart of water. Bring to boil and simmer for 20 minutes. • Serve with olives and pickled lemons.

Mrs. Mohamed M. Benaissa
Wife of the Ambassador of Morocco

QUICK-FRIED CHICKEN WITH PEANUTS   Serves 5

1 pound boneless, skinless chicken breasts	2 tablespoons water
1 tablespoon white wine	1 teaspoon sesame oil
1 teaspoon salt	1 medium-sized green pepper
1 teaspoon sugar	1 medium-sized red pepper
1 egg white	3 cups cooking oil, plus
2 tablespoons cornstarch	4 tablespoons
2 tablespoons light soy sauce	1 cup roasted peanuts (cashews or walnuts)

Cut chicken into bite-sized pieces. Mix wine, salt, sugar, egg white and 1 tablespoon cornstarch. Toss chicken in this mixture and set aside for at least 30 minutes, tossing occasionally. • Meanwhile, make a seasoning sauce with soy sauce, water, sesame oil and remaining 1 tablespoon cornstarch. Set aside. • Chop peppers into bite-sized pieces. Set aside. • Heat 3 cups oil in a large skillet to about 300°. Fry chicken pieces for about 30 seconds, until they change color. Remove chicken pieces and drain. • Remove all of the oil from the skillet and place 4 tablespoons of fresh oil into the same skillet. Stir-fry peppers for about 30 seconds. Add chicken, seasoning sauce and peanuts. Stir quickly until mixed. Remove to a heated platter and and serve.

Mrs. Frederick F. Chien
Wife of the Representative of the Coordination Council for
North American Affairs, Republic of China on Taiwan

CHICKEN "SCAMPI"   Serves 3

"This recipe is an effort to duplicate a wonderful dinner in a little inn in Wales. The original dish included shrimp. You may add it or not, as you wish."

4 tablespoons butter	1½ pounds boneless chicken breasts, cut into bite-sized pieces
2 tablespoons olive oil	
2–3 large cloves of garlic, minced	
1 teaspoon salt	4 tablespoons chopped parsley (optional)
Freshly ground pepper to taste	Lemon wedges

Melt butter and add olive oil, garlic, salt and pepper. Marinate chicken pieces in this mixture for 1–2 hours. • Sauté over high heat for about 5 minutes, turning frequently. Do not overcook. • Sprinkle with parsley if desired. Garnish with lemon wedges. Serve with rice.

Sarah T. Minikes

SPICED MARINATED CHICKEN   Serves 10 to 12

6 chicken breasts, skinned,
   boned and split
2 teaspoons salt
1 teaspoon sugar
½ teaspoon anise seed
¼ teaspoon ground ginger
2 bay leaves

2 tablespoons soy sauce
2 tablespoons olive oil
1 tablespoon vinegar
½ cup flour
4 tablespoons oil
1½ cups hot water
½ teaspoon ground cumin seed

Wash the chicken and place in a wide casserole. Combine next 8 ingredients.
Bring to a boil and pour over chicken. Cover and refrigerate overnight, turning in marinade occasionally. • To cook, remove chicken from marinade and
dust with flour. Sauté in a large skillet in oil until brown. Add hot water to
marinade and pour over chicken. Cover and simmer for 20–30 minutes. Add
cumin seed and continue simmering for another 10 minutes. Serve with rice.

Mrs. Charles J. DiBona

SPICY CHICKEN   Serves 4

1 slice fresh ginger
½ cup soy sauce
½ cup sugar
4 cloves garlic, crushed

6 peppercorns
1 star anise seed
1 2-pound broiler chicken
Oil

In a large bowl, combine ginger, soy sauce, sugar, garlic, peppercorns and
anise seed. Place chicken in a large saucepan and cover with sauce. Simmer
for 45 minutes or until done. Remove from heat and cool. Brush chicken with
oil and cut into pieces. Serve on a bed of vegetables.

Mrs. Buena R. Rabe
Embassy of the Philippines

SZECHUAN CHICKEN STIR-FRY   Serves 2 to 3

5 tablespoons soy sauce
1½ tablespoons white wine
   vinegar
1½ teaspoons sugar
½ teaspoon cayenne pepper
4 chicken breast halves,
   skinned, boned and cut
   into ½-inch pieces

3 tablespoons cornstarch
2 tablespoons vegetable oil
3 cloves garlic, minced
2 scallions, cut on diagonal
Freshly cooked rice

Combine soy sauce, vinegar, sugar and cayenne pepper in a small bowl.

Dredge chicken in cornstarch. Heat oil in a wok or heavy skillet over medium heat. Add chicken and garlic and stir-fry until chicken is opaque, about 5 minutes. Add soy sauce mixture and stir-fry for 30 seconds. Mix in scallions, drain and serve immediately over rice.

Sally D. Collett

TARRAGON CHICKEN SUPREME AU FROMAGE

Serves 6 to 8

1½ cups finely grated Swiss cheese
½ cup finely grated Parmesan cheese
2–3 tablespoons chopped fresh tarragon (less, if dried)

¼ teaspoon white pepper
2 tablespoons cognac
2 egg yolks
4 whole chicken breasts, skinned, halved and boned

In blender, mix cheeses, tarragon and white pepper. Store in a jar in refrigerator until ready to use. • Combine cognac and egg yolks in a flat dish. Dip chicken breasts into egg mixture, then coat with cheese mixture. Place chicken breasts in a shallow baking dish and bake at 375° for 20 minutes. If pale, place under broiler to brown for 1 minute.

Mrs. Porter K. Wheeler

CHICKEN TIKKA

Serves 4

1 3-pound chicken (see note)
1 cup yogurt
1 teaspoon crushed garlic
1 teaspoon crushed fresh ginger

2 tablespoons lemon juice
2 tablespoons ground red pepper
Salt and pepper to taste
2 tablespoons olive oil

Skin and bone chicken and cut into four parts. Prick well with a fork. • In a large bowl, combine yogurt, garlic, ginger, lemon juice, red pepper, salt and pepper. Marinate chicken in this mixture for 2 hours. Thread chicken on skewers and brush with olive oil. Broil for 6 minutes on each side. • Serve with sliced tomatoes, onion rings and lemon quarters on a bed of lettuce.

NOTE: Lamb chops may be substituted for chicken to prepare lamb tikka. Cook lamb chops a little longer than chicken.

Mrs. Arnaz Marker
Wife of the Ambassador of Pakistan

CHICKEN TETRAZZINI   Serves 6 to 8

5 pounds chicken, cut into
  serving pieces
1 onion studded with 2 whole
  cloves
2 stalks celery with leaves
4 tablespoons salt
  (approximately)
½ bay leaf
1 carrot
1 pound spaghettini
10 tablespoons butter
¾ pound sliced mushrooms
1½ tablespoons lemon juice

½ cup sliced almonds
5 tablespoons flour
¼ teaspoon paprika
½ teaspoon white pepper
⅛ teaspoon nutmeg
¼ teaspoon Tabasco sauce
1 egg yolk, lightly beaten
½ cup dry sherry
1 cup light cream
Additional milk or cream
1 cup Parmesan cheese
Paprika to taste
Butter

Place chicken pieces, onion, celery, salt to taste, bay leaf, carrot and 3–4 cups water, enough to cover chicken, in a large pot and bring to a boil. Reduce heat and simmer, covered, for 45–60 minutes, until chicken is tender. Remove chicken from pot and cool. Cut meat from bones and reserve. • Return bones and skin to pot and heat to boiling. Reduce quantity to less than a quart. Strain stock through cheesecloth and set aside. Discard bones and skin. Measure 2 cups stock and set aside. • Place remaining stock in large pot and add enough water to make 6 quarts. Add 3 tablespoons salt and bring to a boil. Add spaghettini and cook approximately 6 minutes, then drain and place in 9 x 13 inch baking dish. • In a large skillet melt 4 tablespoons butter. Sauté mushrooms, which have been sprinkled with lemon juice and ¾ teaspoon salt, until soft. • In another skillet, sauté almonds in 1–2 tablespoons butter. Pour mushrooms and almonds over spaghettini. • Melt 4 tablespoons butter and remove from heat. With a wire whisk blend in flour, paprika, 1½ teaspoons salt, white pepper and nutmeg. • In a large saucepan, bring 2 cups strained chicken broth to a boil and, all at once, add flour mixture, stirring vigorously with whisk until sauce is thickened and smooth. Stir Tabasco into egg yolk and add to sauce. Add sherry, cream and chicken meat. Heat, but do not boil, and pour over spaghettini. At this point, dish may be refrigerated or frozen. • When ready to serve, bring dish to room temperature and heat oven to 350°. Pour a small amount of cream or milk on top of casserole and sprinkle with Parmesan cheese and paprika to taste. Dot with butter and bake for 30–45 minutes, until casserole is heated through.

Karin G. Weber

CHICKEN VINAIGRETTE   Serves 4

"Very low in calories and fat."

4 boneless, skinless chicken
   breast halves
Cooking spray
2 tablespoons Dijon mustard
2 tablespoons minced scallions
2 tablespoons lemon juice

¼ teaspoon salt
½ cup safflower or other
   salad oil
Freshly ground pepper to taste
¼ cup fresh, minced parsley

Preheat oven to 350°. • Wash and trim chicken and cut into generous 1-inch cubes. Dry on paper towels. • Spray a jelly roll pan or other large flat pan with cooking spray. Place chicken on pan. Bake at 350° for 20 minutes, turning after 10 minutes to cook evenly. • While chicken is baking, whisk together mustard, scallions, lemon juice and salt. Add oil in dribbles, beating constantly. Season with pepper. • Discard cooking juices and put warm chicken in vinaigrette. Add parsley and toss several times. Best served slightly warm, but can be served at room temperature or cold.

Mrs. E. Edward Bruce

CHICKEN WITH GINGER   Serves 3 to 4

1 2½- to 3-pound chicken
1 tablespoon sesame oil
4 ounces fresh ginger, thinly
   sliced
2 tablespoons light soy sauce
1 tablespoon dark soy sauce
2 tablespoons sugar

1 tablespoon oyster sauce
1½ cups water
Pinch of salt
Freshly ground pepper
Fresh Chinese parsley
  (cilantro)

Cut chicken into bite-sized pieces. Heat sesame oil in pan. Add ginger and stir. Add chicken and fry for about 2 minutes. • Add light and dark soy sauces, sugar, oyster sauce and water. Simmer for 15–20 minutes. Add salt and pepper to taste. • Serve hot with rice. Garnish with Chinese parsley.

Jenny Tan
Embassy of Singapore

CHICKEN BREASTS WITH CUCUMBER   Serves 6 to 8

*"The unexpected addition of cucumber propels the chicken
to celestial heights."*

1 large cucumber, peeled,
  halved, seeded and cut into
  thin slices
½ cup chicken broth
½ cup dry white wine
6 whole chicken breasts,
  skinned, boned and halved
1½ teaspoons salt
½ teaspoon pepper

3 tablespoons butter
½ cup cognac
⅓ cup thinly sliced scallions,
  white part only
1½ cups light cream
1 tablespoon grated lemon rind
2 tablespoons minced fresh
  parsley

Combine ¼ of cucumber slices, broth and wine in a large saucepan. Bring to
a boil and remove from heat. Let stand for 2 minutes. Strain, reserve liquid
and discard cucumber. • Pound chicken until ½ inch thick and sprinkle with
½ teaspoon salt and pepper. Melt butter in a large skillet and sauté chicken
for 5 minutes. Warm cognac, pour over chicken and ignite. When flame sub-
sides, remove chicken to a platter and keep warm. • Add scallions to skillet
and cover. Cook until tender but not brown. Return chicken to skillet and add
cucumber broth mixture. Cook covered for 5 minutes over low heat. Transfer
to platter and keep warm. • Place skillet over high heat and reduce liquid to
½ cup. Reduce heat and stir in cream, lemon rind and 1 teaspoon salt.
Simmer 3–4 minutes until slightly thickened. Stir in remaining cucumbers.
To serve, pour sauce over chicken and sprinkle with parsley.

*Mrs. Christopher Bond
Wife of the Senator from Missouri*

GRILLED BREAST OF CHICKEN ZUCCHINI AND HERB RAVIOLI

Serves 6

Ravioli:

¼ cup olive oil
1 small onion, chopped
1 garlic clove, crushed
2 zucchini, sliced
2 sprigs thyme
Salt and pepper to taste
¼ pound cleaned spinach

1 bunch cleaned watercress
3 scallions, sliced
½ bunch chives
12 basil leaves
Round wonton skins
Eggwash (to seal ravioli)
2 tablespoons vegetable oil
½ cup chicken stock or water

Chicken:

6 skinless chicken breast
  halves

Seasonings of choice
Olive oil for grilling

Garnish:

Tomato oil
Chervil

Heat olive oil in sauté pan. Sauté onion and garlic until transparent. Add zucchini and cook until very tender, mashing with a fork into a coarse purée. Cook until liquid evaporates. Season with thyme, salt and pepper. Set aside to cool. • Bring a large pot of salted water to boil. Blanch spinach, watercress, scallions, chives and basil. Immediately shock in cold water to stop cooking process. Squeeze out excess water and chop finely. Stir into zucchini purée and season well. • Fashion 18 half-moon ravioli out of the wonton skins, fill with vegetable mixture, seal with egg wash and crimp with fork. Place in refrigerator until cooking time. • Season chicken breasts to taste, rub with olive oil and grill until done. • To prepare ravioli, braise as follows. Heat 2 tablespoons oil in a large skillet. Add ravioli and brown quickly on both sides. Add ½ cup stock or water and bring to a boil. Reduce heat and cook, covered, until done (about 5 minutes). Drain on paper towel. • Arrange three ravioli and one chicken breast on each plate, dribble on a little tomato oil and garnish with chervil.

Patrick Clark, Executive Chef
The Hay Adams Hotel

CHICKEN CUTLETS À LA RUSSE   Serves 4

Cutlets:

2 large whole chicken breasts,   1 large egg
   skinned and boned   1½ cups breadcrumbs
¼ teaspoon nutmeg   1 tablespoon water
Salt and pepper   6 tablespoons butter
5 tablespoons butter, melted   1 teaspoon vegetable oil
½ cup flour, seasoned with
   salt and pepper

Chill a mixing bowl. Finely chop the chicken, or put through a grinder using a fine blade, yielding about 1½ cups of ground meat. (If your market has ground chicken, you can save time — or you can substitute ground turkey.) Place meat in the chilled bowl and add the nutmeg, salt and pepper to taste and the melted butter. Blend well and chill thoroughly. • Place the seasoned flour and the bread crumbs in separate pie plates. • Beat the egg with the water in a small bowl. • Divide the chicken into 8 balls and flatten to ½-inch thickness. Shape into cutlets. Dip each into flour, then the egg, and finally in the breadcrumbs, gently pressing the crumbs into each cutlet. Refrigerate for at least one hour. • In a heavy skillet heat the butter and oil. When very hot carefully add the cutlets. Cook until golden brown on one side, turn and brown the other side. • Serve immediately with paprika sauce.

Paprika sauce:

3 tablespoons butter   3 medium tomatoes, peeled
3 tablespoons finely   and coarsely chopped
   chopped onion   Salt and pepper
¼ cup flour   2 tablespoons sour cream
1 tablespoon paprika

Melt 2 tablespoons of the butter in a skillet. Add the onion and sauté until transparent and soft (do not brown). Stir in the flour and paprika. Add the tomatoes and a dash of salt and pepper. Simmer 15 minutes, stirring frequently. Stir in the sour cream, then swirl in the remaining butter by rotating the pan gently. Taste and season with additional salt and pepper to taste.

Senator and Mrs. John D. Rockefeller IV
(West Virginia)

CHICKEN À LA SMITH   Serves 4

"This is our family's favorite chicken dish and has been for 25 years."

2 large chicken breasts,
  halved
2 pounds fresh broccoli
  (or asparagus in season)

2 cans cream of chicken soup
½ cup mayonnaise
2 tablespoons lemon juice
½ teaspoon curry powder

Preheat oven to 350°. • Simmer chicken in water until done and cut into large chucks. Save broth for cooking rice to accompany the dish. • Cut broccoli into bite-sized pieces and steam until crunchy-tender. Place chicken and broccoli into a shallow baking dish in alternate layers. • Mix soup, mayonnaise, lemon juice and curry powder. Pour mixture over chicken and broccoli, covering completely. • Bake until bubbly. • Serve over rice.

Mary Jo Smith
Wife of Senator Bob Smith (New Hampshire)

CORNISH GAME HENS   Serves 4

2 large Cornish game hens
2 tablespoons butter
Juice and pared rind of
  2 lemons
1 cup chicken stock
Beurre manie (see note)
1 teaspoon chopped parsley
1 teaspoon chopped chives

1 teaspoon chopped mint
Salt to taste
Sugar
Freshly ground pepper
Paprika
Melted butter
Watercress

In an ovenproof pan, heat butter. When foaming (do not burn), add whole hens, lemon rind, most of lemon juice, salt and pepper. Turn to baste hens with liquid. Cover with foil and bake at 350° for 30 minutes. • Remove hens from oven, split the birds and trim away back bones and tidy up wings. Place on an ovenproof serving dish. • Strain the cooking juices from the pan, return to pan and add stock. Thicken with beurre manie a little at a time. Bring to a boil and add parsley, chives and mint. • Sprinkle the hens with lemon juice, salt, sugar and a dusting of freshly ground pepper and paprika. Spoon melted butter over hens and place under broiler for about 5 minutes, until skin of hens is brown and crisp. Spoon stock mixture around hens. Garnish with watercress and serve.

NOTE: Beurre Manie is a liaison of butter and flour and is to be added by degrees to the dish it is required to thicken. Work the flour and butter together on a plate, keeping the proportion of butter slightly greater than the flour.

Anne Green

GAME HENS METTERNICH   Serves 6

Hens:

3 Cornish game hens

3 medium onions, peeled

3 cloves of garlic, peeled

6 slices of bacon

Sauce:

Giblets

2 onions, finely chopped

2 carrots, finely chopped

4 tablespoons butter

2 cups chicken stock

1 teaspoon whole black
  peppercorns

2 bay leaves

1 whole clove

¾ cup red currant jelly

Salt to taste

White pepper to taste

1–2 tablespoons cornstarch
  (optional)

To serve:

1 cup breadcrumbs

4 tablespoons butter

2 bunches of watercress,
  washed and drained

Preheat oven to 450°. • Wash game hens and pat dry. Reserve giblets. Salt and pepper hens inside and out. Place one onion and one clove of garlic inside each hen. Put hens in shallow roasting pan and cover each bird with 2 slices of bacon. Place in oven and immediately reduce temperature to 375°. Roast for approximately 1 hour (20 minutes per pound). • To make sauce, chop giblets and sauté in large saucepan with onions, carrots, and 2 tablespoons butter. When giblets are lightly browned, add stock, peppercorns, bay leaves and clove. Let the sauce simmer, covered, for 45 minutes over very low heat. Strain through a fine sieve and return to pan. Slowly stir in red currant jelly until fully dissolved. Add 2 tablespoons butter and stir until sauce is smooth. Season to taste with salt and pepper. If sauce needs to be thickened, add 1–2 teaspoons cornstarch dissolved in cold water. • Sauté breadcrumbs in 4 tablespoons butter until golden brown. When ready, remove hens from oven. Cover with foil and allow to stand for 5 minutes. Remove bacon, onions and garlic cloves. Split hens in half with sharp knife or poultry shears. Arrange birds on warmed serving platter on a bed of watercress. Spoon some of the sauce over each and sprinkle with breadcrumbs. Serve remaining sauce separately. Serve with buttered noodles and colorful lightly steamed vegetables.

Mrs. Wilfried Platzer

National Cathedral

CROCK POT CORNISH GAME HENS   Serves 6

3 Cornish game hens
8 ounces cornbread
   stuffing mix
¼ cup melted butter

2 tablespoons brown sugar
2 tablespoons lime juice
2 tablespoons dry white wine
2 teaspoons soy sauce

Wash hens and pat dry. • Prepare cornbread stuffing in accordance with package directions and stuff hens. • Combine butter, brown sugar, lime juice, wine and soy sauce in a small bowl and brush sauce on hens. Cook in crock pot on low heat 6–8 hours basting frequently with sauce.

Senator Don Nickles
(Oklahoma)

CHILEAN PIE   Serves 8

"My family looks forward to leftover turkey!"

4 cups cooked chicken or
   turkey, chopped in
   bite-sized pieces
4 onions, chopped
2 tablespoons oil

2 cups pitted black olives
2 cups raisins
2 16½-ounce cans creamed
   corn
2 packages frozen corn soufflé,
   defrosted

Preheat oven to 375°. • Sauté onions over medium-low heat in oil until transparent. Add poultry, olives, raisins and corn. Mix well and transfer to a 9 x 9 inch casserole. • Top with defrosted corn soufflé and bake for 20–30 minutes, until top is golden brown and bubbly. Serve at once.

Maria Gilbert

DIANA McLELLAN'S
CHRISTMAS TURKEY TERRIFICO

Serves 16

"The festive family roast turkey doesn't have to be dry, drab and flavorless. This simple but sophisticated bird drew raves from 16 family members and friends — including a food editor — one Christmas eve. Instead of stuffing, I served wild rice and garbanzo beans cooked in a light chicken stock. (Just before serving, chop and lightly cook 2 bunches of scallions in melted butter, add a few dashes of strong sesame oil, and stir in your cooked wild rice and beans.) On the side: Glazed carrots with prunes, red cabbage cooked in apple juice, and a quick-steamed green vegetable mélange, simply buttered."

1 large turkey
Sea salt
1 or 2 large fresh ginger roots
2 large onions
2 heads garlic
½ gallon jug, or more, cheap
    white wine (a flowery Rhine
    is good)

4 cans condensed chicken broth
Freshly coarse-ground pepper
2 large lemons
2 heaping tablespoons, or more,
    of cornstarch

Start 2–3 days in advance. Thoroughly wash turkey and discard innards. Soak turkey in cold water with sea salt for a couple of hours. • Peel and coarsely chop ginger root, onion and garlic. Place the wine, chopped ginger, onion and garlic and 2 cans of chicken broth in roasting pan into which the turkey will fit tightly. Marinate turkey in pan in refrigerator, breast down, tightly covered for 2 days. • Remove turkey from marinade. Sprinkle inside and outside with sea salt and coarse pepper. • Pour some of marinade into a saucepan, leaving about 1 inch in roasting pan. Scoop out the ginger, onion and garlic and scatter inside the bird. Trickle in some marinade, too. Cut the ends off both lemons, prick all over deeply with a fork and add to the inside of bird. • If you want your turkey good and brown, transfer it and remaining marinade to a flatter pan at this point. Roast, breast-up, uncovered, for length of time suggested on wrapping for unstuffed bird, at 350°. Baste occasionally. • Meanwhile, add the cornstarch and the other 2 cans of chicken broth to the marinade in the saucepan. When turkey is cooked, remove from the roasting pan and put on

a carving platter. Skim most of the fat off the delicious "wine-y" pan juices and add the juices to the saucepan. Boil for a couple of minutes, stirring often, to make a grand gravy. (If you prefer, and don't mind lumps, add saucepan contents to roasting pan instead and boil that.) Make several gravy boats full — they won't be able to get enough. • The turkey should sit about 20 minutes or so before carving. It will be buttery-soft and wonderfully flavorful. • Next day, the carcass and leftover gravy and marinade — and lemons — boiled up, with water and a few bouillon cubes and some white pepper, make the tastiest turkey soup in the world.

Diana McLellan, a reformed gossip columnist,
writes for the "Ladies Home Journal," "Washingtonian"
and various publications here and in Britain.

CAJUN DEEP-FRIED TURKEY   Serves 10 to 12

4 ounces liquid garlic (½ cup)	2 tablespoons liquid crab boil or
4 ounces liquid onion (½ cup)	1 tablespoon Old Bay
4 ounces liquid celery (½ cup)	seasoning
1 tablespoon red pepper	1 poultry or meat injector
2 tablespoons salt	1 10–12 pound turkey
2 tablespoons Tabasco sauce	5 gallons peanut oil

Heat liquid garlic, onion and celery, red pepper, salt, Tabasco and crab boil or seasoning until salt and red pepper dissolve. Fill injector with liquid and inject turkey at breast, wings, drumsticks, thighs and back. Marinate for 24 hours in refrigerator. You may wish to tie turkey legs with ½ inch thick cotton ropes to allow easier removal from oil. • In a 10-gallon pot, bring peanut oil to 350° and deep-fry turkey for 38–42 minutes. Turkey should float to surface after 35 minutes and cooking should continue for an additional 5–7 minutes. • The cooking of fried turkey should be done outdoors. Extreme caution should be taken when placing cold turkey into hot oil.

Mrs. John B. Breaux
Wife of the Senator from Louisiana

The Barns of Wolf Trap

CARIBBEAN TURKEY STEW   Serves 6

2 pounds turkey thighs, skin
  removed
1 tablespoon oil
3 cups thinly sliced onion
½ teaspoon red pepper flakes
½ teaspoon salt
¼ cup sweetened flaked coconut
1 cup reduced-sodium
  chicken bouillon or
  turkey broth

1 16-ounce can stewed
  tomatoes
1½ pounds butternut squash,
  peeled, seeded and cut into
  1-inch cubes
1 pound sweet potato, peeled
  and cut into 1-inch cubes
1 16-ounce can black beans,
  rinsed and drained (see note)

Condiments:

2 medium bananas, sliced
1 bunch scallions, sliced

½ cup sweetened flaked coconut
1 or 2 limes, cut into wedges

Brown the turkey thighs in oil in a 5-quart saucepan over medium-high heat for about 3 minutes on each side. Remove and set aside. • Sauté onion in same saucepan for 2–3 minutes, until translucent. Add red pepper, salt, coconut, broth, tomatoes, squash, sweet potatoes and turkey. Bring mixture to boil, reduce heat, cover and simmer for 1¼–1½ hours, until turkey thighs register 180° to 185° in thickest part. • Ten minutes before serving, remove turkey thighs from stew and strip meat from bones with a fork. Return meat to stew and stir in beans. Heat through. • To serve, spoon stew into bowls and garnish with bananas, scallions and coconut. Squeeze juice of lime over top.

NOTE: If canned black beans are unavailable, soak 8 ounces dried black beans according to package directions. Add beans at beginning of cooking with all other ingredients.

Teresa Farney
Vice President for Consumer Affairs
National Turkey Federation

TURKEY CUTLETS IN VEGETABLE WINE SAUCE

Serves 3

Flour, for dredging
Salt and pepper to taste
¾ pound turkey cutlets
2 tablespoons olive oil
1 onion, chopped
1 clove garlic, chopped
1 cup dry white wine

2 carrots, thinly sliced
1 stalk celery, thinly sliced
½ teaspoon rosemary
1 bay leaf
2 tablespoons chopped parsley
Soft polenta or rice, for serving

Combine flour, salt and pepper and dredge cutlets in the mixture. Heat oil in large nonstick skillet, add cutlets and sauté quickly until they are lightly browned. Remove from skillet and keep warm. Add onion and garlic to skillet and sauté for 3 minutes. Add wine and reduce by half. Add carrots, celery, rosemary and bay leaf. Cover pan, bring to a boil, reduce heat and simmer until vegetables are tender, about 20 minutes. Return cutlets to skillet. Sprinkle with parsley and season with salt and pepper. Serve with soft polenta or rice.

Gail Forman, Columnist
Sunday Magazine, "The Baltimore Sun"

DUCK WITH APRICOTS

Serves 8

2 whole ducks
Salt and pepper to taste
Honey
¾ cup chicken broth
1½ tablespoons cornstarch

30 ounces canned, pitted
   apricot halves (drain and
   reserve liquid)
1 6-ounce can sliced water
   chestnuts

Place ducks, salted inside and out, in pan. Put necks in pan also. Roast at 325° for 2 hours. • Remove ducks from oven and paint with honey. Return to oven and continue baking for 1 hour. • Remove ducks to another pan and keep warm. • Skim 90% of grease from roasting pan, leaving drippings at the bottom of pan. Discard necks. Add chicken broth and simmer, reducing liquid until golden in color. Dissolve cornstarch in 5 tablespoons of reserved apricot syrup and add to pan. Add apricot halves. Simmer for a few minutes, but do not allow apricots to become mushy. Adjust seasoning. Add water chestnuts and cook for 5 minutes. • Strain ⅔ of gravy into serving dish. Pour apricots, water chestnuts and remaining gravy over duck and serve with rice.

Mrs. Jerold J. Principato

ROAST DUCK WITH DUMPLINGS AND SAUERKRAUT

Serves 6

1 7-pound duck	Freshly ground pepper
1 tablespoon salt	1 teaspoon caraway seeds

Dumplings:

2 cups flour	1 egg, beaten
3½ teaspoons baking powder	½ cup milk
½ teaspoon salt	1 tablespoon melted butter

Sauerkraut:

1 quart sauerkraut	1 large onion, chopped
¼ teaspoon caraway seeds	¼ cup chicken or duck fat
2 cups water	1 tablespoon flour

Preheat oven to 400°. • Wash dressed duck and dry thoroughly. Sprinkle with salt and pepper. Place in roaster and sprinkle caraway seeds inside and over duck. Roast, uncovered, for 30 minutes. Reduce oven temperature to 350° and continue roasting for 30 minutes. • To make dumplings: sift flour, baking powder and salt together. Add egg, milk and butter. Form into balls about the size of an egg and drop into a large pot of boiling salted water. Boil for 5–8 minutes, until cooked through. To test, remove 1 dumpling and cut open. • For sauerkraut: drain liquid from kraut, add caraway seeds and water and simmer for 20 minutes. In a skillet, sauté onion in fat until light brown. Add flour and cook for 5 minutes, stirring constantly, until slightly thickened. Add onion and flour to sauerkraut and cook for 5 additional minutes. • To serve: cut duck into serving pieces and arrange on a serving platter with the dumplings and sauerkraut.

Alojz Adamko, Attaché
Former Embassy of Czech and Slovak Federal Republic

ROAST BREAST OF DUCK ON ONION FONDUE   Serves 4
WITH PANCETTA, SPINACH AND SWEET GARLIC

4 breasts of duck with bone	1 cup olive oil
Salt and pepper to taste	4 ounces pancetta, diced
2 stalks fresh rosemary	1 pound fresh spinach
2 stalks fresh sage	1 whole head of garlic,
2 cloves garlic	oven-roasted (see note)
4 white onions, thinly sliced	½ cup stock (duck preferred)

Twenty-four hours before cooking, rub duck with salt, pepper, rosemary, sage and garlic and refrigerate. • When ready to cook, preheat oven to 450° and roast duck until medium rare, about 15 minutes. Remove duck from oven, reduce heat to 300° and return to oven for another 10 minutes. • Meanwhile, sauté onions in some of the olive oil until very tender. In a food processor, purée onions and set aside in a warm place. • Sauté pancetta until crispy, remove from heat and keep warm. • Wash spinach well and sauté in additional oil until crispy. Keep spinach warm. • Peel the cooked garlic cloves and keep warm. • When duck is cooked, remove from baking pan and add stock to pan. Pour a little over duck and pour rest of pan juices through a sieve. Keep warm. • Remove the bones from duck breasts and cut into thin slices. • On each plate, place a spoonful of onion purée (fondue), cover with several slices of duck breast, sprinkle with diced pancetta and garlic cloves and top with fried spinach.

NOTE: To roast garlic, place in 325° oven for 45–60 minutes.

Roberto Donna
Galileo Restaurant

PHEASANT WITH BACON   Serves 2

1 pheasant	1 quarter small onion
Cavender's Greek seasoning	3 strips of bacon
1 celery stalk	Apple wedges
1 lemon wedge	

Sauce:

1 small onion studded with	2 tablespoons butter
3 cloves	1 cup fresh white breadcrumbs
2 cups milk	3 tablespoons heavy cream

Preheat oven to 425°. • Pheasant must be plucked with reasonably unblemished skin. Wash and dry pheasant. Rub inside and out with Cavender's Greek seasoning. Place celery, lemon and onion inside pheasant cavity. Place one strip of bacon over breast lengthwise, then two strips crosswise. Place pheasant in shallow roasting pan and prop upright with apple wedges. Roast for about 20 minutes, until bacon is cooked. • For sauce, place onion in a saucepan with milk and butter. Bring to a boil. Add breadcrumbs and lower temperature. Simmer for 15 minutes. Remove onion and beat sauce until blended. Add cream, stir and serve.

Senator and Mrs. Malcolm Wallop
(Wyoming)

CHRISTMAS ROAST GOOSE   Serves 8 to 10

"When I was growing up in the Soviet Union, Christmas was not observed, and of course there were no ingredients available for a Christmas feast. I was, however, familiar with the idea of Christmas, and roast goose with red cabbage always seemed to me to symbolize a holiday feast. After we came to the West, this was the first thing I asked Galina to prepare in celebration of Christmas."

1 8- to 10-pound goose	3 small hard rolls
Salt and pepper to taste	Stock made from giblets
1 teaspoon marjoram	(optional)
1 small onion	Several small potatoes
3 sprigs dill and 3 sprigs	(optional)
parsley tied together	2 or 3 apples (optional)
with string	

If goose is frozen, defrost in refrigerator for 1 or 2 days, depending on size. • Wash in cold water and pat dry with paper towels. Sprinkle with salt and pepper on outside and inside. Sprinkle with marjoram on outside. Place onion, dill, parsley and rolls inside the cavity. (The rolls are not a stuffing; they absorb the fat as the goose cooks and should be discarded before serving.) • Place goose in baking pan on a rack, breast side up. Tie legs together and tuck under wings. Pierce the skin in several places with a fork. Bake in a 375° oven for 1 hour. (At this point, you can baste with a stock made from the giblets if you desire. This is the only point at which the goose may need basting.) Reduce heat to 325° and bake for an additional 2½ hours, or until the leg joint moves freely. (1¼ hours before goose is done, you may, if you like, put small potatoes and cored apples into the pan to bake with the goose.) • Remove goose from oven, discard rolls and vegetables from the cavity, let cool for about 10 minutes and carve. • Serve with potatoes and apples or with your favorite recipe for red cabbage.

Mstislav Rostropovich, Music Director
National Symphony Orchestra (1977–1994)

GRILLED VIRGINIA QUAIL

Serves 6

12 boneless quail
2 cups goat cheese stuffing
  (recipe follows)
1½ cups roasted garlic
  dressing (recipe follows)

1 pound seasonal field greens
1 pound crispy field onions
Diced tomatoes for garnish

Preheat oven to 450°. • Stuff each quail body with goat cheese stuffing. Season birds and place on the grill until they are marked. Place quail on cookie sheets and finish cooking in oven for approximately 5 minutes. • In a mixing bowl, add greens and garlic dressing and toss until all greens are well coated. • Place greens on chilled salad plates and add crispy onions. Place hot quail on top of salad and garnish with diced tomatoes.

Goat cheese and wild mushroom stuffing:

1 tablespoon butter
1 teaspoon minced garlic
1 tablespoon minced shallots
¼ pound oyster mushrooms,
  sliced
¼ pound shiitake mushrooms,
  sliced

1 teaspoon freshly chopped
  thyme
1 teaspoon freshly cracked
  black pepper
6 ounces goat cheese (chèvre)
Salt to taste

In a skillet, over low-medium heat, melt butter. Add garlic and shallots and sauté lightly, being careful not to brown. Add mushrooms and cook until soft. Transfer mushroom mixture to a bowl and let cool. Add thyme, pepper and goat cheese to mushrooms, mix well and adjust seasoning. Let sit for 2 hours before stuffing quail.

Creamy roasted garlic dressing (Makes 1 cup):

1 garlic bulb
2 teaspoons extra virgin
  olive oil
½ cup sour cream
¼ cup mayonnaise

1 scallion, thinly sliced
1 tablespoon champagne vinegar
¾ teaspoon freshly cracked
  black pepper
½ teaspoon salt

Preheat oven to 300°. • Place garlic on a cookie sheet and slowly roast for 45 minutes, until soft. Remove from oven and allow to cool. • In a mixing bowl, add sour cream and mayonnaise. Squeeze roasted garlic into bowl. Use a rubber spatula to mash garlic into mixture. Stir in scallion, vinegar, pepper and salt. • This dressing may be made a few days in advance.

Chef Michael Patton
Assistant Chef Tom Blundell
1789 Restaurant

Meat

MEDITERRANEAN RABBIT WITH BLACK OLIVES

Serves 4 to 6

1 2½–3 pound fresh rabbit, cut into 7 or 8 pieces
Sea salt and freshly ground black pepper
⅓–½ cup olive oil
4 ounces pancetta, diced
1 small red onion, minced
3 medium carrots, peeled and minced
2 medium stalks celery, minced
10 large sprigs Italian parsley, leaves only, minced
1 clove garlic, minced
1 tablespoon flour

2–3 cups full-bodied red wine, such as Chianti or Dolcetto d'Alba
1 tablespoon sun-dried tomato paste or tomato paste
2 bay leaves
3 tablespoons chopped fresh herbs, such as rosemary, parsley, thyme and sage
1 cup brine-cured black olives, preferably Calamata, pitted
Saffron rice, fresh pasta or polenta, for serving

Season rabbit with salt and pepper. Heat oil in large, non-reactive skillet over medium-high heat. Add rabbit, being careful not to crowd pan as this will prevent browning. Continue cooking until all the rabbit is browned. Remove rabbit from pan and set aside. • Add pancetta, onion, carrots, celery, parsley and garlic to pan, stirring up all brown bits at the bottom of pan. Sauté for 3–4 minutes, until vegetables are softened. Sprinkle with flour and stir to make a thick paste. Add rabbit and stir in wine, tomato paste, bay leaves, herbs and olives. Reduce heat, cover and simmer until rabbit is tender, about 30 minutes. • To serve, remove bay leaves and adjust seasoning. Serve rabbit hot with saffron rice, pasta or polenta.

Ann Harvey Yonkers, President
Les Dames D'Escoffier International

BRAISED VENISON

Serves 10

¾–1 pound bacon or pork
3 pounds frozen venison or reindeer meat

Salt to taste
10 whole allspice
1¼ cups water

Cut bacon or pork into thin strips and brown well in a large pot. Cut frozen venison or reindeer meat into thin strips. Add in small amounts to pot and brown well. Add salt, allspice and water. Cover and cook over low heat until done.

Mrs. Ritva Rantanen
Wife of the Ambassador of Finland

B·E·E·F

BRASATO AL BAROLO
(BRAISED BEEF IN BAROLO WINE)

Serves 8

"This Italian dish is wonderful served with polenta."

1 bottle Barolo or full-bodied
   red wine
2 large onions, chopped
4 large carrots, chopped
8 stalks celery, chopped
3 large garlic cloves, minced
¼ cup chopped parsley

Salt and pepper to taste
1 bay leaf
1 teaspoon thyme
1 rump roast
2 tablespoons olive oil
Beef broth (if needed)

To make marinade, mix wine, vegetables and herbs. • Place meat in large pot. Add wine marinade and leave for 12–24 hours in refrigerator, turning occasionally. • Remove meat from marinade and pat dry. Brown in oil in large Dutch oven. Add marinade, simmer for approximately 2 hours, adding beef broth if needed. • To serve: slice meat, arrange on patter and surround with sauce.

Nina Pillsbury

BOBOTIE AND YELLOW RICE   Serves 6 to 8
(MALAY MEATLOAF)

"This is a recipe brought to South Africa in the seventeenth century by Malay slaves. It has been adapted to suit local conditions."

2–2½ pounds ground beef
2 onions, peeled and chopped
1 apple, peeled, cored and
  chopped
2 tablespoons vegetable oil
2 slices white bread, soaked
  in milk and squeezed dry
2 tablespoons apricot jam
2 eggs, beaten
2 tablespoons vinegar
½ cup seedless raisins,
  soaked in boiling water

2 tablespoons blanched almonds
1 cup milk (using milk from
  soaked bread)
3 stalks lemon grass or bay
  leaves, minced
1 teaspoon turmeric
1 teaspoon curry powder
1 teaspoon ginger
1 teaspoon brown sugar
Salt and pepper

Fry beef, onions and apple in oil until golden brown. Combine with all other ingredients, mix well and pour into a greased pie dish. Bake for 45 minutes at 350°. Garnish with sprigs of parsley and serve with yellow rice and some or all of the following condiments: chopped onion, sliced bananas, chopped tomatoes, chopped green pepper, chutney and shredded coconut.

Yellow Rice:
1 cup long-grain rice
1 tablespoon brown sugar
1 stick of cinnamon
1 tablespoon turmeric

1 teaspoon salt
½ cup seeded raisins
2 tablespoons butter

Bring 3 cups of water to boil. Add rice, brown sugar, cinnamon stick, turmeric and salt. Simmer over low heat, stirring occasionally with a fork. Add raisins when most of the water is absorbed (15 to 20 minutes). Stir in butter and continue cooking over low heat until soft.

Annette Schwarz
Wife of the Ambassador of South Africa

BURGOO   Makes 1 gallon

"This is best made when fresh vegetables are at their peak, but frozen vegetables and canned tomatoes may be used when necessary. It freezes well."

Day 1:

1 4- to 5-pound stewing chicken
1 pound beef stew meat
1 pound veal stew meat
4 large beef or veal knuckle bones
2 or 3 whole celery stalks
1 whole carrot
1 whole onion
Handful of fresh parsley sprigs

1 10-ounce can tomato purée
1 red pepper pod
¼ cup salt
1 tablespoon lemon juice
1 tablespoon Worcestershire sauce
1 tablespoon sugar
1½ teaspoons black pepper
½ teaspoon cayenne pepper

Day 2:

6 onions, finely chopped
2 green peppers, finely chopped
1 medium turnip, finely diced
8–10 tomatoes, peeled and chopped
2 cups shelled fresh butter beans

2 cups thinly sliced celery
2 cups finely chopped cabbage
2 cups sliced fresh okra
2 cups fresh corn (6 ears)
½ unpeeled lemon, seeded

If you make this in 2 parts, on successive days, it is not such a chore. Put all "day 1" ingredients in a large roaster with 4 quarts of water. Bring to a boil and simmer slowly, covered, for about 4 hours. Let cool and strain. • Cut chicken and meat fine, removing all skin, bone and gristle. Return to stock and refrigerate overnight. • The following day, lift off half the fat from stock. Sauté onions and green pepper in bacon fat or butter and add to stock, along with turnip, tomatoes, butter beans, celery and cabbage. Simmer over low heat for 1 hour, covered. Add okra and cook, uncovered, an additional hour, until thick. • Preheat oven to 300°. Cut corn twice, scraping to get milk. Add corn and lemon to simmering pot. Taste and adjust seasoning. • Place roaster in oven and cook, uncovered, for about 2 hours, until burgoo is a thick stew. This will make a gallon. • If made ahead, reheat in oven to avoid scorching. Serve in mugs and sprinkle with chopped parsley.

Senator A. Mitchell McConnell
(Kentucky)

CARBONADA CRIOLLA
(STUFFED PUMPKIN)

1 large onion, diced
4 cloves garlic, mashed
3 tablespoons vegetable oil
2 pounds beef chuck, cut
   into 2-inch squares
1 pound tomatoes, peeled
   and chopped
4 cups beef broth
1 bay leaf
2 tablespoons chopped
   fresh parsley
1 teaspoon oregano
1 teaspoon thyme
1 teaspoon paprika
Salt and pepper to taste

1 large pumpkin or hubbard
   squash
4 tablespoons butter or
   margarine
2 sweet potatoes, peeled and
   cubed (about 1 pound)
¾ cup uncooked rice
1 handful dried apricots
1 handful dried prunes
1 8-ounce can of corn
1 10-ounce package of frozen
   peas
1 16-ounce can peach halves,
   drained

Preheat oven to 350°. • In a large skillet, sauté onion and garlic in oil. Add beef chuck, stir and brown on all sides. Add tomatoes and beef broth, bay leaf, parsley, oregano, thyme, paprika, salt and pepper. Cover and simmer for 20 minutes. • Halve the pumpkin or squash. Remove the seeds, sprinkle with salt and dot with butter. Dampen with a little water and bake for about 20 minutes, until tender. Remove from oven and set aside. • To the skillet, add sweet potatoes and rice. Cover and simmer for an additional 15 minutes, adding more beef broth as necessary. Add the apricots, prunes, corn and peas and simmer for another 10 minutes. • Just before serving, add peach halves to skillet. Turn all of the skillet ingredients into the pumpkin or squash shell and serve.

Embassy of Argentina

BEEF BROCCOLI WITH GINGER SHREDS   Serves 5

1 pound flank steak
1 tablespoon sugar
2 tablespoons soy sauce
1 tablespoon rice wine or
   Chinese cooking wine
1 egg white
1 tablespoon cornstarch

8 tablespoons vegetable oil
½ cup ginger shreds
2 tablespoons oyster sauce
1 tablespoon water
1 teaspoon cornstarch
2 pounds broccoli

Slice beef across the grain into 1-inch square slices. Place in a large mixing bowl. Add sugar, soy sauce, wine, egg white, 1 tablespoon cornstarch and mix well. Add 2 tablespoons vegetable oil and allow to marinate for at least

30 minutes. • Soak ginger shreds in cold water for 30 minutes, in order to make them more tender. In a small mixing bowl, stir oyster sauce, water and cornstarch to make seasoning sauce. • Remove stems from broccoli and cut into pieces about 1-inch long. Place in boiling water and boil for 30 seconds. Remove and plunge into cold water. Drain and dry. • Heat 2 tablespoons oil in frying pan to 300° and stir-fry beef for approximately 20 seconds, until cooked. Remove beef and drain the oil from the pan. • Heat remaining 4 tablespoons of oil in pan. Squeeze water from ginger shreds and quick-fry in hot oil for a few seconds. Add broccoli. Stir quickly over high heat until mixed. Add ginger and broccoli to beef and serve with rice.

Mrs. Frederick F. Chien
Wife of the Representative of the Coordination Council
for North American Affairs, the Republic of China on Taiwan

DAKOTA BEAN STEW   Makes 1 gallon

"This colorful stew goes well with your favorite salad and bread."

1 12- to 14-ounce variety package of dried beans with 5 or more varieties	8 cups water
	2 cans beef consommé
⅓ cup flour	½ cup diced green pepper
Salt and pepper	½ cup diced yellow pepper
1½ pounds beef or pork tenderloin, cut into bite-sized pieces	½ cup diced red pepper
	½ cup white corn, fresh or frozen
¼ cup olive oil	½ cup yellow corn, fresh or frozen
1 cup finely diced celery hearts	½ cup sliced carrots, fresh or frozen
1 cup finely diced red onion	2 cups cooked brown rice
3 large garlic cloves, crushed	

Rinse and soak beans according to package directions. • Put flour with salt and pepper to taste in a brown bag. Add cubed meat and shake well. In a large Dutch oven, heat oil and brown all of the meat. Add celery and onion and cook for 2 minutes. Add garlic and continue cooking until vegetables are soft. Add water and consommé and bring to a boil. Add beans, reduce heat and simmer for about 3 hours, until beans are tender, adding water if needed. Add peppers, corn and carrots and simmer for an additional 30 minutes. Fold in rice and heat thoroughly. (Freezes well.)

Mrs. Larry Pressler
Wife of the Senator from South Dakota

FEIJOADA
(BRAZILIAN BLACK BEANS)

3 cups black beans
1 pound carne seca (sun-
cured salted beef) which
has been soaked in water
overnight and cut into
1½ inch squares
2 pounds raw smoked tongue,
peeled and cut into large
cubes

½ pound linguiça defumada
(Portuguese sausage)
½ pound chuck beef cut
into ½-inch slices
½ pound salt pork cut into
½-inch slices
Salt and pepper to taste
2 large cloves of garlic, chopped
2 teaspoons shortening

Wash beans well and soak overnight in cold water to cover. Drain, add 6 cups
of water and simmer, covered, adding water as needed, until the beans are
tender (about 2½ hours). As beans come to a boil, begin adding meats as they
are prepared, beginning with the carne seca. • Cover tongue with water, bring
to a boil and simmer for 10 minutes. Drain and add to beans. • Prick sausages
with a fork, cover with water and boil for a few minutes, drain, and add to
beans. • Season beef and pork with salt and pepper and add to beans. •
When beans are tender, brown garlic lightly in shortening in a medium frying pan. Add 1 cup of beans to garlic, mash well and return mixture to large
pot. Adjust seasoning. • Remove meat from beans and place on a large platter. Turn the beans into a chafing dish or bowl. We serve with rice, onions in
sauce, sweetened orange slices, pepper sauce, collard greens and braised
pork loin.

Mrs. María Luiza Penna Moreira
Embassy of Brazil

FILLET OF BEEF CHERNIAVSKY   Serves 6 to 8

1 3–4 pound fillet of beef, trimmed and tied
Salt and pepper to taste
1 tablespoon oil
3 cups veal stock
2 shallots, cut in pieces
4 ounces lean bacon, sliced and cut into pieces
1 pound mushrooms, finely chopped
2 pounds tomatoes, peeled, seeded and chopped
8 medium tomatoes
2 tablespoons arrowroot or potato starch
8 tablespoons Madeira wine
1 bunch of watercress

Preheat oven to 450°. • Sprinkle the beef with salt and pepper. Heat oil until very hot and brown meat on all sides. Place meat in oven and roast for 11 minutes. After roasting, remove meat from pan and set aside to cool. • Discard any fat from pan. Add half the veal stock and boil, stirring to dissolve pan juices. Strain juices back into remaining stock. Set aside. • To make stuffing; chop shallots and bacon to a paste in a food processor. (If chopping by hand, chop as finely as possible.) Heat the paste in a frying pan and brown for 1–2 minutes, stirring constantly. Add mushrooms, chopped tomatoes, salt and pepper and cook over high heat, stirring occasionally, until all liquid has evaporated, for 15–20 minutes. Taste for seasoning and allow to cool completely. • When meat is cool, discard strings and slice meat ¾-inch thick, cutting almost through the meat but allowing the underside to remain attached. • Spread a tablespoon of mushroom stuffing between each slice and press fillet back into its original shape. Reserve the remaining stuffing. • Wrap beef in two layers of aluminum foil. • Core the 8 tomatoes. Cut off tops to form a lid and slice the base so tomatoes will sit upright. Set tomatoes in an oiled baking dish. Place a tablespoon of reserved mushroom stuffing on each tomato and cover with tomato lid. Set aside. • Bring the remaining stock to a boil. Make a paste of the arrowroot and 2 tablespoons Madeira wine and whisk into stock to thicken. Add remaining Madeira and adjust seasoning. • At this time, meat, tomatoes, stuffing and sauce may be kept for 24 hours in refrigerator if stuffing was cold before adding to beef. • Roast the beef wrapped in foil at 425° until a skewer inserted in the center comes out warm to the touch (140° on a meat thermometer) or for about 25 minutes for medium rare. Add 10 minutes for medium well. Bake the tomatoes in the same oven for 15–20 minutes, until tender. • Transfer the beef to a heated serving dish and remove foil. Allow the beef to rest briefly before serving. Arrange the tomatoes alongside meat on one side of dish. Just before serving, bring sauce to a boil and spoon a little over beef. Serve remaining sauce separately. Garnish with watercress.

Anne Willan
President, École de Cuisine La Varenne
(Wife of Mark Cherniavsky, for whom this recipe is named)

BEEF GOULASH
(RINDSGULYAS)

Serves 4 to 6

5 medium onions, sliced
3 tablespoons butter
1 teaspoon paprika, or more
   to taste
2 pounds round steak or beef
   chuck, cut into 2-inch cubes
1 tablespoon vinegar

½ teaspoon caraway seeds
Marjoram to taste
Beef broth (to cover)
Salt to taste
Flour (if needed)
½ teaspoon paprika heated
   in 1 teaspoon butter

Slice onions and sauté in butter until golden. Add 1 teaspoon or more paprika and stir well. Add beef, vinegar, caraway seeds and marjoram and stir. Barely cover with beef broth or water and season lightly with salt. Simmer, covered, until meat is tender. If desired, thicken gravy with a little flour diluted with cold water into a paste. • Just before serving, pour paprika heated in butter over goulash. Serve with boiled potatoes or dumplings.

The Ambassador of Austria
and Mrs. Tuerk

HAMBURGERS AU POIVRE

Serves 4

2 pounds chopped beef
4 teaspoons coarsely ground
   black pepper
Salt
4 teaspoons butter
Tabasco sauce to taste

Worcestershire sauce to taste
Lemon juice to taste
2 tablespoons cognac or
   brandy (optional)
Chopped parsley
Chopped chives

Shape beef into 4 patties. Sprinkle each on both sides with pepper and press in with heel of hand. Let stand for 30 minutes. • Sprinkle a light layer of salt over a heavy skillet and place on high heat. When salt begins to brown, add hamburgers. Cook until well browned on one side and turn. • For rare hamburger, cook for 30 seconds on high, lower heat to medium and cook 1 more minute. Adjust heat and time for greater degree of doneness. • Place a teaspoon of butter on each patty. Add Tabasco, Worcestershire and lemon juice. Ignite warmed cognac and pour over patties. Transfer patties to serving plate and keep warm. • Lower heat and swirl sauce left in skillet. Pour over meat. • Sprinkle parsley and chives over each patty and serve.

Ingeborg Silton

JIM WRIGHT'S BARBECUE

Serves 10 to 12

Soy sauce
Lemon juice
Wine or beer
1 4- to 5-pound beef brisket
8 tablespoons margarine
1 clove garlic, minced
1 white onion, finely diced
2 jalapeño peppers, seeded,
  skinned and finely diced
1 medium can tomatoes or
  tomato sauce

Dash Tabasco sauce
Worcestershire sauce to taste
1 can beer (use more beer or
  coffee for thinning sauce)
Hickory or mesquite chips or
  oak bark
Seasonings: salt, lemon pepper,
  paprika and cayenne pepper
  and garlic powder (optional)

Combine equal parts of soy sauce, lemon juice and wine or beer. Marinate brisket in this mixture overnight. • In a large pan, melt margarine. Add garlic, onion, jalapeño peppers, tomatoes, Tabasco and Worcestershire. Bring to a slow boil, add 1 can of beer and allow to simmer for at least 2 hours. If sauce becomes too thick, thin from time to time with beer or coffee. Sauce should be thin for basting. The residue will thicken when heated a bit and can be used at table. • Make a fire using charcoal and heat until coals are white with ash. Soak hickory or mesquite

chips or oak bark in water for 30 minutes, then sprinkle on coals from time to time to promote smoke. Place aluminum foil under the brisket to avoid burning. Brisket must be at least 12 inches above the fire. Cook with grill cover closed. Top should have a small enough vent to allow smoke to accumulate. If fire flames, douse with water or beer. It is the smoke that makes the barbecue. • Baste and turn brisket every 15 minutes for the first hour. At each turn, sprinkle with a mixture of salt, lemon pepper and paprika plus cayenne pepper and garlic powder, if desired. Then baste and turn every 20 minutes. Brisket should smoke for 2½–3 hours.

The Honorable Jim Wright
Former Speaker of the House of Representatives

MOUSSAKA

Serves 8 to 10

4 medium eggplants or
    potatoes or both
3 large onions, peeled and
    minced
8 tablespoons butter
2 pounds ground beef
3 teaspoons tomato paste
½ cup dry red wine (optional)
1 cup chopped fresh parsley
¼ teaspoon cinnamon

Salt and freshly ground
    pepper to taste
8 tablespoons butter
2 tablespoons flour
1 quart hot milk
4 eggs
Nutmeg to taste
1 cup fresh breadcrumbs
1 cup Parmesan cheese

Peel eggplant and cut into slices, ½ inch thick. If using potatoes, slice to ¼ inch thick. Heat 4 tablespoons butter in a heavy skillet and brown eggplant or potato slices. Do not overcrowd. Remove from skillet and drain on paper towels a few at a time. Add 4 tablespoons butter to skillet and sauté onions over medium heat, stirring occasionally, until brown. Add beef and cook for 10 minutes, stirring occasionally. • In a bowl, combine tomato paste, wine, parsley, cinnamon, salt and pepper. Stir into meat mixture and bring to a boil. Reduce heat and simmer, stirring often, until all liquid is absorbed. Remove from heat. • To make the white sauce, heat butter in a heavy saucepan. Stir in flour and make a smooth paste. Cook over moderate heat, stirring constantly for 3–4 minutes. Add hot milk and, whipping constantly with a wire whisk, cook until thick and smooth. Remove from heat and cool. • When sauce is cool, beat in eggs, one at a time, beating hard after each addition. Stir in nutmeg. • Preheat oven to 400°. • Grease a 13 x 9 x 2 inch pan. Lightly cover the bottom of pan with breadcrumbs. Arrange alternate layers of eggplant and meat mixture over breadcrumbs. Sprinkle each layer with Parmesan cheese and breadcrumbs. Pour sauce over all. Shake the pan so sauce can filter down. • Bake for 1 hour, until top is golden brown. Remove from oven and cool for 20–30 minutes before serving. • Cut into squares to serve. • Moussaka improves with standing, and, if desired, can be refrigerated for 24 hours and reheated before serving.

The Ambassador of Greece and Mrs. Tsilas

KOREAN GRILLED BEEF   Serves 6

1½ pounds boneless sirloin steak
2 teaspoons sesame seeds
1 bunch scallions, trimmed and sliced thinly
4 cloves of garlic, minced

2 tablespoons peeled and finely chopped ginger root
4 tablespoons soy sauce
1 tablespoon rice vinegar
2 teaspoons vegetable oil
1½ teaspoons sugar
Black pepper

Remove fat from meat. Score beef with a sharp knife, almost cutting through to other side, in a diamond pattern on both sides. Tenderize meat by pounding lightly with a mallet. • To prepare sesame seeds, heat a skillet to medium-high. Place seeds in bottom and toast, tossing until they brown—do not allow to pop. Using a mortar and pestle, crush with a dash of salt. • Combine remaining ingredients in a shallow baking pan. Add steak and turn to coat. Refrigerate in marinade for at least 2 hours and up to 6 hours, turning occasionally. • Prepare grill to white hot. Remove meat from marinade and grill for about 4 minutes per side. Slice into thin strips and serve.

Mrs. William H. Darden

GRILLED BOHEMIAN TERIYAKI BEEF   Serves 4 to 6

½ cup soy sauce
¼ cup brown sugar
2 tablespoons olive oil
2 tablespoons plum jelly
1 teaspoon dry ginger

¼ teaspoon lemon pepper
¼ teaspoon garlic salt
2 pounds top sirloin, cut 1 inch thick
Plum jelly

In a large bowl, combine soy sauce, brown sugar, olive oil, plum jelly, ginger, lemon pepper and garlic salt to make marinade. • Cut sirloin into strips ¼ inch wide and marinate in the refrigerator for 2 hours. • Place meat, accordion-style, on skewers. Cook over hot grill. Keep turning meat and brush with marinade until done, about 8–10 minutes. Serve with plum jelly as a condiment.

Senator and Mrs. J. James Exon
(Nebraska)

LIGHT AND LEAN BEEF BROIL   Serves 4 to 6

Served July 8, 1983 at the wedding luncheon of
Suzanne and Larry Craig in Midvale, Idaho.

½ cup soy sauce
¼ cup water
2 tablespoons lemon juice
2 tablespoons honey
1 teaspoon instant minced onion

¼ teaspoon garlic powder
1½ pounds beef sirloin, top
  round, flank steak or brisket
Sesame seeds

Combine soy sauce, water, lemon juice, honey, onion and garlic powder in a non-metallic pan. Add beef and marinate 24–48 hours in refrigerator, turning occasionally. • Remove meat from marinade and broil until cooked to medium rare. Slice beef across the grain into thin slices. Sprinkle with sesame seeds.

Mrs. Larry E. Craig
Wife of the Senator from Idaho

NORTH TEXAS CHILI   Serves 8 to 10

2 pounds lean ground meat
2 16-ounce cans stewed
  tomatoes
1 green pepper, diced
1 onion, diced
Chili powder to taste

Salt to taste
2 15-ounce cans dark red
  kidney beans
Grated colby longhorn cheese
Corn chips

In a large skillet or pot, brown meat. Drain off grease. Add tomatoes, green pepper, onion, chili powder and salt. Also add a small amount of water. • Let the mixture simmer over low heat for 1½ hours. Taste and adjust seasonings. Add kidney beans and simmer for another 30 minutes. • Serve with grated cheese and corn chips.

Jim Lehrer, Associate Editor and Co-anchor
"The MacNeil/Lehrer Newshour"

SOUTHERN BARBECUE BRISKET   Serves 6 to 8

1 large beef brisket
  (4–5 pounds)
1 5-ounce bottle Liquid
  Smoke

1 5-ounce bottle Worcestershire
  sauce
1 bottle of your favorite
  barbecue sauce

Marinate the brisket overnight in the Liquid Smoke and Worcestershire sauce. • Cover brisket and bake in a 225° oven for 7 hours. • Remove brisket from oven and pour off most of marinade, leaving only a few tablespoons. Slice the brisket against the grain and arrange on bottom of cooking pan. Pour barbecue sauce over brisket, cover and return to oven for 30 minutes. Serve warm.

Sandra C. Lee

MY FAVORITE BRISKET   Serves 8 to 10
(NOT TOO GEDEMPTE FLEYSCH)

2 teaspoons salt
Freshly ground pepper to taste
1 5-pound brisket of beef,
    shoulder roast of beef,
    chuck roast or end of steak
1 garlic clove, peeled
2 tablespoons vegetable oil
3 onions, peeled and diced
1 10-ounce can tomatoes
    (see note)
2 cups red wine

2 stalks celery with leaves,
    chopped
1 bay leaf
1 sprig fresh thyme
1 sprig fresh rosemary
¼ cup chopped parsley
6–8 carrots, peeled and sliced
    on the diagonal
Farfel, noodle kugel or potato
    pancakes, for serving

Preheat oven to 325°. Sprinkle salt and pepper over beef and rub with garlic. Sear beef in oil and then place, fat side up, on top of onions in a large casserole. Cover with tomatoes, red wine, celery, bay leaf, thyme and rosemary. Cover and bake for about 3 hours, basting often with pan juices. • Add parsley and carrots and bake, uncovered, for 30 minutes, until carrots are cooked. To test for doneness, stick fork in the flat (thinner or leaner) end of beef. When there is a light pull on the fork as it is removed from the meat, it is "fork tender." Cool and refrigerate. • This dish is best prepared in advance and refrigerated so that fat can easily be skimmed from the surface of the gravy. • When ready to serve, remove meat from sauce and trim all visible fat. Then place meat on a cutting board, on what was fat side down. Look for the grain—that is, the muscle lines of the brisket—and with a sharp knife, cut across the grain. • Preheat oven to 350°. • Skim fat off gravy and reheat. Put the sliced beef in a roasting pan, pour hot gravy over meat, cover and reheat in oven for 45 minutes. • Serve with farfel, noodle kugel or potato pancakes.

NOTE: Try substituting sun-dried tomatoes for canned tomatoes for a more intense flavor.

Joan Nathan, Author
"Jewish Cooking in America"   Les Dames d'Escoffier

BEEF RENDANG   Serves 4 to 6
(A MALAYSIAN CURRY)

4 tablespoons oil
10 dried chili peppers
10 black peppercorns
½ thumbsized piece ginger
½ thumbsized piece turmeric
5 cloves of garlic
10 small shallots

4 stalks lemon grass
4 candlenuts (macadamia nuts
　may be substituted)
2 pounds beef, cut into
　2-inch cubes
Salt to taste
5 cups canned coconut milk
Juice of 1 lime

Heat oil in a frying pan over low heat until smoking slightly. Pound together chilies, peppercorns, ginger, turmeric, garlic, shallots, lemon grass and nuts and place in oil. Fry until fragrant, about 3–4 minutes. • Add meat and salt and fry for another 2–3 minutes. Slowly add 4 cups coconut milk, waiting after each addition for the liquid to be absorbed. Continue cooking until meat is tender, stirring constantly. Add last cup of coconut milk and simmer over very low heat. Do not boil. Add lime juice and cook for an additional 1–2 minutes. • Serve with hot rice.

Renée Talalla
Wife of the Ambassador of Malaysia

RABADA MINEIRA DA FAZENDA
(OXTAILS IN THE STYLE OF MINAIS GERAIS)

Marinade:

3 medium-large onions
8 large garlic cloves
2 bay laurel leaves
6 black peppercorns

2 tablespoons salt
1 cup rice vinegar or white
　vinegar (not sweetened)

4 oxtails, trimmed of all fat

Stew:

4 tablespoons tightly packed
　minced garlic
1½ tablespoons salt
4 tablespoons Portuguese or
　sweet olive oil
2½ teaspoons urucum
　(annato), (see note)

⅓ cup cachaca (Brazilian
　alcohol), (see note)
6–8 cups water
1½ tablespoons tomato paste
5 scallions with green tops,
　finely chopped

Twenty-four hours before serving, place onions and garlic cloves in food processor and chop finely. Place in a large pot and add bay leaves, peppercorns, salt and vinegar. Add the oxtails and cover with water. Bring to a rolling boil. Boil for 3 minutes, turn off heat and allow to cool in marinade for at least 5 hours and preferably overnight. • Remove oxtails and discard marinade. • For the stew, crush garlic with 1½ tablespoons salt in a mortar until it is a smooth paste. In a large pot, heat olive oil and sauté garlic salt mixture with urucum until garlic is crisp. Add cachaca and allow to cook down over medium heat. Add pieces of oxtail and stir well so that each piece is coated with oil and garlic. • To 2 cups water, add tomato paste and scallions and add to oxtail mixture. Bring to a boil and stir well. Place mixture in a 350° oven and cook, covered. After 1 hour add more water and scrape the sides of the pot. Check the pot every hour and add water to be sure the meat is partially covered. Cook for about 3 hours. Adjust seasoning. Serve with Angu a Mineira.

NOTE: Cachaca is available in liquor stores and annato is available at Latin American grocery stores.

Angu A Mineira Da Fazenda:
(Provincial Corn Meal Mush)

8 cups water
4 garlic cloves, thinly sliced
2 teaspoons salt
3 tablespoons Portuguese
  olive oil

2 cups finely ground corn meal
¾ cup roasted manioc flour
(see note)

Place 4 cups water, garlic, salt and olive oil in pot and bring to a boil. Blend other 4 cups water with corn meal. When water in pot boils, add cornmeal, water, stirring constantly. Cook over medium high heat, stirring, until mixture thickens. Remove from heat and whisk in manioc flour until mixture is thick and somewhat dry. Adjust seasoning. Serve immediately.

NOTE: If you cannot find roasted manioc flour, place regular manioc flour in a pan and roast gently stirring often, until golden brown. Cool.

Mrs. Paulo Tarso Flecha de Lima
Wife of the Ambassador of Brazil

BEEF STEW WITH FRENCH BREAD   Serves 8

4 pounds beef, cut into
  1-inch cubes
Flour
Butter
Oil
2 quarts boiling water
2¼ cups V8 juice
2 pounds small red potatoes,
  peeled

1 pound carrots, scraped
  and sliced
2 pounds turnips, peeled
  and cubed
1½ pounds pearl onions, peeled
1 cup red wine, or more
Salt and pepper to taste
Parsley, chopped (optional)

Place beef cubes in a plastic bag with flour and shake. • Sauté beef in a little butter and oil until brown. Transfer beef to a large pot and cover with two quarts boiling water. Add V8 juice and cover pot. Simmer for 1 hour on top of stove or in oven at 325°. • Add potatoes, carrots, turnips, onions and red wine. Add salt and pepper and continue cooking until vegetables are tender. • Sprinkle with chopped parsley just before serving. Serve with a green salad and individual baguettes of French bread for each person.

Mrs. Frank N. Ikard

STEAK AND KIDNEY PIE   Serves 8 to 10

"A Scottish favorite, nicely enhanced."

2½ pounds fillet of beef or
  boneless top sirloin
Salt and freshly ground
  pepper
Nutmeg
4 veal kidneys, trimmed of
  fat
4 tablespoons butter
½ pound mushrooms, washed
  and thinly sliced
¼ cup chopped shallots
1 tablespoon finely minced
  garlic
1 tablespoon dried tarragon

3 medium tomatoes, diced or
  1 cup canned tomatoes,
  drained
1 cup white wine
1½ cups brown sauce or
  1 10¾-ounce can of beef
  gravy
1 teaspoon finely chopped
  fresh thyme or
  ½ teaspoon dried thyme
5 hard-boiled eggs
Pastry (recipe follows)
1 egg
1 tablespoon water

Cut fillet into 12 equal slices or cut top sirloin into 1-inch cubes. Sprinkle lightly with salt, pepper and nutmeg. • Cut kidneys into approximately 24 bite-sized pieces. Sprinkle lightly with salt and pepper. • Heat half of butter in a large skillet and cook beef on both sides until brown. Remove meat and reserve in a warm place. Add kidneys to skillet in which beef was cooked and brown on all sides. Remove kidneys to a separate dish to drain. Add mushrooms and remaining butter to same skillet and cook until soft. When mushrooms are limp, add shallots, garlic, tarragon, tomatoes and wine. Stir in brown gravy and thyme. Bring to a boil, stirring. Add beef and kidneys and cover. Simmer

for 10 minutes or until meat is tender. • Pour into a 2½- to 3-quart casserole or deep-dish pie dish, preferably one with a rim around edge. Allow to cool until lukewarm. The meat should protrude slightly above gravy. If there is too much gravy, spoon some out and reserve. • Preheat oven to 450°. Arrange hard-boiled eggs cut into fours lengthwise over meat. Place a metal or glass funnel in the middle of dish to help hold the pastry up and provide an escape for steam. • Cover pie with pastry, allowing a double thickness around rim. Do not stretch pastry. Decorate around funnel opening (or cut a slash if funnel is not used) with pastry leaves cut from trimmings. Brush with egg and water. Bake for 15 minutes or until pastry is set and lightly browned. Reduce oven heat to 350° and bake for 30 minutes or until pastry is cooked. Serve with reserved gravy.

NOTE: A touch of Madeira may be poured onto each hot portion as it is served.

Pastry:

2 cups flour   **¾ cups butter**
½ teaspoon salt   **Cold water to mix**

Sift flour and salt together. With a palette knife or pastry blender, flake and distribute butter into flour (do not use your hands). Continue until mixture is crumbly. Add enough cold water to form a dough that leaves the bowl clean, using your hands to gently bring it all together. Wrap in aluminum foil or plastic wrap and chill for 30 minutes. • Roll out to a size to cover pie dish or casserole, leaving some for double edging and decorative leaves.

Mrs. Stuart C. Davidson

STUFFED FLANK STEAK   Serves 6

¼ cup butter, plus 2
   tablespoons
½ cup chopped onion
2 large cloves of garlic
1¼ cups cooked rice
½ cup chopped parsley
½ cup freshly grated
   Parmesan cheese
½ teaspoon salt
¼ teaspoon freshly ground
   pepper

2-pound flank steak
2 tablespoons soy sauce
½ teaspoon freshly ground
   pepper
½ cup condensed beef broth
½ cup water
1 tablespoon chopped
   crystallized ginger
Sprigs of parsley
Broiled tomatoes (optional)

Melt ¼ cup butter in a large frying pan. Add onion and 1 crushed clove of garlic and sauté until onion is golden. Remove from heat. Stir in rice, parsley, Parmesan cheese, salt and pepper. • Wipe the steak with a damp towel. With a sharp knife, score both sides lightly into diamonds. Rub steak on both sides with remaining clove of garlic. Brush each side with soy sauce and pepper. Lay steak flat and spread with 1 tablespoon of butter. Place rice mixture over steak, leaving 1½ inches of steak showing around edges (see note) • Roll steak, starting at narrow end, around the rice mixture. Fasten the edges with skewers. Tie the steak roll in two or three places with twine. Cover tightly and refrigerate until 30 minutes before cooking. • Before placing in oven, spread remaining 1 tablespoon butter over surface of rolled steak. Place in roasting pan. Dilute broth with water and pour over steak roll. Sprinkle with ginger and roast at 350° for 45–60 minutes, basting occasionally with pan juices. • Transfer steak to warm platter, remove twine and skewers. Garnish platter with sprigs of parsley and, if you wish, broiled tomatoes. Pour pan

juices into a bowl to serve with meat.

NOTE: If you cannot use all of rice mixture in flank steak, bake remaining rice in a small ovenproof dish and place around steak roll on serving platter.

Belinda McKenzie

BEEF TENDERLOIN WITH DIJON RUB   Serves 4 to 6

1½- to 2½-pound trimmed
   beef tenderloin
⅔ cup flour
½ pound butter, at room
   temperature

½ cup Dijon mustard
¾ teaspoon salt
½ teaspoon freshly ground
   pepper

Have meat at room temperature. Pat dry with paper towel. • Combine remaining ingredients in a food processor and spread generously over meat. • Preheat oven to 425°. Place roast in a heavy baking dish. • Roast meat for 20–25 minutes for rare, 25–30 minutes for medium-rare, and 35 minutes for well done. Remove pan from oven and immediately remove meat to a cutting board to cool. After about 15 minutes, slice and serve.

Marcia Fox, Owner
The World of Cuisine

TEX-MEX TORTILLA CASSEROLE   Serves 8

1 cup nonfat cottage cheese
1 egg or 2 egg whites
1 pound very lean ground beef
⅓ cup finely chopped onion
1 8-ounce can tomato sauce
1 1½-ounce package taco
   seasoning
8 ounces tortilla chips

1½ cups grated mozzarella
   cheese
1 6-ounce can black olives,
   sliced
1 4½-ounce can green chiles
1 cup grated cheddar cheese
½ cup salsa, mild or hot

Preheat oven to 350°. • Combine cottage cheese and egg or egg whites in a bowl and set aside. • In a large skillet, brown beef and onion. Drain off fat. Add tomato sauce and taco seasoning and stir well. Bring to a boil. • Place ⅓ of the tortilla chips in an 11½ x 8 x 2 inch baking dish. Cover with half of meat mixture. Continue layering with half of cottage cheese, half of mozzarella, half of olives and half of chiles, in that order. Repeat and top with cheddar cheese. Cover and bake for 30 minutes, until bubbling.

Mrs. Porter K. Wheeler

TOMATO BEEF   Serves 4 to 6

1 2- to 3-pound sirloin, top
   round or flank steak
½ pound fresh mushrooms
1 large or 2 small onions
1 large or 2 small green
   peppers
4 tomatoes

1 tablespoon oil
2 tablespoons sugar
2 tablespoons sherry
2½ tablespoons soy sauce
1½ teaspoons cornstarch
½ cup water

Slice beef into strips 2 inches long and 1 inch thick, cutting across the grain. Slice mushrooms. Cut onion, green peppers and tomatoes into large chunks. • In a hot skillet (390° in an electric skillet), sauté mushrooms in oil. When mushrooms are partially cooked, add onion and cook quickly. Push mushrooms and onion to the side of skillet and add steak and 2 pieces of tomato. Mash tomatoes to give flavor to sauce. Brown the steak quickly and sprinkle with sugar, sherry and soy sauce. Add green peppers and remaining tomatoes. • In a small bowl, make a paste of cornstarch and water and add to skillet. Cook 3 more minutes and serve with hot rice.

Senator and Mrs. Harris Wofford
(Pennsylvania)

BIFF RYDBERG   Serves 4

8 medium potatoes
2 tablespoons butter
2 yellow onions, finely minced
1 pound beef tenderloin, cut
   into ½-inch cubes

2 teaspoons salt
Pinch freshly ground black
   pepper
Pinch freshly ground white
   pepper

Sweet, strong mustard sauce:
3–6 tablespoons heavy cream
4 teaspoons dry mustard

3 tablespoons sugar

Use 2 frying pans. • Pare the potatoes and cut them into cubes, not too large. Place the cubes in boiling, salted water. Let simmer approximately 5 minutes. Drain well and dry on a clean dish towel. • Fry potato cubes slowly for about 5 minutes in 1 tablespoon browned butter over medium heat until they are soft on the inside and brown on the outside. Mix in the minced onions and fry for another 5 minutes. (An alternative would be to fry the onions by themselves and serve separately on the serving plate.) • Brown the remaining tablespoon butter in the second frying pan, add the beef cubes and quickly brown them. They should not be completely cooked. Due to the quality of the meat, this does not take long. Add salt and pepper to taste. • To make the mustard sauce, whip the cream, combine the mustard and sugar, and stir into the whipped cream until the sugar has dissolved. • Place the potato and onion mixture and beef cubes in separate mounds on a serving plate and serve with the mustard sauce. • A green salad completes the meal nicely.

Ingmar Bjorksten, Cultural Counselor
Embassy of Sweden

TOURNEDOS TERLECKYJ   Serves 4

"Dedicated to Maestro Terleckyj."

4 large fresh artichokes
4 beef fillets, ¾-inch thick

Café de Paris sauce:
4 tablespoons butter, at   1 tablespoon chopped
**   room temperature   fresh parsley**
1 clove garlic, pressed

Steam artichokes for 40 minutes. Remove leaves and choke. Keep artichoke bottoms warm. • Prepare Café de Paris sauce by combining butter, garlic and parsley. Form into 4 dollops and refrigerate. • Sauté fillets over high heat for about 10 minutes or until desired redness is reached. Top each fillet with an artichoke bottom, concave side up. Fill with café de Paris sauce and serve immediately.

John Harbert, M.D.

VINAIGRETTE BEEF   Serves 6 to 8

Salt   Oregano
1 onion   2 bay leaves
1 carrot   3 stalks celery
Parsley sprigs   1 2½-pound eye of round

Sauce:
6 garlic cloves, chopped   Salt and pepper
3 tablespoons capers   1 cup vinegar
2 tablespoons chopped parsley   1 cup olive oil
4 hard-boiled eggs, sliced   ½ cup water from meat

Cover salt, onion, carrot, parsley, oregano, bay leaves, celery and beef with water and bring to a boil. Simmer for 2½ hours and allow to cool on the stove. Remove meat from pot. • Mix all of the sauce ingredients thoroughly and coat meat with the sauce. Refrigerate for at least one day, preferably two, before serving.

Mirta Londero

SWISS STEAK

Serves 6 to 8

¼ pound suet, chopped
2-pound bottom round or
    boneless chuck, 2-inches
    thick
Flour, for dredging
1½ teaspoons salt
1 teaspoon black pepper
1 large onion, diced
1 green pepper, diced
2 celery stalks, diced
1 large carrot, diced

1 teaspoon basil
1 bay leaf
1 teaspoon thyme
1 tablespoon Worcestershire
    sauce
2 dashes Tabasco
3 cups beef stock
3 cups chopped canned
    tomatoes and juice
3 tablespoons chopped parsley

Brown suet in a large Dutch oven or deep skillet. Remove suet from fat. •
Dredge meat in flour seasoned with salt and pepper. Pound to tenderize.
Brown the meat, remove from fat and set aside. Add vegetables, herbs,
remaining salt and pepper, Worcestershire and Tabasco to the pan and simmer until onion is transparent. Add beef stock and tomatoes and simmer for
5 minutes. Return meat to the pot, cover and simmer for 1 hour or until meat
is fork tender. Add parsley and stir. • Serve with buttered egg noodles, rice
or mashed potatoes.

Mrs. Eugene B. Casey

V·E·A·L

BLANQUETTE DE VEAU   Serves 6

4 cups water
1 teaspoon salt
2 pounds veal
1 large onion
2 whole cloves
2 small carrots, sliced
Pinch of thyme
½ cup celery leaves
1 clove garlic
1 tablespoon chopped parsley
1 bay leaf

5 peppercorns
7 tablespoons butter
12 small white onions
½ pound mushrooms
Salt and pepper
2 tablespoons flour
½ cup white wine
¼ cup dry vermouth
1 cup cream or milk (optional)
1 teaspoon lemon juice

Bring water to boil and add salt. Add veal slowly so water continues to boil. Add onion, cut in half and each half stuck with a clove. Add carrots, thyme, celery leaves, garlic, parsley, bay leaf and peppercorns. Cover, reduce heat and simmer until tender, about 1½ hours. • While veal cooks, melt 3 table-spoons butter in a saucepan, add small white onions and cook until lightly browned. Lower heat and simmer until tender, about 30 minutes. • Sauté mushrooms in 2 tablespoons butter for about 6 minutes. Season with salt and pepper. • When veal is tender, remove pieces to a serving casserole. Add onions and mushrooms and keep warm. Strain broth, discarding solids, and set aside two cups. • In a saucepan or skillet, melt remaining 2 tablespoons butter and gradually blend in 2 tablespoons flour. Do not let flour brown. When roux is blended, add 2 cups strained broth, wine and vermouth. Stir until smooth and thickened. Bring to boiling point, lower heat to simmer. Add cream or milk, if desired, and lemon juice. • Add veal, onions and mush-rooms. Reheat and return to casserole. Sprinkle with parsley and serve with rice and green peas.

Mrs. Donald W. Jeffries

ALSATIAN MEAT TART   Serves 8

"One of my 'star' recipes."

Pastry:

2½ cups flour
Salt to taste
8 tablespoons butter, frozen

6 tablespoons well-chilled
   olive or corn oil
6 tablespoons cold milk
   (approximately)

Meat Filling:

1 pound lean ground
   veal (shoulder or leg)
½ pound lean ground pork
Salt and freshly ground
   pepper to taste
⅛ teaspoon grated nutmeg
2 teaspoons butter
⅓ cup finely chopped onion

1½ tablespoons finely chopped
   shallots or scallions
¾ cup finely chopped fresh
   mushrooms
1 egg
1 egg yolk
1 cup heavy cream

To make pastry: In the bowl of a food processor, combine flour and salt. Add butter and cut into flour until mixture is like coarse cornmeal. Gradually add oil and then milk. As soon as dough forms a ball, it is ready. Wrap in wax paper and chill for at least 30 minutes. • Remove dough from refrigerator and place on a lightly floured surface. Roll out into a rectangle measuring about 12 x 6 inches. Fold a third of dough over toward center and fold the other side of dough over toward center to form a three-layered package of dough. Cover and refrigerate for about 30 minutes. • Roll out dough into a rectangle once more on lightly floured surface, sprinkling surface with additional flour as needed. Fold dough into thirds, as before, cover and chill. • Roll out dough into a circle and line a 10-inch quiche pan with removable bottom. Chill. • Preheat oven to 375°. • To make filling: sprinkle veal and pork with salt, pepper and nutmeg. Heat butter in a skillet and sauté onions and shallots or scallions until wilted. Add mushrooms and cook for 5 minutes, stirring frequently. Add veal and pork and stir until meat is broken up. Cook until meat is grey and most of liquid evaporates. • Beat egg and egg yolk with a fork until blended. Add cream, salt and pepper and blend well. Pour egg mixture into meat and stir well. • Pour contents of skillet into prepared pie shell and bake for 15 minutes. Reduce heat to 350° and continue baking for 30–35 minutes, until custard is set. Remove from oven and let stand. Serve lukewarm or at room temperature.

Loni Landfield

VEAL CUTLETS PARMA STYLE — Serves 6

6 veal cutlets
Salt
4 tablespoons butter
¼ pound prosciutto (Parma
　ham), finely chopped

2–3 sprigs parsley, chopped
¼ cup Parmesan cheese
2½ tablespoons Marsala wine

Pound veal lightly to flatten. Sprinkle with salt and brown in butter in heavy frying pan on both sides until golden. Put a little prosciutto, parsley and Parmesan cheese on each cutlet and sprinkle with Marsala. As soon as cheese begins to melt, remove from heat and serve immediately, pouring sauce over cutlets.

Anna Maria Via

DICED VEAL IN CREAM SAUCE (ZÜRCHER GESCHNETZELTES) — Serves 4 to 6

1¼ pounds tender boneless
　veal, diced
Dash of flour
Salt and pepper to taste
4 tablespoons butter

1 onion, chopped
½ cup diced mushrooms
　(optional)
7 ounces white wine
7 ounces heavy cream

Dust veal in flour seasoned with salt and pepper and sauté in small quantities in butter. Remove from skillet and keep warm. • Sauté onion until tender and transparent. Add mushrooms, if including them, and continue cooking, covered, for 3 minutes. Stir in wine and continue cooking to reduce amount. Mix in cream and simmer for 3 minutes. Return veal to skillet and warm. • Serve at once with rice or rösti. (See rösti recipe in "Vegetables" section.)

The Ambassador of Switzerland and Mrs. Jagmetti

OSSO BUCO MILANESE   Serves 6

This recipe is topped with gremolada—a piquant garnish generally made by mixing grated lemon grind, garlic, and chopped parsley.

6 slices shank of veal, 2½ to
  3 inches thick
Flour
6 tablespoons butter
½ cup dry white wine
1 14-ounce can peeled Italian
  tomatoes
Salt and pepper

Hot stock or water, if needed
1 clove garlic, minced
Grated rind of ½ lemon
3–4 sprigs fresh parsley,
  finely chopped
1–2 anchovy fillets, finely
  chopped

Dust veal in flour, shaking off excess. In a large pan, brown veal on all sides in butter. Add wine and simmer for 15 minutes. Add tomatoes and season with salt and pepper to taste. Cover and cook for 2 hours over low heat, until meat is very tender. If necessary, hot stock or water may be added during cooking. • Prepare a gremolada by mixing garlic, lemon rind, parsley and anchovy fillets. Sprinkle over the veal a few minutes before serving. Serve with rice, preferably risotto alla Milanese with saffron.

Anna Maria Via

PETTO DI VITELLO RIPIENO   Serves 8 to 10
(STUFFED VEAL BREAST)

1 4- to 5-pound breast of
  veal with bones
3 slices of white bread
2 cups of cold water
2 tablespoons butter
2 tablespoons oil
1 large onion, coarsely
  chopped
1 pound ground meat (veal,
  pork and beef mixed)
½ cup Parmesan cheese,
  freshly grated

Pinch of thyme
½ cup cooked spinach, dried
  and chopped
½ cup shelled pistachio nuts
Salt and freshly ground pepper
1 egg
5 hard-boiled eggs
1½ inch thick slice of boiled
  ham
Water
2 carrots
2 leeks

Wash the veal repeatedly in cold water to keep it white. Pat dry and lay meat flat, bone side up. With a very sharp, small knife, remove the bones, cutting as close as possible to the meat. Keep the bones. If there are holes in the meat, cut small pieces from edges and fill in. • Soak bread in cold water. • Melt butter in a skillet and add oil. Add onion and sauté until transparent. • Place ground meats in a mixing bowl and add cooked onion, Parmesan cheese, thyme, spinach and pistachio nuts. Squeeze bread to remove excess water and add to mixture. Season with salt and pepper, keeping in mind that veal is bland and needs quite a bit of both. Add egg and mix well, kneading lightly with your hands. • With veal breast flat in front of you, place the ground meat mixture in the center of veal breast. Flatten slightly with your hands. Place hard-boiled eggs end to end on meat mixture. Cut the slice of boiled ham into 5 or 6 strips and place over and beside eggs. Roll the veal over this mixture like a jelly roll. Tuck in stray ends and tie veal with string, once lengthwise, then in 4 or 5 places horizontally. Some of the filling may show at either end. • Wrap the meat that is now tied like a sausage in two layers of cheesecloth. Make a knot at each end. • In an heatproof pan that is close to the shape of the meat, bring about ½ inch water to boil. As soon as the water boils, place the veal roll in it. The cheesecloth ends should hang over the edges at either end of the pan. Place the carrots and leeks around the veal roll. Add the veal bones and cover the pan. Simmer over low heat for 1½ hours. • Allow meat to cool in its cooking liquid. • Lift meat roll from pan, using the ends of the cheesecloth as handles. Place on a platter. • Reduce the cooking liquid to half the quantity. Let cool and strain into a jar and refrigerate. Discard the bones, carrots and leeks. • Place a wooden board on top of meat and weigh with a heavy object. Place in refrigerator overnight or for at least several hours. • When ready to serve, unwrap veal carefully and slice. Arrange slices on a platter, displaying the stuffing to best advantage. • Fit a pastry bag with large nozzle. Take the jellied liquid from jar in refrigerator and place in pastry bag. Gently squeeze gelatin over the top and around the edges of the stuffed veal.

Flavia Biancheri
Wife of the Ambassador of Italy

WIENER SCHNITZEL   Serves 6 to 8
(VIENNESE VEAL CUTLETS)

1 3-pound leg of veal	1 cup breadcrumbs
Salt to taste	1 cup butter or butter/oil
¾ cup flour	combination
2 eggs, beaten	1 lemon, sliced

Have butcher cut and flatten veal into thin cutlets. Make incisions at edges after trimming to prevent curling when cooking. Salt. Dip veal cutlets into flour, then into egg and finally into breadcrumbs. • In a large skillet, fry cutlets on both sides in hot butter until golden brown. Remove from skillet and drain on paper towel. Decorate with lemon slices.

Monika Tuerk
Wife of the Ambassador of Austria

ROAST VEAL LOIN STUFFED WITH SPINACH, MUSHROOMS AND PROSCIUTTO

Serves 5 to 6

Stuffing:

½ pound fresh spinach
4 tablespoons olive oil
6 shallots, finely chopped
Salt and pepper to taste
½ pound fresh chanterelle
   mushrooms (or any firm-
   fleshed mushrooms)

¼ pound prosciutto, thinly
   sliced
2 ounces Parmesan cheese,
   grated
Cheesecloth

Remove stems from spinach and wash thoroughly. Heat 2 tablespoons of the oil in a large skillet. Add shallots and sauté 1 minute. Add spinach and dust with salt and pepper. Cook until spinach is just cooked and place in a cheesecloth, wringing out excess moisture. Cool to room temperature. Wash mushrooms and cut into quarters. Heat remaining oil in the skillet and sauté mushrooms over medium heat until cooked, about 7–8 minutes. Season with salt and pepper and set aside. Trim any fat from prosciutto and julienne into thin strips. Combine prosciutto with the Parmesan cheese, spinach and mushrooms. Mix thoroughly.

Veal:

1 3-pound veal loin (weight
   after butcher has removed
   all fat and sinew)

Salt and pepper
Butcher's twine

Preheat oven to 400°. Using a long, sharp knife, make a slit through the middle of the veal, going from one end to other lengthwise (make opening large enough to accommodate the stuffing). On a piece of plastic wrap, form the stuffing into a cylindrical shape that will fit easily into the veal loin. Roll the stuffing in the plastic wrap and twist each end so it is secure. Season inside the cavity of the veal with salt and pepper. Work one end of the stuffing, still wrapped in plastic, through the cavity until all the stuffing is surrounded by veal. Untwist one end of the plastic and pull the other end while trapping the stuffing in the veal with your free hand. Tie the veal with butcher's twine to hold stuffing in and keep the shape of the meat. Brown veal quickly on all sides and place in oven for

25–30 minutes, or until interior temperature reaches 120°-130°. Untie veal and allow to rest on a warmed serving platter for 7–10 minutes, then serve with sauce.

Sauce:

1 cup white wine   **1 cup veal stock**
1 sprig thyme

Pour off any fat from roasting pan and deglaze pan with the wine over medium heat, reducing liquid by half. Add thyme and veal stock and simmer for 5 minutes. Strain and serve over veal.

Brian McBride, Executive Chef
Melrose Restaurant, Park Hyatt Hotel

VEAL PAPRIKA   Serves 6 to 8

2 pounds veal, pounded very   **2 tablespoons paprika**
    thin   **½ cup white wine**
Salt and pepper to taste   **½ cup chicken broth**
2 tablespoons Crisco oil   **1½ cups sour cream**
4 tablespoons butter   **¼ cup half and half (optional)**
3 shallots, chopped

Cut veal into small strips, approximately ½ inch x 2 inches, and sprinkle with salt and pepper. Heat oil and 2 tablespoons butter in skillet and brown veal quickly on high heat. Transfer to a casserole. • To the skillet add remaining 2 tablespoons butter and sauté shallots until tender. Stir in paprika and add wine. Cook until liquid is almost completely reduced. Add broth and reduce for 5 minutes. Gradually stir in sour cream. Adjust salt and pepper to taste. • Pour the sour cream sauce over the veal and heat, but do not boil. Thin sauce with half and half, if desired. • Serve with buttered noodles.

Mrs. Jerold J. Principato

L·A·M·B

BARBEQUED LEG OF LAMB   Serves 6 to 8

1 leg of lamb, boned and
   butterflied
1 cup oil
¼ cup wine vinegar

¼ cup soy sauce
2 cloves garlic, crushed
1 tablespoon salt
Black pepper

Hot barbeque sauce:
2 teaspoons Tabasco sauce
2½ cups chili sauce
1 teaspoon minced chili
   peppers
¾ cup oil
½ cup lemon juice
2 tablespoons tarragon
   vinegar

2 cups chopped onions
2 cloves garlic, minced
1 tablespoon brown sugar
1 bay leaf, crumbled
1 teaspoon dry mustard
1 teaspoon salt
½ cup water

Marinate lamb for at least 2 hours at room temperature in a mixture of oil, vinegar, soy sauce, garlic, salt and pepper. • To make barbeque sauce combine all ingredients. Bring to a boil, reduce heat and simmer for 15 minutes. Keep covered in refrigerator. • Broil or barbeque lamb for approximately half an hour per side, basting with hot barbeque sauce.

Sarah T. Minikes

FRENCH LAMB STEW

2 pounds lamb, cubed
2 tablespoons butter
1 clove of garlic, chopped
1 onion, chopped
2 bay leaves
1 teaspoon salt
¼ teaspoon pepper
¼ teaspoon marjoram
2 tablespoons parsley,
   chopped

14½ ounces chicken broth
½ cup white wine
3 carrots, cut or
   1 package frozen carrot tips
8 small white onions or
   1 package frozen
3 potatoes, peeled and cubed
Parsley sprigs

Brown lamb in butter and remove lamb to a platter. Add garlic and onion to pan and brown. Pour off fat and add lamb. Add bay leaves, salt, pepper, marjoram, parsley, chicken broth, and wine. Cover and simmer over low heat for 20 minutes. Add carrots, onions and potatoes and continue cooking for about

15 minutes. Check seasoning. Sprinkle with fresh parsley. Serve with French garlic bread and a green salad.

Mrs. Jerold J. Principato

HONEY MUSTARD PECAN ROAST RACK OF LAMB   Serves 4

¼ cup Dijon mustard
1 tablespoon honey
1 tablespoon molasses
2 cloves garlic, minced
½ cup pecans, toasted

3 tablespoons breadcrumbs
1 teaspoon rosemary
2 tablespoons olive oil
2 racks of lamb

Preheat oven to 375°. • Mix mustard, honey, molasses and garlic. Set aside. • In a food processor, combine pecans, breadcrumbs and rosemary until mixture resembles a fine meal. • In a heavy skillet, heat oil over high heat. Add first rack of lamb and brown on all sides, turning frequently, about 5 minutes. Transfer to roasting pan and coat with mustard mixture on all sides. Repeat with second rack. • Arrange lamb with rounded sides up and sprinkle with pecan mixture. Bake until medium rare, about 25–30 minutes. Cut between bones and serve.

Embassy of New Zealand

NEW ZEALAND LAMB CASSEROLE "ITALIAN"   Serves 4 to 6

1½ pounds lamb, cubed
2 tablespoons butter
2 onions, chopped
2 cloves garlic, minced
1 teaspoon sage, dried or
    fresh
½ cup dry white wine
½ cup water
2 tablespoons chicken stock

1 egg yolk
1 tablespoon cornstarch
Juice of 1 large lemon
Rind of 1 large lemon, cut
    in strips
2 tomatoes, chopped
Rosemary, chopped
Parsley, chopped

In a large skillet, brown lamb cubes in butter. Add onion and garlic. Cook until onion is transparent. Add sage, wine, water and chicken stock. Simmer for 1½ hours, until tender. • Mix egg yolk, cornstarch, lemon juice and lemon rind with a little of the liquid from lamb. Add to lamb mixture and cook until sauce thickens. Do not boil. • Place lamb mixture in a casserole, sprinkle with tomatoes, rosemary and parsley. Serve in casserole.

Chef Warren A. Neame
Embassy of New Zealand

LAMB SHANKS DIVINE   Serves 2

"Tastes even better the second day. A great favorite of men."

2 lamb shanks
1 small cabbage, thinly sliced
1 eggplant, peeled and cut
   in ¾-inch cubes

1 14½-ounce can of tomatoes
1 cup uncooked rice
Salt to taste

Preheat oven to 325°. • Rinse shanks and cut off excess fat. Do not skin (skin and fat add to flavor). • Place in a large covered casserole. Cover with cabbage, tucking it around sides. Cover cabbage with eggplant and also pack around sides. Break up tomatoes and pour with liquid over all. • Bake, covered, for 2–2½ hours. Pour rice into liquid around lamb shanks and continue cooking for 1 hour.

Mrs. Alan K. Simpson
Wife of the Senator from Wyoming

RACK OF LAMB ASSYRIAN   Serves 6

Marinade:
1 large onion
2–3 cloves garlic
1 teaspoon dried basil leaves
½ cup pomegranate juice
   (or less of concentrate)

¼ cup dry red wine
½ teaspoon salt
½ teaspoon pepper

2½ lamb racks, each with
   8–9 ribs (see note)

In a blender or food processor, purée the marinade ingredients. Rub the marinade well into the racks. Place the racks in a shallow glass or enameled pan and pour the remaining marinade over them. Marinate in the refrigerator overnight or at cool room temperature for 6–8 hours. (If meat has been kept in the refrigerator, let it come to room temperature — about 45 minutes — before roasting.) • Preheat oven to 450°. • When ready to cook, wipe off any excess marinade and roast the racks for 15–20 minutes for medium rare, longer if you like lamb done to a greater degree.

NOTE: Ask the butcher to remove the chine bone and the lifter meat and to French-cut the rib bones.

Narsai M. David, Author
"Monday Night at Narsai's"

LAMB PAPRIKA   Serves 4

1 pound lamb, cubed
3 tablespoons flour
6 slices bacon, cut in small
  pieces
½ cup chopped onion
2 cups diced potatoes
1 tablespoon paprika
½ teaspoon caraway seeds

¼ teaspoon crushed fresh
  rosemary
½ teaspoon salt
¼ teaspoon white pepper
1 cup diced and drained
  tomatoes
½ cup beef broth
½ cup red wine

Dredge lamb cubes in flour. • In a deep skillet sauté the bacon and onion until brown. Add the potatoes and meat and brown lightly. Sprinkle with paprika, caraway seeds, rosemary, salt and pepper. Add tomatoes, broth and wine and simmer, covered, for 40 minutes. Serve hot.

Mrs. Eugene B. Casey

LAMB CHOPS WITH CHESTNUTS   Serves 4

1½ pounds fresh chestnuts
4 shoulder lamb chops,
  trimmed of fat
Butter for browning lamb
  chops
1 onion, finely chopped
5 or 6 cloves

1 teaspoon cinnamon
6 sprigs flat-leaf parsley
Salt and freshly ground
  pepper to taste
¼ cup molasses
1½ cups water, plus more
  as needed

Glaze:
2 tablespoons unsalted butter   2 tablespoons molasses

Boil chestnuts in water for about 30 minutes and drain. Remove shells and inner skin and set aside. • In a large skillet, brown lamb chops in butter on both sides. Add onion and continue cooking for a few minutes. Add cloves, cinnamon, parsley, salt, pepper, molasses and 1 cup water; cover and simmer for about 20 minutes or until chops are half done. Add chestnuts and remaining ½ cup water and simmer for about 20 minutes, until chestnuts are tender and lamb is cooked. As they cook, maintain the liquid level. Remove chops and chestnuts to a platter and keep warm. • Strain the sauce and simmer gently to reduce and thicken. Adjust seasoning. • Meanwhile, make the glaze. In a small skillet, melt 2 tablespoons butter. Stir in 2 tablespoons molasses and allow to caramelize slightly. Return chestnuts to skillet and glaze with this mixture on all sides. Remove from heat. • Return the lamb and chestnuts to large skillet of simmering sauce. When thoroughly heated, arrange lamb and chestnuts on warmed plates, and cover with sauce. Serve immediately.

The Ambassador of Turkey and Mrs. Kandemir

DOLMA DARPIS
(GRAPE LEAVES WITH LAMB)

Serves 8 to 10

*"Recipe from my mother, Mrs. J.P. Sayad,
all the way from Azerbaijan, Iran (67 years ago)!"*

3 pounds boned lamb (or
  beef)
1 cup long-grain rice,
  partially cooked
1 bunch fresh dill, chopped or
  2 heaping tablespoons dry
  dill weed
1 green pepper, finely
  chopped
1 medium onion, finely
  chopped

1 bunch scallions, finely
  chopped
2 cloves garlic, minced
1 tablespoon paprika
Salt to taste
3 jars of grape leaves
1 cup butter
Sour cream (or yogurt)
Paprika butter (recipe follows)
½ cup chopped fresh cilantro

Paprika butter:
½ cup finely chopped onion
½ cup of butter

1 teaspoon paprika

Cut meat into small pieces and sauté in 3 tablespoons of butter until nicely browned. Add rice, dill, green pepper, onion, scallions, garlic and 1 tablespoon paprika. Stir over medium heat until well mixed. Remove from heat , season with salt to taste, and set aside. • Rinse grape leaves thoroughly. Place 1 heaping teaspoon of meat mixture in the center of each grape leaf. Fold edge of leaf toward the center, tucking in ends, to form into rolls. Repeat with all grape leaves and meat. Layer in a roasting pan or casserole dish 14 x 9½ x 3½ inches, folded sides down, packed closely. Add remaining butter and boiling water to within an inch of the top of pan. Cover and bake at 350° for 1½–2 hours, until leaves and rice are tender. Check after 1 hour and add boiling water if necessary. Remove lid and continue cooking for 10 to 15 minutes. • To make paprika butter, sauté onion in butter. Add paprika and simmer gently until onions are transparent and tender. • To serve, spoon 1 tablespoon sour cream on each grape leaf packet, top with 1 teaspoon paprika butter and sprinkle with cilantro.

Mrs. Charles W. Barker

P·O·R·K

ANNETTE'S STUFFED PORK CHOPS   Serves 4

4 tablespoons butter
1 small onion, minced
Dash Worcestershire sauce
½ cup Pepperidge Farm
   herb stuffing mix

¼ ounce blue cheese, crumbled
Salt and pepper to taste
4 pork chops, at least ½ inch
   thick

Preheat oven to 350°. • In a medium skillet, heat butter and sauté onion until transparent. Add stuffing mix, Worcestershire sauce, blue cheese and salt and pepper. Mix lightly. • Cut pockets in pork chops and stuff with blue cheese mixture. Secure with toothpicks. Place in a lightly greased ovenproof dish and cover lightly with aluminum foil. Bake for about 45 minutes, until pork chops are brown on top. • Serve with wild rice and a salad.

Annette Shelby

ROAST PORK WITH ARTICHOKE MUSTARD SAUCE

Serves 6

"Sauce is good on steaks, lamb, pork, chicken, turkey or grilled fish."

3 pounds boned, rolled pork loin	2 cloves garlic, slivered
	Salt and pepper
1–1½ cups white wine	½ teaspoon dried thyme

Preheat oven to 350°. • Place pork loin in a shallow pan and rub with some wine. Cut slits in pork and insert garlic slivers. Work salt, pepper and thyme into pork. Roast for 2¼ hours, basting occasionally with pan juices. If dry, add wine to pan after 1 hour. • When pork is cooked, remove from oven and allow to sit for 10 minutes. Carve and cover slices of pork with pan juices. Serve with artichoke mustard sauce.

Artichoke mustard sauce (makes 2 cups):

¼ cup Dijon mustard	2 teaspoons lemon juice
6 tablespoons boiling water	1 14-ounce can artichoke
¾ cup olive oil	hearts, drained and coarsely
Ground pepper to taste	chopped

In a food processor or electric mixer, place mustard and boiling water. Beat constantly until well blended. Add oil in a steady stream while mixing until sauce becomes creamy. Add pepper and lemon juice. Stir in artichoke hearts. • May be used immediately or refrigerated for later use with steak, lamb, pork, chicken, turkey or grilled fish. If refrigerated, bring sauce to room temperature before serving.

Mrs. Richard S. Morehouse

MARINATED PORK TENDERLOIN

4 tablespoons soy sauce	2 teaspoons light brown sugar
1 clove garlic, minced	2 tablespoons olive oil
½ teaspoon freshly ground pepper	1 teaspoon grated fresh ginger
	Pork tenderloin

In a bowl, mix soy sauce, garlic, pepper, brown sugar, oil and ginger and pour over tenderloin. Cover and refrigerate for 4 hours. • Bring pork to room temperature and preheat broiler. Broil tenderloin in marinade for 12–15 minutes, 4 inches from broiler.

Paula Jeffries

CONDUCTOR'S STEW   Serves 6

Hearty and delightfully different. The symphony orchestra conductor who originated it chooses to remain anonymous.

2 cups dried lentils	2 pounds sausage (sweet
Salt to taste	Italian, Kielbasa, knockwurst,
1 medium onion, chopped	etc.—choose 2 or 3)
2 tablespoons oil	1 bay leaf
2½–3 cups canned tomatoes	1 tablespoon sugar
Garlic salt	Freshly ground black pepper

Wash lentils and place in deep saucepan. Cover with salted water and bring to a boil. Simmer for about 20 minutes, until tender but not mushy. Drain, reserving liquid. • Sauté onion in oil until soft. Stir in tomato and a few dashes of garlic salt. Continue cooking until slightly thick. • Remove casings from sausages and cut into 1-inch pieces. Place sausages, lentils, tomato mixture and seasonings in a large casserole. Add a little of the liquid from lentils. • Bake for 30 minutes, covered, at 350°. Add more liquid as needed if it becomes too dry. • This dish is best made ahead and reheated.

Anonymous

BONELESS PORK ROAST

Boneless pork tenderloin	Soy sauce
Minced garlic	Ginger

Preheat oven to 350°. • Place pork on a large sheet of aluminum foil. Spread with garlic and sprinkle with ginger. Pour soy sauce over meat and wrap tightly with foil. Place package in baking pan. Bake 1–1½ hours or until done. To serve, slice tenderloin and spoon some of the cooking juices over each portion.

Sarah T. Minikes

GOUDSE PORK LOIN   Serves 4

1 pound pork loin
Salt and pepper to taste
4 tablespoons butter
4 Golden Delicious apples,
   peeled, cored and halved
Brown sugar
1 potato (around 3 ounces)

⅓ cup white wine
3 ounces mature Gouda cheese
1 tablespoon flour
3 tablespoons cream
Parsley sprigs
1 8-ounce can mandarin
   oranges

Rub pork with salt and pepper. In a deep skillet (which has a lid), sear quickly in hot butter on all sides. Fill the halved apples with brown sugar. Add apples, potatoes and wine to skillet, sprinkle with salt and allow to simmer, covered, for 30 minutes. • Preheat oven to 275°. • Remove pork from skillet and cut in four large pieces almost all the way through meat. Fill the spaces between with slices of cheese (cheese should be showing above meat). • Place pork in an ovenproof dish, surrounded with apples and potatoes. Place in oven until the cheese has melted about 5 minutes. • While pork is in oven, combine flour with cream and mix well with a fork. Add cream mixture to cooking liquid in skillet and heat until thickened. • Remove pork from oven and garnish with parsley and mandarin oranges. Place sauce in a separate serving dish.

Monique Fein
Wife of the Ambassador of the Netherlands

MENUDO   Serves 6
(A Zesty Pork Stew)

1 cup sliced pork
1½ cups water
1 teaspoon minced garlic
4 tablespoons chopped onions
½ cup chopped tomatoes
1 large piece chorizo sausage,
   sliced
⅓ cup sliced pork liver

1 cup pork broth
1 15-ounce can peas, reserve
   liquid
½ cup cubed potatoes
½ cup sliced red peppers
Scant 2½ teaspoons salt
Dash of pepper
1 tablespoon oil

Cook pork in water for 15 minutes. Extract fat from pork. • Sauté garlic, onions, tomatoes, chorizo and pork liver for 5 minutes. Add pork broth and liquid drained from peas. Bring to boil. Add potatoes and red peppers. Cook for 12 minutes. Add peas and continue cooking for 3 minutes longer. Season with salt and pepper and serve.

Cultural Attaché
Embassy of the Philippines

ANNIE GLENN'S HAM LOAF

Serves 4 to 6

1 pound ground cured ham
½ pound ground fresh ham
1½ cups dry breadcrumbs
2 eggs, beaten
¾ cup milk

Pepper to taste
¼ cup water
¼ cup vinegar
¼ cup sugar
1 tablespoon mustard

Preheat oven to 350°. • Combine hams, breadcrumbs, eggs, milk and pepper, form into loaf and place in baking pan. • Heat together water, vinegar, sugar and mustard and stir until dissolved. Pour ¾ of mixture over ham loaf. Bake for 1½ hours, basting frequently. Add additional sauce as needed. Can be served hot or cold.

Annie Glenn
Wife of Senator John H. Glenn (Ohio)

PORK LOIN ON MINTED ZUCCHINI

Serves 4

2 medium zucchini
3 tablespoons honey
Salt and pepper to taste
2 teaspoons chopped mint
  leaves
2 teaspoons chopped basil
  leaves

1 tablespoon balsamic vinegar
4 slices boneless pork loin,
  ½–¾ inch thick
Paprika
Chopped mint and basil, for
  garnish

Preheat broiler. Place oven rack 2 inches from heat and line broiler pan with foil. • Trim ends off zucchini and cut in half lengthwise. Brush insides lightly with a little honey, salt and pepper. Place on grill rack and broil until browned and bubbly, about 5–6 minutes. Remove and cool on a cutting board until cool enough to slice. Slice very thin and place in a medium bowl. Add mint, basil and vinegar and toss. Keep warm while pork cooks. • Place pork slices on the same broiler pan, brush tops and sides lightly with honey and sprinkle with salt, pepper and paprika. Broil for about 5–6 minutes, until lightly browned. Turn over, drizzle other side with honey and sprinkle with salt and pepper. Broil another 5 minutes. Slices should be browned and quite firm to the touch but not hard. • To serve, place an equal portion of zucchini on each plate to form a bed. Top with a slice of pork. Garnish with additional mint and basil. Serve immediately.

Rita Calvert, Author
"Plain and Fancy Mustard Cookbook"
and columnist for the "Baltimore Sun"

IOWA STUFFED PORK CHOPS   Serves 2

½ cup whole kernel corn
½ cup breadcrumbs
Pinch of salt and pepper
¾ tablespoon parsley
Pinch of sage

½ tablespoon finely chopped
  onion
½ cup diced apple
1 tablespoon milk
2 Iowa pork chops, thick cut

Basting sauce:
¼ cup honey
¼ cup mustard
¼ teaspoon rosemary

½ teaspoon salt
Pinch of pepper

In a bowl, combine corn, breadcrumbs, salt, pepper, parsley, sage, onion, apple and milk until well mixed. • Cut a slit into the side of each pork chop and stuff with the mixture. • In a separate bowl, combine basting ingredients until smooth. • Brown stuffed pork chops on both sides in a skillet and transfer to a baking dish. Bake for 1 hour at 350°, basting often.

Senator Tom Harkin
(Iowa)

COUNTRY HAM BAKED IN CIDER

1 whole 12-pound smoked
  country ham
1 quart apple cider
2 teaspoons ground cloves
½ cup light brown sugar

1 teaspoon dry mustard
Apples baked with apple
  jelly and ginger
Sprigs of watercress for
  garnish

Scrub ham thoroughly with a stiff brush. Place in large, deep roasting pan or stockpot and cover completely with cold water. Soak at room temperature for 12–48 hours, changing water a couple of times. • Preheat oven to 300°. • Discard soaking water and place ham in deep roasting pan, fat side up. Set aside 3 tablespoons apple cider. Pour remaining cider into pan and add enough water to barely cover ham. Set pan on lowest rack of oven and bake for 2 hours. Do not allow liquid to exceed a quiet simmer or ham will be tough. Turn ham to ensure even cooking. Bake for 2 hours longer. (It takes 20–25 minutes per pound to cook a tender ham.) A thermometer inserted in the center but not touching the bone should read 170°. • Remove from oven and leave in liquid to cool overnight in a cool place to keep ham moist. (At this point, ham can be removed from liquid, wrapped and refrigerated and kept for up to 1 week. Bring ham to room temperature before proceeding.) • Preheat oven to 425° and remove ham from all liquid. Using a sharp knife, remove skin from ham and trim fat all over to ¼ inch. • Return ham to roasting pan, fat side up. Stud fat with cloves. Blend brown sugar, mustard and reserved 3 tablespoons

apple cider to make a thick paste. Rub paste over fat. Roast for 20–25 minutes, until ham has a beautiful golden glaze. Allow to cool. • Carve by cutting a thin slice from bottom to allow ham to sit flat. Turn and cut a wedge from hock end. With a long, thin knife, carve very thin vertical slices, then slide knife horizontally against bone to release slices. Surround ham with apples baked with apple jelly and ginger and sprigs of watercress.

Chef Michael Patton
1789 Restaurant

ROAST PORK PORTUGUESE STYLE   Serves 4 to 6
(CARNE DE PORCO À PORTUGUESA)

"This is a very traditional dish from Alentejo Province
in the south of Portugal."

2½ pounds cockles or clams
1¼ pounds pork loin
Salt and pepper to taste
Massa de pimentão (red pepper pulp)
2½ pounds new potatoes, peeled
1 tablespoon butter

Oil, for frying pork and potatoes
1 bay leaf
5 cloves garlic, minced
1 bunch parsley, roughly chopped
Juice of 1 lemon

Wash clams thoroughly and set aside. • Cut pork into cubes and season with salt, pepper and pepper pulp. Cut potatoes, if large, and set aside. • Heat butter and oil in a large skillet and sauté pork with bay leaf until golden. Remove pork and sauté garlic and half of the parsley. Add clams. When clam shells open, add pork and simmer. • In a separate skillet, fry potatoes in very hot oil until cooked through. Drain on paper towels. Place potatoes, meat and clams in large serving dish and mix well. Season with lemon juice and sprinkle with remaining parsley. Serve hot.

Rita Cardoso Pinto
Portuguese Embassy

PERNIL DE COCHINO HORNEADO   Serves 20
(Venezuelan Pork Roast)

2 large onions, cut in chunks
17 cloves garlic, cut coarsely
½ cup oil
3 teaspoons Worcestershire
   sauce
7 teaspoons salt, plus
   additional to sprinkle on
   pork before serving
1¾ teaspoons black pepper
¼ cup wine vinegar

2 teaspoons fresh marjoram or
   1 teaspoon dry marjoram
1 sprig thyme
1 bay leaf
2 cups orange juice
1 12–14 pound pork thigh
   (fresh ham)
1 lemon
½ cup sweet muscatel or
   Madeira wine
1 teaspoon flour (optional)

One day before roasting the pork thigh, place onions, garlic and oil in food processor and blend well. Add 2 teaspoons Worcestershire sauce, 7 teaspoons salt, 1½ teaspoons pepper, vinegar, marjoram, thyme, bay leaf and orange juice and blend again. • Remove excess fat from pork and rub well with lemon. Wash the pork, dry it well and rub with 2 teaspoons salt. Rub the pork with above onion mixture and refrigerate until following day, turning occasionally and bathing with marinade a couple of times. • Remove pork from refrigerator at least 30 minutes before roasting. Preheat oven to 400°. Place pork in large roasting pan and completely cover with aluminum foil. Roast for 4 hours (20 minutes per pound) until meat starts detaching from the bone. Increase oven temperature to 450° and uncover pork. • Continue roasting, basting once in a while with pan juices, to brown. Turn and, still basting, brown underside of pork for a total of about 1 hour. Remove pork from pan and set aside. • To make a sauce, remove excess grease from the pan. Heat pan juices over medium heat, scraping bottom and sides. Add wine, remaining ¼ teaspoon pepper, remaining 1 teaspoon Worcestershire sauce and flour to thicken, stirring well. If necessary, correct seasonings. Bring sauce to a boil and cook for 10 minutes. Strain. • Allow pork to cool for 2 hours before cutting into thin slices. Sprinkle lightly with salt and serve with warm sauce.

Embassy of Venezuela

SAUSAGE AND PEPPER RAGOUT   Serves 4

1 pound Italian sausage,
  sweet or mild
1 tablespoon olive oil
1 garlic clove, minced
2 onions, peeled and cut
  in strips
1 red bell pepper, cut into
  strips

1 green bell pepper, cut into
  strips
¾ cup red wine
4 tablespoons tomato paste
2 teaspoons dried basil
¼ teaspoon salt
¼ teaspoon crushed red pepper

Cut sausage into 1-inch rounds. Heat oil over medium heat and, when hot, add sausage. Turn sausage to brown all sides for 12–15 minutes. • Drain all but one tablespoon of fat from skillet. Increase temperature of skillet to high. Add garlic, onions and peppers and brown for about 5 minutes, stirring frequently. • Pour in wine and scrape bottom of pan. Add tomato paste, basil, salt and pepper flakes and continue cooking for about 5 minutes, stirring constantly. (If the sauce seems too thick, add a little water and mix well.) • Serve hot with rice.

Elena Schupp Darden

PORK TENDERLOIN JAVANESE   Serves 4 to 6

2 pounds pork tenderloin
6 Brazil nuts, grated
1 cup minced onion
2 cloves garlic, minced
¼ cup lemon juice

¼ cup soy sauce
2 tablespoons brown sugar
2 tablespoons ground coriander
¼ teaspoon crushed red pepper
¼ cup olive oil

Trim excess fat from pork and cut into 1-inch cubes. Combine remaining ingredients. Marinate pork cubes for half an hour. • Prepare grill or preheat broiler. Place pork on skewers, reserving marinade. Grill over hot coals or broil for 6–8 minutes, brushing once with marinade. Turn, brush again with marinade and cook until done. Serve with saffron rice.

Katie Hunnicutt

SWEET AND SOUR PORK   Serves 3 to 4

1 pound tenderloin of pork
¼ teaspoon white pepper
½ teaspoon salt
1 tablespoon soy sauce

1 tablespoon white wine
1 tablespoon cornstarch
1 tablespoon flour
1 cup oil

Sauce:

1 teaspoon chopped garlic
1 teaspoon chopped scallion
1 teaspoon chopped ginger
1 tablespoon white wine
2 tablespoons sugar

3 tablespoons vinegar
4 tablespoons ketchup
5 tablespoons water
1 teaspoon cornstarch

Cut pork into bite-sized strips. Sprinkle with pepper, salt, soy sauce, wine, cornstarch and flour. Mix thoroughly and marinate for at least 10 minutes. • Place oil in skillet and, when hot, add pork mixture. Sauté for 3–5 minutes, until brown. Remove meat to a plate. Drain off all but 2 tablespoons of oil from skillet. • For sauce, sauté garlic, scallion and ginger in remaining oil. Mix wine, sugar, vinegar, ketchup, water and cornstarch. Add to garlic mixture in skillet and stir over medium heat for 15–20 seconds. • Return pork to skillet, coat well with sauce and cook for about 10 seconds, until hot. • Good served with rice

Mrs. Frederick F. Chien
Wife of the Representative of the Coordination Council
for North American Affairs, Republic of China on Taiwan

Eggs and Cheese

CHILE RELLENO CASSEROLE

Serves 6 for dinner or 10 for buffet

"A favorite Campbell family recipe. This recipe is ideal for buffet-style gatherings where you would like to serve rellenos for many, without the trouble of making each individual relleno."

3 7-ounce cans whole green chiles or fresh poblano chiles, roasted peeled, with seeds and stems removed
1 small yellow onion, diced
2 cups shredded Jack cheese (may use jalapeño Jack)
2 cups shredded cheddar cheese
Salsa, to taste

4–6 corn tortillas, cut into wide strips
8 eggs
½ cup milk
½ teaspoon salt
½ teaspoon pepper
½ teaspoon ground cumin
½ teaspoon garlic powder
1–2 sprigs fresh cilantro, minced
Paprika

Cover the bottom of a well-greased, 9-inch square baking dish with ⅓ of chiles, opened flat. Cover with a layer of onion, layers of the cheeses, sprinkle lightly with salsa, and cover with a layer of tortilla strips. Repeat to build three layers. • Beat eggs, milk, salt, pepper, cumin and garlic powder. Stir in cilantro and sprinkle with paprika for color. Pour egg mixture evenly over casserole and bake, uncovered, at 350° for about 40 minutes, until puffy and set in the center when lightly touched. • Let stand for 10 minutes before serving.

Senator Ben Nighthorse Campbell
(Colorado)

CHEESE GRITS

1 cup grits
1 cup grated sharp cheddar cheese
4–8 tablespoons butter
2 eggs, beaten
¼ teaspoon garlic powder

1 tablespoon Worcestershire sauce
Salt (hickory smoked salt preferred)
Pepper to taste

Preheat oven to 350°. • Cook grits according to directions on package. Remove from stove. • Add cheese and butter while grits are hot. Allow to cool somewhat. Add eggs and seasonings. • Bake in greased casserole dish for 1 hour. Allow to sit 10–15 minutes before serving.

Elliott Jones

CHEESE MONKEY   Serves 6 to 8

Swiss cheese (Gruyère),
   cubed (see note)
Sourdough French bread,
   sliced (see note)
1½ cups milk

½–¾ cup heavy cream
4–6 eggs, well beaten
½–¾ cup white wine
½ teaspoon salt
½ teaspoon dry mustard

Alternate layers of cheese and bread in a round or rectangular casserole to make a total of 4 layers. • Combine milk, cream, eggs, wine, salt and mustard and pour over bread and cheese to cover. • Bake for 45 minutes at 375° or until liquid is almost completely cooked away. • Serve as you would cheese soufflé. This one will never fall. It is even better the next day as leftovers.

NOTE: I use a ratio of approximately 1½ cheese to 1 loaf of bread.

Val Cook

MIGAS   Serves 4 to 6
(MEXICAN SCRAMBLED EGGS)

½ cup chopped onion
½ cup chopped tomatoes
1 pickled jalapeño pepper,
   seeded
½ cup corn oil
12 corn tortillas

12 eggs
½ cup milk
Flour tortillas
Picante sauce
1 avocado, chopped (optional)

Sauté onion, tomatoes and jalapeño pepper in ¼ cup hot oil. • Remove tomato, onion and pepper and add remaining oil to pan. Heat oil. Cut corn tortillas into strips and sauté until soft (this happens very quickly). Remove tortilla strips and drain on paper towels. • Beat eggs and milk. Scramble softly and add cooked vegetables. Fold in tortilla strips. Serve immediately with heated flour tortillas and picante sauce and chopped avocado, if desired.

Mrs. John E. Chapoton

FLIPPED WHALE (AN APOCRYPHAL RECIPE)   Serves 4
OMELETTE AU HOMARD

"It seems entirely proper in the present mixed state of the world and its recipes to consider not only the design and manipulation of ingredients but also who eats whom and how. The usual accounts of the adventures of the prophet Jonah have him consumed, though temporarily, by a 'great fish,' 'sea monster' or 'dragon.' Flipping it all around, one can easily conjure up a situation in which Jonah is the eater and the monster the eaten. Carrying it a step further, the fish-dragon-monster becomes the 'homard noble' and the eaters, we and our guests.

"Our recipe for such an 'homard noble' was inspired by more than one visit to Mont San Michel and the kitchen of Mère Poulard. Although we never saw her recipe for omelette, we can still hear the din of the egg beaters and see the splendid golden concoction enter the oven in a skillet, to reappear shortly as a finished delicacy long to be remembered. Some years ago, following an entire week of lobster-eating on the coast of Maine, we had a plentiful quantity of meat remaining, and no heart for leaving it behind. Instead it became the basis of a quickly improvised and uncommonly good omelette."

2 cups cooked lobster meat, cubed	Salt and white pepper, to taste
2 tablespoons sweet butter	4 tablespoons heavy cream
8 eggs, separated	1 tablespoon grated Parmigiano-Reggiano cheese

Preheat oven to 375°. • Sauté the lobster in melted butter in a 10-inch iron skillet. Remove from burner and keep warm. • Whisk egg yolks with salt and pepper and add cream. • Beat egg whites until firm and fold into egg yolks and cream. Fold eggs with warm lobster meat in a skillet. Return to burner for 1 minute on moderate heat. Sprinkle with the grated cheese. • Place in oven. Serve when puffed and brown (about 15 minutes). Bon appétit!

W. D. Knight

POACHED EGGS WITH CAVIAR-LEEK CREME ON PUFF PASTRY, SMOKED SALMON AND ASPARAGUS

Serves 4

Cream sauce:

4 shallots, sliced
½ leek, white part, washed
  and chopped
¼ teaspoon butter
1 cup white wine
1½ cups heavy cream

¼ cup leeks, green part,
  washed and cut into small
  julienne strips
2 tablespoons caviar (beluga,
  osetra, sevruga or lumpfish)

Eggs, pastry and garnish:

Frozen puff pastry, cut into
  3- to 4-inch diamond shapes
  and baked according to
  directions on box
8 thin slices smoked salmon
12 asparagus spears, peeled
  and blanched

8 poached eggs
2 teaspoons chopped chives
  for garnish
1 tablespoon chopped tomatoes,
  for garnish

To make sauce, sauté the shallots and white part of leek in butter, without browning. Add wine, bring to a boil and reduce until only 2 tablespoons are left. Add cream, bring to a simmer (do not boil) and reduce by ¼ (until thick enough to coat a spoon). Strain through a fine sieve. Set aside. • Blanch green part of leek in boiling, salted water until tender. Drain. Add to cream sauce. Gently add caviar (stirring too hard will break the delicate eggs). • To assemble, for each serving split puff pastry diamond in half lengthwise (giving you a top and a bottom) and place on a plate. Using the bottom half as a raft, cradle these elements in the following order: 2 slices smoked salmon topped with 3 pieces of asparagus, then 2 poached eggs coated with caviar-leek cream. Offset the puff pastry lid on top and garnish with chopped chives and tomatoes.

Chef Michael Patton
1789 Restaurant

SEARED LOBSTER, BASIL AND TOMATO FRITTATA

Serves 2

2 ounces lobster, chopped
Salt and pepper
1 tablespoon clarified butter
Pinch of salt
4 eggs
1 tablespoon basil chiffonade
  (cut into thin strips)

¼ cup seeded and diced
  tomatoes
1 tablespoon Parmesan cheese,
  grated

Have all ingredients ready to go so eggs do not overcook. Turn on broiler. • Season lobster meat with salt and pepper and sear over high heat in clarified butter. • Add pinch of salt to eggs and beat until frothy. Quickly add to an 8-inch cast iron skillet and scramble until soft. Throw in basil and tomato and dust top generously with cheese. Run under broiler until cheese starts to brown and eggs are firm to the touch.

Chef Michael Patton
1789 Restaurant

ALSATIAN ONION TART

Serves 10

1 pound white onions, peeled
  and thinly sliced
½ cup butter
½ tablespoon vegetable oil
1 tablespoon flour
1⅓ cups half and half
3 eggs, well beaten

Pinch of salt
Freshly ground pepper
Nutmeg to taste
2 9-inch uncooked pie shells
6–8 slices bacon, julienned,
  browned and drained
½ cup grated Swiss cheese

In a large saucepan, sauté onions in butter and oil over low heat until soft but not colored. Sprinkle with flour and, stirring continuously, cook for 2 minutes more. Remove from heat and add half and half, blending well. Cool mixture for a few moments before adding eggs. Season with salt, pepper and nutmeg. Pour mixture into pie shells and sprinkle with bacon and cheese. Bake at 350° for approximately 30 minutes.

Edmond Foltzenlogel
Le Caprice Restaurant

SPINACH CHEESE BAKE

Serves 8 to 10

2 10-ounce packages frozen
   chopped spinach, thawed
1 pound bulk Italian sausage
1 8-ounce can tomato sauce
2 cups cream-style cottage
   cheese

½ cup grated Parmesan cheese
1 egg, slightly beaten
1 8-ounce package shredded
   mozzarella cheese

Drain spinach thoroughly, squeezing out liquid. • Cook sausage until brown; drain fat. Stir in tomato sauce. Set aside. • In a large bowl, combine drained spinach, cottage cheese, Parmesan cheese and egg. Spread mixture in the bottom of an 11 x 7 inch baking dish. Spoon sausage mixture over the top and sprinkle with mozzarella cheese. • Bake at 350° for 40 minutes.

Melissa Lindsay

Winter on the C & O Canal

ENGLISH LEEK PIE   Serves 6 to 8

"Easy but looks special."

5–6 leeks	1 cup heavy cream
6 tablespoons butter	4 ounces Swiss cheese,
Salt and pepper to taste	sliced or grated
1 uncooked pie shell	

Cut greens off leeks. Cut white of leeks lengthwise, then slice. Sauté leeks in butter until lightly brown, about 20 minutes on low-medium heat. Add salt and pepper. Place leeks into pie shell to fill. Cover with cream. Cover with cheese. Bake at 350° for about 1 hour, until brown.

Susan Lloyd

ZUCCHINI AND HAM QUICHE   Serves 6 to 8

¼ cup finely chopped onion	4 large eggs
1 small clove garlic, finely	¾ cup milk
minced	½ cup heavy cream
2 tablespoons butter	1 uncooked pastry shell
1¼ pounds zucchini, trimmed	(optional)
and sliced	¼ cup each grated Parmesan
Salt and pepper to taste	and cheddar cheese, mixed
¼ pound sliced boiled ham,	
finely diced	

Preheat oven to 375°. • Sauté onion and garlic in butter, stirring, until translucent. Add zucchini, salt and pepper. Continue cooking, stirring gently and shaking pan, for about 5 minutes. Stir in ham and remove skillet from heat. • In a mixing bowl, beat eggs and add milk and cream. Add salt and pepper to taste. Fold into zucchini mixture. • Pour mixture into an ovenproof glass pie plate (or a 10-inch quiche pan lined with pastry). Sprinkle with cheeses and place on a baking sheet which has been covered with brown paper. Place a small pan of water on bottom shelf of oven beneath the baking sheet. • Bake for 30 minutes. Reduce heat to 350° and continue baking for 15 minutes.

Mrs. Malcolm Price

Pasta and Rice

Street Festival in Adams-Morgan

MUSHROOM SAUCE WITH SPINACH LINGUINE

Serves 6 to 8

1 cup butter
9 cloves of garlic (crushed
  or cut very small)
1 red pepper, cut into thin
  strips
2 pounds medium mushrooms,
  sliced

⅓ cup beef broth
1 can undiluted mushroom soup
  (strain out mushrooms)
¾ cup heavy cream
Salt and pepper to taste
Spinach linguine

In a large pan combine butter and garlic and brown lightly. Stir in red pepper and mushrooms. Cook for 10 minutes. Add the beef broth and soup and cook for 10 minutes. Pour in cream and cook for another 10 minutes. Serve over linguine or other pasta.

Mrs. Eugene B. Casey

BROCCOLI PASTA

Serves 4

1¼ pounds broccoli
8 ounces thin spaghetti
¼ cup olive oil

1 large garlic clove, minced
¼ cup grated Parmesan cheese,
  plus extra for serving

Cut florets from broccoli stalks so they are in small, even-sized clusters. You should have about 4 cups. Steam until tender and drain. • Cook spaghetti according to package directions and drain. • Heat oil and garlic and toss with broccoli and spaghetti. Top with Parmesan cheese and serve at once as a first course, passing additional Parmesan. • This can become a main dish by adding shrimp or scallops to the oil and garlic and sautéing, before tossing with remaining ingredients.

Karin G. Weber

CHÈVRE, SUN-DRIED TOMATOES AND ROASTED GARLIC PIZZA

Serves 2 to 3

10–12 garlic cloves
½ cup olive oil
Fresh or frozen pizza dough
2 cups shredded mozzarella
2 cups crumbled chèvre or
  other goat cheese
12 sun-dried tomatoes in olive
  oil, well drained and slivered

¼ cup fresh minced parsley
Salt and freshly ground pepper
  to taste
¼ cup freshly grated Parmesan
  cheese

Toss whole garlic cloves with 3 tablespoons olive oil and place in a baking dish. Cover and bake at 300° until garlic is tender, about 30 minutes. Remove from oven and cool, peel, chop and set aside. • Increase oven temperature to 500°. • Follow directions on pizza dough. Brush dough thoroughly with olive oil. Top with mozzarella and chèvre, leaving ½ inch around edges. Sprinkle with garlic, tomatoes, parsley, salt and pepper. Drizzle with olive oil. Place pizza on pizza screen or baking stone and bake for 10–15 minutes, until crust is golden brown. Sprinkle with Parmesan cheese and serve.

JoAnn Mason

FETTUCCINE FREDDE ALLA PRONTO (COLD PASTA)   Serves 4

"Prepare in advance to enhance flavor."

6 tablespoons olive oil
2 cloves garlic, finely minced
2 ounces pignoli (pine nuts)
1 cup tomatoes, skinned, seeded and roughly chopped
1 pound fresh fettuccine
1 cup tuna, cut into rough pieces
½ red pimento, cut into thin strips

6 black olives, pitted and roughly chopped
1–2 tablespoons chopped parsley
2 tablespoons red wine vinegar
Salt and pepper to taste
Additional parsley for garnish

Heat olive oil in a skillet. Add garlic and pignoli. Sauté over low heat for 5 minutes, or until garlic becomes translucent and pignoli are golden. Add tomatoes and continue cooking for 1 minute. Turn mixture into a large bowl and cool. • Cook fettuccine in 6–7 quarts of rapidly boiling salted water. When pasta is al dente, stop boiling by adding a glass of cold water. Drain. • Add the cooked pasta to the bowl containing oil, garlic, pignoli and tomatoes and toss gently to coat. • Add the tuna, pimento, olives, parsley and vinegar. Turn with two large spoons to blend. Season with salt and freshly ground pepper. Sprinkle additional parsley on top and serve at room temperature.

Mrs. Elizabeth Beach Rea

SPAGHETTINI "TRICOLORE"   Serves 2

1 medium onion, chopped
1 red pepper (hot), chopped
4 cloves garlic, chopped

⅓ cup olive oil
Handful of chopped parsley
½ pound spaghettini

In an 8-inch skillet, sauté onion, red pepper and garlic in oil over low heat for at least 15 minutes, until onion is translucent but not brown. Stir in parsley. • Cook spaghettini al dente according to package directions and drain well. Toss with onion mixture and serve immediately.

Mrs. John C. Gore

FETTUCCINE WITH THREE CHEESES   Serves 4

8 ounces egg fettuccine
8 ounces spinach fettuccine
½ cup chopped walnuts
2 cups heavy cream, at room
  temperature
8 ounces whole milk
  mozzarella, shredded
6 ounces sweet Gorgonzola
  cheese, crumbled
  (sweet Gorgonzola is milder
  than aged) or, if unavailable
  4 ounces aged Gorgonzola

3 tablespoons freshly grated
  Parmesan cheese
3 tablespoons finely chopped
  Italian (flat leaf) parsley
2 tablespoons finely chopped
  fresh basil
1 tablespoon finely chopped
  fresh oregano or
  ½ tablespoon dried oregano
1 tablespoon finely chopped
  fresh chives
Additional Parmesan for serving

Bring 3 quarts of salted water to a boil. Add fettuccine and cover. Return to a rapid boil, uncover and stir. Cook, uncovered, until tender but still firm, for 2–4 minutes if fresh fettuccine (cook 5–8 minutes if dried). • While fettuccine is cooking, heat a small skillet over medium heat. When empty skillet has reached temperature that will evaporate a bead of water on contact (about 1 minute), add walnuts and toast, stirring constantly, until fragrant, about 2 minutes. Remove from heat and reserve. • As soon as fettuccine has cooked, drain well. Pour cream into pot in which fettuccine was cooked and heat to boiling. Boil for 1 minute, add fettuccine, mozzarella, Gorgonzola, 3 table-spoons grated Parmesan, parsley, basil, oregano and chives. Continue heating, stirring occasionally, until sauce is well blended and slightly thickened, about 2 minutes. • Remove to a warm platter. Sprinkle with toasted walnuts and Parmesan to taste. Serve immediately.

Nan Snyder

DAN DAN NOODLES

Serves 8

1 pound fresh Chinese wheat
   noodles, preferably West
   Lake brand lo mein noodles
   made with egg
2 tablespoons peanut oil
8 dried shiitake mushrooms

⅓ cup dried tree ear mushrooms
   (the very small ones)
½ cup scallions, thinly sliced
   diagonally
½ bunch cilantro, leaves only

Sauce:

2 tablespoons very finely
   grated fresh ginger
1 clove garlic, minced
3 tablespoons soy sauce
2 tablespoons soy sauce paste,
   preferably Wan Ja Shan
   brand
2 tablespoons light rice vinegar

2 tablespoons Chinkiang vinegar
1–3 teaspoons chili paste with
   garlic
1 tablespoon dark sesame oil
⅓ cup toasted sesame seeds,
   crushed
1 teaspoon sugar

Garnish:

½ red bell pepper, diced
½ cup scallions, thinly sliced
   diagonally
½ bunch cilantro, leaves only
Thinly sliced plum tomatoes
   (optional)

Blanched broccoli florets
   (optional)
Hydroponic cucumber, scored
   and thinly sliced (optional)

Cook the noodles in plenty of salted boiling water until just al dente. Drain and rinse in cold water until cool, drain thoroughly and toss with peanut oil. • Soak shiitake and tree ear mushrooms in very hot water until softened. Drain, squeeze out excess water, stem and slice shiitake mushrooms. The tree ears do not need cutting. • Combine ingredients for the sauce and stir thoroughly. Taste for balance of hot, sour, salt, ginger and garlic. Add more of any of these to taste. • Toss the noodles with the sauce and add shiitake, tree ears, scallions and cilantro and mound on a platter. Top with red pepper, scallions and cilantro leaves. Tuck tomato slices or broccoli or cucumbers around the edge of noodles and serve at room temperature.

Sharon Farrington
Specialist in Asian Food and global food history

SPINACH AND GOAT CHEESE LASAGNA

5½ ounces goat cheese
4 ounces cream cheese
1 teaspoon dried basil (more
  if fresh)
15 ounces frozen spinach,
  defrosted and drained (1½
  10-ounce packages)
½ cup heavy cream
Salt, pepper and nutmeg to taste

½–¾ pound spinach or plain
  lasagna (depending on
  desired thickness)
1 tablespoon olive oil
2 cups chopped tomatoes
  (fresh or canned)
12 ounces shredded mozzarella
  cheese

In an electric blender, combine goat cheese, cream cheese and basil. Remove and set aside. • Combine spinach, cream, salt, pepper and nutmeg. Cook lasagna according to instructions on package and drain, immerse in cold water to stop cooking and drain again. • Coat the bottom of a 9 x 13 inch baking dish with olive oil and cover with a layer of lasagna. Next spread on half of the tomatoes, half the spinach mixture and all of the goat cheese mixture. Then sprinkle half the mozzarella over this. Top with the remaining lasagna, spinach, tomatoes and, finally, the rest of the mozzarella. Bake for 1 hour at 350°.

Dorothy B. Wexler

NUTTY PASTA   Serves 12

6 tablespoons Italian-style
  seasoned breadcrumbs
¼ cup pine nuts
1–1½ cups olive oil
6 garlic cloves, chopped
2 pinches cayenne pepper
Salt to taste
2 pounds fresh linguine

Freshly ground pepper
½ cup freshly chopped parsley
6 tablespoons grated Pecorino
  Pepato cheese (if unavailable,
  use Pecorino or Parmesan
  cheese with freshly ground
  pepper)

Preheat oven to 350°. • Place breadcrumbs and pine nuts in separate baking pans and toast until golden brown, about 5 minutes for breadcrumbs and 8 minutes for pine nuts. • Heat oil in large, heavy skillet over medium-low heat. Add garlic and cayenne and sauté until garlic is golden brown. Remove garlic using slotted spoon and discard. Reserve oil and salt lightly. • Cook linguine in large pot of boiling salted water until tender but firm. Drain. Season linguine generously with pepper, parsley, and reserved oil. Sprinkle with breadcrumbs, pignoli and cheese.

Anastasia Shaw

PENNE WITH ASPARAGUS   Serves 2

1 pound asparagus
1 red pepper
8 ounces penne
2 tablespoons olive oil
3 teaspoons grated lemon peel

¼ cup fresh lemon juice
6 tablespoons toasted pine nuts
Salt and pepper to taste
8 tablespoons freshly grated
  Parmesan cheese

Trim asparagus and microwave in ¼ cup of water for 3–4 minutes, until tender but still crisp. Cut spears into 1-inch lengths on the diagonal. Preheat broiler. • Roast whole red pepper under broiler, turning carefully with tongs to brown all sides evenly. Remove, place in a plastic bag, seal well and allow to sit for 10 minutes. Chop when cool. • Cook penne according to package directions and drain. Place penne in a large, warm serving bowl. Add oil and toss. Add asparagus, red pepper, lemon peel, lemon juice, pine nuts, salt and pepper. Toss gently. Add Parmesan cheese and toss again. Serve immediately.

Elena Schupp Darden

ROTINI CASSEROLE   Serves 4

8 ounces rotini
1 pound ground beef
1 cup chopped onion
1 small green pepper, chopped
½ small red pepper, chopped
1 28-ounce can tomatoes,
  drained and roughly chopped
2 6-ounce cans tomato paste
1 4-ounce can sliced
  mushrooms, undrained

1 teaspoon salt
½ teaspoon basil
½ teaspoon oregano
¼ teaspoon garlic powder
¼ teaspoon cayenne pepper
2 cups grated shredded
  mozzarella cheese

Cook rotini according to package directions. Drain. • In a large skillet, sauté beef, onion and peppers. Drain excess fat. Add tomatoes, tomato paste, mushrooms and seasonings and simmer for 20 minutes. • Combine rotini with meat sauce. Spoon half of rotini and meat into a 3-quart casserole. Top with 1 cup mozzarella. Repeat layers. • Bake at 350° for 35 minutes.

Roberta Anschuetz

DIET PITA PIZZAS   Serves 3

2 half chicken breasts
3 6-inch whole-wheat pita
   breads
1 can artichoke hearts,
   drained and diced

2 tomatoes, diced
½ cup chopped scallions
6 slices Muenster cheese

Preheat oven to 400°. • Poach chicken breasts gently for 15 minutes. Remove chicken, discard skin and cut into marble-sized chunks. • Split pita breads around the edges making 6 whole rounds. • Portion ingredients evenly on pita rounds. • Heat for 10–15 minutes, until cheese has melted. Serve two rounds per person with a salad.

Chris Hunter

PASTA WITH SUN-DRIED TOMATO,   Serves 6
GORGONZOLA AND ROASTED GARLIC SAUCE

1 pound fresh pasta
   (pappardelle or fettuccine)
2 cups half and half
1 cup crumbled Gorgonzola
   or blue cheese
⅔ cup sliced sun-dried
   tomatoes packed in oil,
   with a little of the oil

4 heads roasted garlic,
   separated into cloves
1 2-inch sprig rosemary
Salt and freshly ground black
   pepper
⅓ cup coarsely chopped, toasted
   walnuts

Put pasta water on to boil. • Pour half and half into a large skillet. Add cheese, tomatoes, ¾ of the garlic and rosemary. Place over low heat and slowly heat contents of pan, smashing garlic cloves with the back of a wooden spoon and stirring occasionally, for about 10 minutes. Add salt and pepper to taste. • Add salt to boiling water and cook pasta al dente. Drain pasta and transfer to the skillet. Add remaining garlic cloves. Toss pasta well and serve in warm serving bowls. Garnish with walnuts and a little freshly ground pepper.

Susan Belsinger
Food Writer and Photographer

NOODLES ROMANOFF   Serves 8 to 10

1 8-ounce box wide egg
   noodles
1½ cups large-curd cottage
   cheese
1 clove garlic, minced
1 teaspoon Worcestershire
   sauce

1 cup sour cream
1 large onion, finely chopped
¼ teaspoon Tabasco
½ cup grated Parmesan cheese

Cook noodles according to directions on box and drain. • Combine cooked noodles, cottage cheese, garlic, Worcestershire sauce, sour cream, onion and Tabasco. Turn into unbuttered casserole. Sprinkle with grated Parmesan. • Bake in 350° oven just until hot and bubbly (about 20 minutes).

Mrs. Lewis R. Townsend

PISTACHIO RICE PILAF   Serves 6

¼ cup currants
1 cup long-grain brown rice
2 cups water or vegetable
   broth

¼ cup dried apricots, cut
   into strips
½ cup unsalted pistachio nuts
Cinnamon

Soak currants for 15 minutes in warm water. Drain and set aside. • Wash rice and drain. Place rice in a skillet over medium heat and stir until dry and lightly browned. Place rice in 1½-quart saucepan and cover with water or broth. Bring to a boil, reduce heat to low, and cover with a tight fitting lid. Simmer for 25 minutes, add currants, apricots and pistachio nuts. Do not stir. Return the lid and continue cooking for 20 minutes, until rice is tender and all water is absorbed. Remove from heat and let stand for 2 minutes. Turn into a serving dish and sprinkle with cinnamon.

Mrs. Joseph I. Lieberman
Wife of the Senator from Connecticut

SPANISH OR MEXICAN RICE   Serves 4

"It's colorful, easy and very good."

3 tablespoons oil
1 cup rice
¼ cup chopped onion
2 cloves of garlic, minced

1½ cups water
2 tomatoes, peeled, seeded
  and chopped
Salt and pepper to taste

Heat oil in iron pan. Add rice and brown lightly. Add onion and garlic. Cook for 1 minute. Add water, tomatoes, salt and pepper. Cover and simmer for 25 minutes. Stir lightly. Serve in a heated terra cotta dish.

Mrs. John E. Chapoton

WILD RICE CASSEROLE   Serves 6 to 8

1½ cups wild rice or
  mixture of brown and
  white rice
1 pound fresh mushrooms,
  sliced
1 cup butter

2 tablespoons flour
1 cup heavy cream
Salt and ground black pepper
  to taste
1 cup good sherry
Buttered bread crumbs

Cook rice in salted water according to package directions. Drain and steam dry. • In a large skillet, sauté mushrooms in butter until golden. Add flour and, stirring constantly, add cream. Add the cooked rice and stir in the sherry. Turn into a well-greased casserole and top with buttered bread crumbs. • Put in a moderate oven (325°) until heated through and light brown on top.

Betsy Rea

WISCONSIN WILD RICE   Serves 4

1 cup wild rice
2 tablespoons butter
½ cup finely chopped onions

½ cup finely chopped celery
1 cup chicken broth, plus
  more if needed

Preheat oven to 325°. • Wash rice thoroughly. Add to large quantity of rapidly boiling water and boil for 20–25 minutes, until kernels pop and show some white. Drain and rinse with hot water from tap. Drain again. Sauté the onions and celery in butter while rice is cooking. • Place rice, onions, celery, and chicken broth in a casserole and bake covered for 1 hour. Stir occasionally and add more broth if rice looks dry.

Chris Hunter

Vegetables

ALOO ACHAR   Serves 5
(Spicy Potatoes)

4 medium potatoes, boiled
  and peeled
1 cup sesame seeds
Green chilies, chopped
  (optional)
½ teaspoon turmeric

1 tablespoon corn oil
¼ teaspoon fenugreek seeds
¼ cup lemon juice
Salt to taste
Sprig of parsley, chopped

Cut potatoes into bite-sized pieces and place in a large bowl. Set aside. • Toast sesame seeds in a frying pan until dark brown . Remove from heat and let cool. Grind sesame seeds to a powder with mortar and mix with potatoes. If desired, add chilies. Add turmeric. • Heat oil in skillet and fry fenugreek until it becomes black. Pour over potatoes. Add lemon juice and salt and mix well. Sprinkle with parsley. (OPTIONAL: Add ½ cup water and adjust seasoning if you want a little gravy.) Serve with rice.

Royal Nepalese Embassy

ARTICHOKE HEARTS WITH DILL   Serves 4

4 large artichokes
Salt
Lemon halves
⅓ cup lemon juice
1 tablespoon flour
3 large shallots, finely chopped

1 cup water
6 tablespoons fine olive oil
Pinch of salt
1 teaspoon sugar
¾ cup chopped, fresh dill

Remove outer leaves of artichokes and cut off stems. Slice off inner leaves almost down to heart. Pare artichokes as if paring an apple, removing green parts down to white heart. Scoop out fur and rub artichoke hearts with salt and lemon halves to prevent discoloration. • Place artichoke hearts in a saucepan of water with 2 tablespoons lemon juice and flour. Bring water to a boil and simmer for 5 minutes. • Remove artichoke hearts and place in a shallow pan. Spoon ¼ of shallots on each artichoke. Mix water with olive oil, salt, sugar and 2 tablespoons lemon juice and pour over the artichokes. Cover and simmer for 30 minutes, adding water as necessary to maintain level of liquid, until artichokes are very tender. Sprinkle with ½ cup dill and continue cooking for a few minutes. Remove from heat and cool. • Serve cold sprinkled with remaining dill and lemon juice.

The Ambassador of Turkey
and Mrs. Kandemir

JOHN McCAIN'S BAKED BEANS   Serves 8

"This dish is perfect for a barbecue. Enjoy!"

1 medium onion, chopped
1 teaspoon butter
1 16-ounce can red kidney
  beans
1 16-ounce can B & M baked
  beans

1 cup ketchup
1 cup packed brown sugar
1 teaspoon vinegar
1 teaspoon mustard
4 strips fried bacon, cooled
  and crumbled

Preheat oven to 350°. • In a skillet, sauté onion in butter. In a large baking pot, combine kidney beans, baked beans, ketchup, brown sugar, vinegar, mustard and bacon. Stir well. Add onions and stir. • Cover pot and bake for 35 minutes, until piping hot.

Senator John McCain
(Arizona)

TENNESSEE BARBECUED BEANS   Serves 4 to 6

"Great with hamburgers or fried chicken."

1 16-ounce can B & M baked
  beans
1 small onion, chopped
1 green pepper, chopped
1 jalapeño pepper, chopped
1 tablespoon prepared mustard
1 tablespoon chili powder

1 teaspoon Worcestershire
  sauce
½ cup brown sugar
¼ cup ketchup
¼ cup bottled barbecue sauce
4 strips bacon, cut into
  2-inch pieces

Combine all ingredients, except bacon. Pour into an ovenproof casserole and top with bacon pieces. Bake, uncovered, for one hour at 350°.

Mrs. Ben F. Dixon, IV

CORN SOUFFLÉ   Serves 4

⅔ cup flour
½ cup sugar
4 teaspoons baking powder
4 eggs, beaten

½ cup butter
2 11-ounce cans whole kernel
  corn, drained

Combine flour, sugar and baking powder. Mix in eggs, melted butter, milk and corn. Pour into a greased 3-quart casserole and bake at 350° for 45 minutes, until top is crusty golden brown and center is firm.

Sarah T. Minikes

BROCCOLI PURÉE

2 pounds cooked broccoli
   stems and florets (fresh
   or frozen)
½ cup heavy cream
1 teaspoon salt
Freshly ground pepper

½ teaspoon nutmeg
4 tablespoons butter, cut into
   pieces
1 tablespoon fresh parsley
⅓ pound Swiss cheese, grated

In a food processor, purée broccoli. Add cream and process. Add salt, pepper, nutmeg, butter, parsley and half of the Swiss cheese and run food processor. Pour into a buttered casserole and top with remaining cheese. Bake at 350° for 20 minutes, until bubbling hot.

Sarah T. Minikes

CARROT AND BROWN SUGAR CASSEROLE   Serves 6

1 small onion, chopped
5 tablespoons butter
5 cups shredded carrots
¾ cup orange juice

1½ teaspoons lemon juice
2 teaspoons dry mustard
Salt to taste
2 tablespoons brown sugar

In a large skillet, brown onions in 2 tablespoons butter until translucent. Add carrots and toss. Cook for 5 minutes. Add orange juice, lemon juice, mustard and salt. Mix well. Place carrot mixture into a casserole. Sprinkle with brown sugar, dot with remaining 3 tablespoons butter. Bake for 45 minutes at 325°-350°.

Mrs. G. William Miller

CARROT LOAF   Serves 8

2 pounds carrots, peeled
   and cut into ¼-inch slices
10 tablespoons unsalted butter
¼ pound mushrooms, sliced
½ pound spinach, cleaned
   with stems removed

5 eggs
4 ounces grated Swiss cheese
½ teaspoon salt
1 teaspoon freshly ground
   pepper

Sauté carrots slowly in 4 tablespoons butter until tender. Chop coarsely and reserve in a large mixing bowl. • Over high heat, sauté mushrooms in 2 tablespoons butter for 2 minutes. Chop coarsely and add to carrots. • Sauté spinach in 2 tablespoons butter. Chop coarsely and reserve separately. When spinach is cool, add 1 egg and mix thoroughly. • Beat together remaining eggs and cheese. Combine this mixture thoroughly with the carrots and mushrooms. Add salt and pepper. Correct seasoning, if necessary. • Line an

8½ x 4½ x 2½ inch loaf pan with aluminum foil. Butter foil with remaining 2 tablespoons butter and fill pan with half carrot mixture. Cover with spinach and top with remaining carrot mixture. Place in a pan of hot water and bake at 400° for 1 hour and 15 minutes, or until a knife plunged into center comes out clean. • Invert onto a warm serving platter and remove foil. Slice and serve immediately.

Katie Hunnicutt

CARROT RING WITH BROCCOLI FLORETS   Serves 4 to 6

1 large onion, chopped
2 tablespoons butter
2½ cups (1 pound) shredded carrots
¾ cup fresh orange juice
1½ teaspoons fresh lemon juice

2 teaspoons dry mustard
2 tablespoons brown sugar
2 eggs, well beaten
1 tablespoon flour
Salt to taste
Steamed broccoli florets or another green vegetable

Preheat oven to 350°. • Amply butter a 1-quart ring mold and lightly dust with flour. • Sauté onions in butter. Add shredded carrots and cook for 5 minutes. Add all remaining ingredients, except broccoli, stirring vigorously. Spoon into prepared mold. • Place mold in a shallow pan of hot water and bake until firm, about 45 minutes. Unmold and fill center with broccoli or another green vegetable and serve.

Adriana Miller

MIXED CREAMED VEGETABLES

½ cup each of five of your favorite vegetables (such as green beans, carrots, broccoli, cauliflower, zucchini)

1 can cream of celery soup
¼ cup milk
6 ounces Velveeta cheese

Preheat oven to 325°. • Parboil vegetables and drain well. Mix vegetables with other ingredients and pour into a greased casserole. Bake for 1½ hours.

Mrs. William T. Hunter, Jr.

CORN AND CHEESE SOUFFLÉ (CHIPA GUAZU)

"A fine Paraguayan specialty"

12 large ears of yellow corn or   1 teaspoon salt
   3 cups canned yellow corn,   ½ cup milk
   drained   4 eggs, separated
1 medium onion, finely chopped   8 ounces Muenster or Swiss
½ cup butter or margarine   cheese, cubed
½ cup water

Preheat oven to 350°. • Scrape kernels off ears of corn or drain canned corn. Grind the corn. • In a skillet, sauté onion in butter until translucent. Add water and salt. Cover and simmer for 10 minutes. Remove from heat and cool. Then add milk. Beat egg yolks and add to onion mixture. Add corn and cheese and stir well. • Beat egg whites until they form soft peaks. When ready to bake, fold egg whites into corn mixture. Do not overmix. • Place in a lightly greased casserole or baking dish and bake for about 1 hour, until a knife inserted in the middle comes out dry. Serve with meat, poultry or fish.

Francoise Martinez Mendieta
Embassy of Paraguay

CORN RISOTTO   Serves 8

8 cups fresh corn kernels   6 cups or more chicken stock
   cut from cob   1 cup Arborio rice
8 tablespoons butter   ½ cup dry white wine
6 tablespoons finely chopped   1 cup Parmesan cheese
   shallots   Salt and pepper

Purée 6 cups of corn kernels in blender and set aside. Melt 6 tablespoons butter and add shallots. Cook over low heat until soft. Meanwhile, heat stock to just under a simmer. Add the rice to shallots and stir to coat. Cook over medium heat until rice begins to change to opaque. Add wine and cook until all liquid is absorbed. Begin adding stock, about 1 cup at a time. Starting with the first cup of stock, cook until nearly all liquid is absorbed, then add more stock, repeating the process. Total cooking time is between 18 and 22 minutes. The final addition of stock should be just as the rice is becoming tender. There should be some liquid that is not absorbed at the end so that the rice is thick and creamy looking. Stir in the corn purée and corn kernels. Add remaining butter and cheese. Correct seasoning with salt and pepper if necessary. Serve immediately.

Carol Mason
Catering Director, Dean & DeLuca

CREAMY MASHED POTATOES   Serves 6

10 medium potatoes
2 3-ounce packages cream
  cheese, softened
1 cup sour cream or plain
  yogurt
2 teaspoons onion salt

1 teaspoon garlic salt
Pepper to taste
2 tablespoons butter
Grated cheddar or Parmesan
  cheese
Paprika

This must be made at least 12 hours before serving. • Peel and quarter potatoes, boil until tender and drain. Mash until smooth. • Add cream cheese, sour cream, onion and garlic salts and pepper. Beat well. • Refrigerate for 12 hours or more. • When ready to bake, place potatoes in greased casserole. Dot with butter, top with cheese and paprika and bake, uncovered, at 350° for 30–45 minutes.

Frankie Swenholt

CAROL'S CREOLE BLACK BEANS   Serves 6 to 8

"A real gourmet will start from scratch, cook black beans with ham bone."

1 large green pepper, chopped
Bacon fat
1½ large onions, chopped
¾ teaspoon minced garlic
Andouille or tasso sausage
  cut into 1-inch slices
  (Italian sausage if others
  are unavailable)

3 cups cooked black beans,
  canned or home-made
1 cup extra virgin olive oil
¼ teaspoon cumin
1 teaspoon vinegar

Sauté green pepper in bacon fat until soft, add onions and let brown slowly. Add garlic and continue cooking. • While cooking onion, sauté sausage in separate skillet until completely cooked. • To the onion and green pepper, add beans, olive oil and cumin. When meat is cooked, add to bean mixture and stir well, simmering over low heat. Add vinegar and continue simmering for another 5 minutes. To thicken mixture, mash beans. • Remove from heat and let settle overnight. Reheat just before serving.

NOTE: You may add other meats such as ham, pork, smoked meat or even smoked turkey.

Senator Carol Moseley-Braun
(Illinois)

FENNEL CABBAGE

1 small head of cabbage	2½ cups water
3 rashers of bacon, chopped or	1½ tablespoons wine vinegar
4 tablespoons olive oil	Salt and pepper
(lower cholesterol)	1 teaspoon fennel seeds

Wash, drain and shred cabbage. • Heat a pan large enough to hold all of cabbage. Fry bacon until the fat runs or heat oil. Add cabbage, water, vinegar, salt, pepper and fennel seeds. Cook, uncovered, over low heat until cabbage is tender and most of liquid has evaporated, about 25–30 minutes.

Mrs. John K. Walker

GREEN BEAN BUNDLES   Serves 8

8 ounces haricots verts or other tiny, young green beans	1 clove garlic, minced
	¼ teaspoon crushed dried tarragon leaves or
1 yellow squash, about 1½ inches in diameter	1 teaspoon minced fresh tarragon leaves
1 tablespoon olive oil	Salt and pepper (optional)

Place beans in a colander and rinse well. Snap off ends and arrange in 8 stacks, about 10–12 beans per stack. • Cut 8 ½-inch thick slices off squash, hollow each within ¼ inch of rind. Thread each stack of beans through a piece of squash as if it were a napkin ring. • To steam, place steamer basket in a large stockpot or saucepan and add 1 inch of water. (Water should not touch the bottom of steamer basket.) Place bean bundles in steamer, cover and bring to a boil on high heat. Steam for about 4 minutes, until beans turn bright green and are crisp-tender. • If you prefer to microwave, place bean bundles in a rectangular glass baking dish and add 2 tablespoons water. Cover with vented plastic wrap and microwave on high for 4 minutes, until beans turn bright green and are crisp-tender. • Meanwhile, heat oil in small sauté pan. Add garlic and tarragon and cook until garlic is soft but not brown. • Or place oil, garlic and tarragon in a 1-cup glass measure and microwave for 1 minute. • To serve, transfer bean bundles to a serving plate and pour garlic oil over top. Season with salt and pepper, if desired.

CiCi Williamson
Syndicated Newspaper Columnist and cookbook author

HOPPIN' JOHN   Serves 8

2 cups fresh or frozen
   black-eyed peas
¼ pound slab of bacon

2 small pods red peppers
2 cups uncooked rice
Salt to taste

Cover peas with water. Add bacon and peppers. Simmer in a covered pot over low heat for 1–1½ hours, until tender. Add rice, cover and reduce heat to low. Continue cooking for 20–25 minutes, until rice is cooked. Stir frequently. If needed, add water during cooking. Salt to taste and serve.

Senator Mitch McConnell
(Kentucky)

HOT SPINACH CASSEROLE   Serves 4–6

2 10-ounce packages frozen
   chopped spinach
3½ tablespoons butter
2–3 tablespoons chopped onion
2 tablespoons flour
½ cup evaporated milk
¾ teaspoon celery salt
¾ teaspoon minced garlic

1 teaspoon Worcestershire
   sauce
Dash of cayenne pepper
Black pepper
1 6-ounce roll jalapeño cheese
Croutons or bite-sized squares
   of bread

Cook spinach according to directions and drain well. Save ½ cup of cooking liquid. • In a skillet, melt butter and add onion. Sauté onion until tender. Add flour and mix well. Add evaporated milk and the liquid saved from cooking the spinach. Season with celery salt, garlic, Worcestershire sauce, cayenne and black pepper. • Cut jalapeño cheese into small squares and add to skillet. Cook until cheese has melted. Add the drained spinach and stir well. Place the mixture in an ungreased baking dish. • In a small skillet, sauté croutons in ½ tablespoon of butter. Top casserole with croutons. • Bake at 350° for about 30 minutes, until bubbly.

Lynda J. Robb

MOIN-MOIN
(Nigerian Baked Black-Eyed Peas)

Serves 10 to 12

2 cups black-eyed peas
2 medium onions
2 large red peppers
1 red chile (optional)
4 bouillon cubes (beef or
  chicken)

½–1 cup warm water
8 tablespoons vegetable oil
Salt to taste

Soak black-eyed peas in water for 20 minutes. Wash off skin and soak again for 1 hour. • Chop onions, red peppers and chile and add drained peas. Place a small amount of pea mixture into a blender and purée to a smooth paste, adding small amounts of warm water as necessary. Repeat until all peas are blended. Pour paste in a bowl and add bouillon cubes dissolved in warm water. Add oil and salt, beating with a wooden spoon or wire whisk. Add additional water if necessary to make good consistency. • Oil a large baking pan. Drop the purée by tablespoons onto baking pan. Cover tightly. Put some water in a pot large enough to hold the baking pan and bring water to a boil. Put pan with purée into pot so that water reaches ⅔ of the way up the sides. Cover the pot and steam on top of stove for 40–60 minutes. Moin-moin is ready when a fork inserted in the middle of purée comes out clean. • Serve with main course. Could also be cut into small pieces and served as an hors d'oeuvre.

Mrs. Amina Ahmadu
Wife of the Ambassador of Nigeria

MUSHROOM SOUFFLÉ

Serves 6

½ pound firm white
  mushrooms, finely chopped
1 medium onion, finely
  chopped
5 tablespoons butter
2 cups milk

4 tablespoons Cream of Wheat
½ teaspoon marjoram
Dash of pepper
½ teaspoon salt
3 eggs, separated

Preheat oven to 300°. • Sauté mushrooms and onions in butter. • Scald milk and sprinkle in Cream of Wheat. Stir until thick and add mushroom mixture. Add marjoram, pepper, salt and beaten egg yolks. • Beat egg whites until stiff but not dry and fold into mixture. Pour into well-greased 1½-quart baking dish. • Bake for 1 hour. Serve immediately.

Mrs. Donald W. Jeffries

PISTO   Serves 6

3½ tablespoons olive oil
1 large onion, coarsely
   chopped
2 green peppers, diced
2 cloves garlic, chopped
1 large eggplant, peeled
   and diced
1 teaspoon salt

Pepper
1 teaspoon oregano
6 tomatoes, peeled and chopped
Additional olive oil, if served
   cold
Squeeze of lemon juice, if
   served cold

Heat oil in a large ovenproof pan over medium heat. Sauté onion, green pepper and garlic for about 5 minutes, until tender. Add eggplant and continue cooking until oil has been absorbed. Season to taste with salt, pepper and oregano. Add tomatoes, stir and cover. Continue cooking on medium heat about 15 minutes, until all vegetables are tender. Remove cover and cook to evaporate liquid. • If this is to be served cold, add a little olive oil and a squeeze of lemon immediately before serving.

Josu Zubikarai
Taverna Restaurant

POMMES DAUPHINE   Makes 14 to 16 puffs

1 cup water
4 tablespoons unsalted
   butter, cut into pieces
¼ teaspoon salt

1 cup flour
4 large eggs
2 cups plain mashed potatoes
1 cup vegetable oil

Place water, butter and salt in a saucepan. Bring to a boil. When butter has melted, remove from heat. Add flour all at once and mix rapidly. Return to very low heat and stir constantly with a spatula, 5–6 minutes. When ready, the dough should be soft and not stick to your fingers. • Transfer the dough to a clean bowl and add the eggs, one at a time, mixing after each addition. Mixture should be smooth and shiny and as thick as mayonnaise. • Add an equal amount of mashed potatoes to the mixture. • Heat 1 cup of oil in large skillet. Put potato mixture by teaspoonfuls into skillet and fry for 8–10 minutes. Drain on paper towels and season with salt.

Christine van Mulders

VEGETABLES PICANTE

Serves 6 to 8

3 tablespoons margarine
1 large onion
¼ pound green beans
2–3 medium-sized potatoes,
  cooked and sliced
1½ cups thinly sliced zucchini
4 tomatoes, thinly sliced

½ teaspoon salt
1 can of cheese soup
¼ pound extra sharp cheddar
  cheese, thinly sliced
¼ cup picante sauce
1 cup bread cubes

Preheat oven to 325°. • Grease an ovenproof casserole with 1 tablespoon margarine. Slice the onion vertically and separate into slivers. Sauté onion in 1 tablespoon of margarine until tender. • Cut the green beans into bite-sized pieces and steam or boil until barely tender. • Place a layer of potatoes in casserole. Cover with a layer of onion, a layer of green beans, a layer of zucchini and finally a layer of tomatoes. Repeat until all vegetables are in casserole, ending with a layer of tomatoes. Sprinkle with salt. • Combine cheese soup and picante sauce and pour over casserole. Cover with layer of cheese slices. Cover casserole and bake for 30–35 minutes. • Sauté bread cubes in remaining tablespoon of margarine. Sprinkle bread cubes over casserole and bake for an additional 10–15 minutes, uncovered.

Mrs. Carl Swan Shultz

ROASTED SHALLOT FLAN

Serves 12

"Use as a vegetable accompaniment or as a garnish for a clear soup or broth."

16 shallots
⅓ cup peanut oil
5 eggs
3 egg yolks
1 cup heavy cream

1 cup half and half
Sea salt
White pepper
Nutmeg to taste

Prepare 12 2-ounce molds by buttering well and placing in refrigerator. Preheat oven to 300°. • Roast shallots in peanut oil until soft. Cool and remove outer skin. Purée in an electric blender. Set aside. • In a large bowl, beat eggs and egg yolks together and gradually add cream and half and half, beating constantly. Whisk in shallot purée and strain, pressing hard with a wooden spoon. Season with salt, pepper and nutmeg. • Ladle shallot custard into chilled molds about ⅔ full. Cover each mold tightly with plastic wrap and set in a large pan with 1 inch or so of hot water. Bake for approximately 40 minutes, or until set. • Remove molds from pan and allow to rest for 5 minutes. Unmold onto small serving plates.

Janet E. Terry, Executive Chef
The Grand Hotel

RÖSTI

2¼ pounds potatoes   **4 tablespoons butter**
Salt and pepper to taste   **2 tablespoons oil**

In a large pot, boil potatoes in their skins until tender. Cool for several hours or overnight. Peel and cut coarsely. Season with salt and pepper. • In a large non-stick skillet, heat butter and oil. Add potatoes, pressing them together to form a large cake. Cook over medium heat for about 20 minutes, until a golden crust forms on the bottom. Turn cake over and add more butter. Cook for another 10 minutes. Serve with veal.

The Ambassador of Switzerland
and Mrs. Jagmetti

SPINACH SQUARES HOLLANDAISE   Serves 12

3 10-ounce packages frozen
  chopped spinach
½ cup finely chopped onion
2 tablespoons butter or
  margarine
4 eggs, beaten
2 cups milk
3 cups fresh breadcrumbs

1 pound cooked ham, diced
  (3 cups) or
½ pound cooked bacon,
  crumbled
½ teaspoon seasoned salt
Hollandaise sauce (your
  favorite recipe)
4 hard-boiled eggs, diced

Preheat oven to 350°. • Cook spinach according to package directions and drain well. • Sauté onion in butter until tender. Combine, spinach, onion, eggs, milk, breadcrumbs, ham and seasoned salt. • Spread evenly into an ungreased 11 x 7 x 2 inch baking dish. Bake for 40–45 minutes, until set. • Prepare hollandaise sauce and stir in chopped eggs. • Cut spinach into squares and serve with hollandaise sauce.

Diane Harris

SPINACH WITH ARTICHOKES   Serves 6 to 8

2 10-ounce packages of
  frozen chopped spinach,
  defrosted
½ cup butter or margarine,
  melted
1 8-ounce package cream
  cheese, softened

3 tablespoons lemon juice
1 10-ounce package frozen
  artichoke hearts, defrosted
Bread crumbs
Additional butter or margarine

Preheat oven to 350°. • Drain defrosted spinach until quite dry. With an electric beater, mix melted butter, softened cream cheese and 1½ tablespoons lemon juice. Stir in spinach. • Place mixture in a shallow, greased baking dish. Place defrosted artichoke hearts on top of spinach mixture, scatter with breadcrumbs and dot with additional butter. Pour remaining lemon juice over top and bake for 20–30 minutes.

Mrs. Arthur Wexler

TIMBALLO DI CRESPELLE E ZUCCHINI   **Serves 6 to 8**
(ZUCCHINI AND CRESPELLE MOLD)

*"Serve as a first course, followed by a meat dish, or as a light lunch.
Looks beautiful on a buffet."*

Zucchini:

6 medium-sized zucchini,
  washed
⅓ cup olive oil
1 clove of garlic

Salt and pepper to taste
Pinch of nutmeg, freshly grated
¾ cup freshly grated Parmesan
  cheese

Crespelle (Makes 6 crespelle)
(Thin Pancakes):

1 cup milk
¾ cup flour, sifted
1 teaspoon salt
½ cup water
3 eggs

Pinch of nutmeg, freshly
  grated (optional)
1 tablespoon butter, or more
  as needed

Cut zucchini in half lengthwise and slice ⅓ inch thick. • Heat oil in a large skillet. Sauté garlic until golden, then remove and discard. Add zucchini slices to oil. Season with salt and pepper and cook over medium-high heat until al dente (about 20 minutes), stirring frequently so they do not stick. Add nutmeg and ½ cup Parmesan cheese. • To make crespelle, mix milk, flour, water and salt in a large bowl. Add eggs, one at a time, beating well after each addition. Add nutmeg, if desired, and let mixture stand for at least 30 minutes. • Butter an 8-inch omelette or crêpe pan and place over fairly high heat. Pour ⅓ cupful of batter into pan. Tilt pan in all directions so batter coats as much surface as possible, to make a crespella about 6½ inches in diameter. When the batter starts bubbling and the edge begins to turn golden, loosen edge with a spatula and shake pan to loosen crespella. Turn and fry on other side. Turn crespella onto a platter. Rub the pan with buttered paper towel and repeat process to make next crespella. • Zucchini and crespelle may now be assembled. Preheat oven to 350°. • Butter an 8-inch soufflé mold. Place 1 crespella on the bottom of mold and line sides with 4 of the remaining crespelle, making sure they cling to the sides of mold. Fill mold with zucchini mixture. Fold the edges of the crespelle over the center and cover with the remaining crespella. Sprinkle the remaining Parmesan cheese on top (or wait until unmolded to sprinkle on remaining Parmesan). Bake for 10–15 minutes, until Parmesan has melted. Remove mold from oven and allow to cool for 3–4 minutes. Place a large round platter over top of mold and invert.

Flavia Biancheri
Wife of the Ambassador of Italy

WHITE BEAN PURÉE   Serves 6 to 8

1 pound dry Great Northern
  white beans
6 garlic cloves
1 large onion
4 whole cloves
1 bay leaf

1 teaspoon freshly ground
  pepper
3 tablespoons butter
¾ cup heavy cream
Salt to taste

Cover white beans with cold water and boil for 2 minutes. Remove from heat and allow to sit, covered, for 1 hour. Add garlic, onion stuck with cloves, bay leaf and pepper and bring to a boil, covered. Reduce heat and simmer for 2 hours, until beans are tender. Drain in a colander and discard bay leaf and cloves. • Purée bean mixture in an electric blender. Beat in butter, cream and salt. Reheat in a clean saucepan.

Elena Schupp Darden

FESTIVE POTATOES   Serves 8 to 10

"Do ahead mashed potatoes."

8–9 baking potatoes, baked
  or boiled and peeled
¼ cup hot milk
2 3-ounce packages cream
  cheese
1 cup sour cream

2 tablespoons butter
2 teaspoons onion salt
1 teaspoon salt
¼ teaspoon pepper
Butter to dot on top
Paprika to sprinkle on top

Cream potatoes with hot milk. Add all remaining ingredients and put into a 2-quart buttered casserole. Dot with butter and sprinkle with paprika. • Can prepare ahead of time to here and refrigerate. • Return to room temperature, before baking at 350° until bubbly.

Melissa Lindsay

FRESH GREEN BEANS, CHINESE-STYLE   Serves 4

1 tablespoon soy sauce
1 teaspoon sugar
1 tablespoon pale, dry
  sherry or
  dry white wine
1 chicken bouillon cube
⅔ cup chicken broth

1 pound fresh green beans,
  with ends snapped off
1 tablespoon peanut oil
2 tablespoons butter
4–6 cloves garlic, minced
2 scallions, chopped

Mix soy sauce, sugar and sherry and set aside. • In a large saucepan, dissolve bouillon cube in the chicken broth over a high heat. Add the beans and simmer until nearly all liquid has evaporated (about 5–8 minutes), stirring constantly. Drain the beans and set aside. • In a wok or skillet, heat the oil and butter. Add garlic and scallions and stir-fry for about 30 seconds or until just softened. Add the beans and toss until coated. • Sprinkle soy-sugar-sherry mixture over beans and stir-fry for 1 minute. Serve hot.

Dotty Wexler

ONION-NUT BRUSSELS SPROUTS   Serves 4

1 large onion, thinly sliced
1 tablespoon olive oil
Pinch of salt
Freshly ground black pepper
½ cup water

1 cup dry white wine
½ cup chopped walnuts
1 pound fresh Brussels sprouts,
  outer leaves and bottoms
  removed and cut in half

Place the onion, oil, salt, pepper and water in a saucepan. Simmer, partially covered, over medium heat, stirring occasionally, until caramelized. This will take about 1 hour. • Uncover the pan and add the wine to the onion. Raise the heat to high and boil rapidly until almost all the wine has evaporated (5–10 minutes). Toss the walnuts with the onions. • About 15 minutes before the onion is done, steam the Brussels sprouts in a vegetable steamer for about 5 minutes, or until tender. Toss the onion and walnuts with the sprouts and serve.

Dotty Wexler

HOTCH-POTCH WITH RICE   Serves 4

2–3 onions, finely chopped
½ cup vegetable oil
1 cup rice
2 peppers, chopped
Salt
Paprika

Black pepper
3–4 tomatoes, sliced
½ cup of water
4 eggs
2 cups yogurt

Brown the onions in a little of the oil, add the rice and the peppers, brown a little, add a little salt and, by way of seasoning, some paprika and black pepper. • Arrange ingredients in layers in a casserole, with tomatoes on top. Pour 3–4 tablespoonfuls of oil and ½ cup water on top of hotch-potch and put into a 400° oven. When the vegetables are well cooked, pour over them the beaten eggs mixed with the yogurt and put back into the oven until a fine brown crust is obtained.

Embassy of the Republic of Bulgaria

ROASTED VEGETABLE MELANGE   Serves 4 to 6

1 bunch small carrots, peeled
and cut into 1-inch lengths
12 small new potatoes, cut
into quarters
2 leeks, white part only,
quartered
4 cloves garlic, mashed
6 scallions, white part only,
halved

¼ cup olive oil
4 large tomatoes, cut into
bite-sized chunks
¼ cup fresh chopped basil
leaves
2–3 tablespoons balsamic
vinegar
Salt and coarsely ground
fresh pepper

Preheat oven to 425°. • Put carrots, potatoes and leeks into a large bowl with garlic, scallions and olive oil. Toss and put in roasting pan. • Roast for 35–40 minutes or until soft. Stir from time to time to make sure leeks don't burn. • Remove veggies from oven and let cool slightly. Put in serving bowl. Add tomatoes and basil. Sprinkle with vinegar, salt and pepper. • Can sit for an hour or two before serving.

Dotty Wexler

VEGETABLES PICHELSTEINER (GEMÜSEPICHELSTEINER)

Serves 6 to 8

2 tablespoons butter or
  margarine
2 pounds seasonal vegetables
  to include as many of the
  following as possible:
  4 carrots, scraped and sliced
  1 small knob celery root,
    peeled and diced
  2 leeks, washed and sliced
  1 small cauliflower, broken
    into florets
  ½ pound green peas
  ¼ pound string beans, cut
    into 1-inch pieces
  ¼ head of white or savoy
    cabbage, sliced as for cole
    slaw

1½–2 pounds potatoes, peeled
  and sliced
Salt to taste
2 cups water or stock
Minced parsley

Melt butter or margarine in a 3-quart casserole or stew pot and add vegetables in layers, beginning with carrots, celery root, and leeks. Sprinkle lightly with salt and continue to layer with cauliflower, peas, string beans, cabbage and, finally, potatoes. Sprinkle with salt again. Add water or stock. • Cover tightly and bring to a boil. Reduce heat and simmer for 1 hour, until vegetables are thoroughly cooked. • When ready to serve, season with salt, if necessary, and sprinkle with minced parsley.

Embassy of the Federal Republic of Germany

VEGETABLE PILAF   Serves 8
(SABZI PULAO)

"A delicious low-fat recipe from Pakistan"

4 tablespoons butter
1 medium onion, sliced
1 clove garlic, minced
1 teaspoon ginger
1 tablespoon curry powder
¼ teaspoon tumeric
½ teaspoon chili powder
2 potatoes, peeled and cubed
⅔ cup sliced carrots
1 small eggplant, cubed
1 cup fresh cauliflower florets
1 small green pepper, chopped

⅔ cup peas
2 cups canned, chopped plum
   tomatoes
¾ cup chicken broth
1 teaspoon salt
2 cups cooked Basmati rice
1 tablespoon slivered almonds,
   lighted toasted
2 cups yogurt with 2–3
   tablespoons freshly minced
   cilantro (optional)

Preheat oven to 325°. • Melt butter and sauté onion, garlic and ginger. • When onion is golden, add other spices and stir constantly for about 1 minute more. • Add the vegetables one by one, stirring well with each addition. Pour in broth and bring to a boil. Add salt, reduce heat and simmer for 25 minutes, or until the vegetables are tender. • Layer rice and vegetable mix in a well-greased, ovenproof dish, beginning and ending with the rice. Cover and bake for 25 minutes. • Sprinkle with the almonds and serve, accompanied by yogurt-coriander side dish, if desired.

Sara Knight

Salads and Salad Dressings

JUMBO LUMP CRAB SALAD WITH CITRUS, GINGER AND SOY VINAIGRETTE

Serves 4 to 6

Salad:

½ cup diced wakame
  seaweed
1 thinly sliced hot house
  cucumber
1 package dikon sprouts

1½ tablespoons julienned
  pickled ginger
3 scallions, thinly sliced on
  the bias
2 cooked Dungeness crabs
  (cleaned)

Vinaigrette:

2 tablespoons chopped
  shallots
2 tablespoons chopped ginger
¾ cup rice wine vinegar
4 tablespoons soy sauce

2 tablespoons sesame oil
1 cup extra virgin olive oil
Juice of 2 oranges and 2
  limes

Garnish:

Scallions
Chives
Chervil

Crispy ginger
Toasted sesame seeds

To prepare salad, soften seaweed in warm water, then dice. In a large bowl, combine the cucumber, dikon sprouts, ginger, scallions and seaweed. Add crabmeat. • Prepare vinaigrette by putting all ingredients in a bowl and whisking briskly. Pour over crab mixture and toss very gently, taking care not to break up the crabmeat. • To serve, place salad in mounds on oriental-style plates and garnish with scallions, chives, chervil, ginger and sesame seeds.

Patrick Clark, Executive Chef
The Hay-Adams Hotel

"NEW" POTATO SALAD   Serves 6 to 8

6 medium potatoes
2 chopped hard-boiled eggs
2 tomatoes, diced
1 red or green pepper,
  chopped
2 scallions, minced
1 cucumber, chopped
½ cup chopped fresh parsley

½ cup alfalfa sprouts
½ cup toasted cashews
¼ cup mixture of toasted
  sunflower and sesame seeds
Spinach leaves, washed and
  drained
Lemon wedges for garnish

Dressing:
¾ cup mayonnaise
1 teaspoon salt
Freshly ground pepper
Dash Worcestershire sauce
½ cup cider vinegar

½ teaspoon dry mustard
½ teaspoon tarragon
1 teaspoon prepared
  horseradish

Boil potatoes in their skins until tender for 15–20 minutes. Drain, cool and dice. Combine with eggs, tomatoes, pepper, scallions, cucumber, parsley, alfalfa sprouts, cashews, sunflower and sesame seeds. • Make dressing by combining mayonnaise, salt, pepper, Worcestershire sauce, vinegar, mustard, tarragon and horseradish. Pour over potato mixture and combine well. Chill. • Serve on spinach leaves with lemon wedges.

Toni Walker

ARABIC DAOUD PASHA SALAD   Serves 6

¼ cup olive oil
1½ tablespoons wine vinegar
Juice of 1 lemon
Salt and pepper to taste
Sugar
Garlic
Parmesan cheese
Cumin
Oregano

Onions
Lime juice
6 large tomatoes, peeled
  and sliced
Kasseri or Kefalotyri cheese
  (see note)
Butter
Choice of bread, cut into
  triangles and toasted

Combine oil, vinegar, lemon juice, salt, pepper, sugar, garlic, Parmesan cheese, cumin, oregano, onions and lime juice (vary amounts of the 8 last ingredients accordingly to your fancy) and pour over sliced tomatoes. Marinate for 8 hours. • Fry the Kasseri or kefalotyri cheese in butter. Serve tomatoes with fried cheese and triangles of toast.

NOTE: These are Greek cheeses, available at Greek markets.

Theodosia Craig

ARTICHOKE SALAD   Serves 4

"Makes a wonderful red and green salad for the holidays."

1 14-ounce can water-packed artichoke hearts	¼ teaspoon dry mustard
1 cup chopped celery	¼ teaspoon black pepper
2 scallion tops, finely sliced	1 teaspoon sugar
1 2-ounce jar pimento strips	2 tablespoons white wine vinegar
½ cup chopped fresh parsley	5 tablespoons vegetable oil

Drain artichoke hearts and cut into quarters. In a bowl, combine artichoke hearts, celery, scallions, pimento and parsley. • Make dressing in a jar by combining mustard, pepper, sugar, vinegar and oil. Shake well. Pour dressing over artichoke mixture and toss gently. • Marinate in refrigerator overnight.

Mrs. E. Edward Bruce

ASPARAGUS SALAD   Serves 6 to 8

3 pounds asparagus	⅓ cup soy sauce
2 cloves of garlic, minced	1 egg yolk
2 tablespoons minced fresh ginger	1 whole egg
2 tablespoons rice wine vinegar	1 tablespoon lemon juice
2 tablespoons light brown sugar	2 tablespoons Dijon mustard
	¼ cup sesame oil

Cut off bottoms of asparagus and slice each stalk diagonally into 2 or 3 pieces. Steam asparagus tips for about 2 minutes and steam stalks until crisp, about 3 minutes. Remove from heat to a platter. • Place garlic, ginger, vinegar, brown sugar and soy sauce in a saucepan. Bring to a boil over medium-high heat, then reduce heat and simmer sauce until it is reduced to ½ of original amount. Place egg yolk, egg, lemon juice and mustard in an electric blender and mix on high speed for 15 seconds. Slowly, add sesame oil while blender is on. Add soy sauce mixture while blender is on. Pour sauce over asparagus and toss. Refrigerate for 2 hours before serving.

Elena Schupp Darden

RONALD BRASO'S CAESAR SALAD   Serves 6

2 heads of romaine lettuce   ½ teaspoon dry mustard
2 eggs   ½ tablespoon cracked pepper
1 cup croutons   Juice from 1 lemon
½ cup Parmesan cheese   8 anchovies, chopped
¼ cup olive oil   2 cloves of garlic, crushed

Wash and cut lettuce and place in a large wooden bowl. Boil eggs for 3 minutes and add to bowl. Top with croutons and Parmesan cheese. Make the dressing by combining oil, mustard, pepper and lemon juice. Mix well. Add anchovies and garlic. When well combined, pour over lettuce, toss and serve.

Ronald Braso

CARROT AND RAISIN SALAD   Serves 8

2 pounds carrots, washed,   ½ cup oil
   peeled and diced   2 cups water
1½ cups seedless raisins   1 clove garlic, crushed
1 teaspoon ginger   ⅓ cup honey
¼ teaspoon salt   1 teaspoon cinnamon
½ teaspoon saffron

In a large saucepan, cook the carrots, raisins, ginger, salt, saffron, oil, water and garlic over moderate heat for 15 minutes. Add honey and cinnamon and simmer for another 5 minutes. • Serve right away or cool and serve.

NOTE: Two pounds sweet potatoes, peeled and cut into 1-inch squares, may be substituted for carrots.

The Ambassador of Morocco
and Mrs. Benaissa

CHICKPEA (CHANNA) SALAD   Serves 5

3 16-ounce cans chickpeas
1 cucumber, chopped into
    small pieces
2 tomatoes, chopped into
    small pieces
1 small piece fresh ginger,
    chopped
2 onions, diced

1 green pepper, diced
1 sprig parsley, chopped
Green chilies, diced (optional)
½ cup olive oil
¼ cup lemon juice, or to taste
Salt and pepper to taste
½ teaspoon sesame seeds

Drain chickpeas thoroughly. In a medium-sized bowl, mix chickpeas, cucumber, tomatoes, ginger, onions, green pepper, parsley and chilies, if desired. • In a jar, mix olive oil, lemon juice, salt and pepper and sesame seeds. Shake well. • When ready to serve, pour dressing over salad. Serve chilled.

The Royal Nepalese Embassy

BONNIE BRYAN'S CHICKEN AND RICE SALAD

1½ cups cooked rice
¼ cup minced onion
1 tablespoon vinegar
2 tablespoons oil
1 teaspoon curry powder
2 cups diced cooked chicken

1 cup diced celery
1 cup diced green pepper
¾ cup Miracle Whip or
    mayonnaise
Salt and pepper to taste

Mix rice with onion, vinegar, oil and curry. Add remaining ingredients and chill. Miracle Whip adds a tangy flavor; however, mayonnaise may be substituted.

Mrs. Richard H. Bryan
Wife of the Senator from Nevada

GIRL OF THE GOLDEN WEST SALAD   Serves 6 to 8

4–5 cups chicken, cooked
and diced
2 teaspoons finely chopped
onion or scallions
1 cup chopped celery
1 cup chopped green pepper
½ cup chopped red pepper
¼ cup sour cream

⅔ cup mayonnaise
1 teaspoon salt
⅛ teaspoon pepper
2 tablespoons vinegar
⅔ cup slivered almonds, toasted
1 8-ounce can mandarin
orange sections

Combine chicken, onion, celery, and peppers. • Mix sour cream with mayonnaise until smooth. Add salt, pepper and vinegar. Blend with chicken mixture. Cover and refrigerate. • Place almonds on a cookie tray and brown for 10 minutes in 300° oven. • When ready to serve, decorate chicken with mandarin orange segments and sprinkle with almond slivers.

Phyllis Cowen

CHICKEN POTATO SALAD

3 cups cooked and cubed
chicken
2 cups cooked and cubed
potatoes
½ cup coarsely chopped
dill pickles
3 hard-boiled eggs, peeled
and coarsely chopped
1 teaspoon salt
⅛ teaspoon white pepper
¾ cup mayonnaise

¾ cup sour cream
1 tablespoon finely chopped
fresh dill
3 tablespoons capers, drained
and patted dry
12 green olives
12 ripe olives
2 tomatoes, peeled and cut
lengthwise
1 head of Boston lettuce

Combine chicken, potatoes, pickles and eggs. Sprinkle with salt and pepper. Toss lightly. • In a small bowl, beat together the mayonnaise and sour cream. Stir half of mayonnaise mixture into chicken salad. Taste for seasoning. Mound salad onto a platter, mask with remaining mayonnaise dressing. Sprinkle with dill and capers. Garnish with olives, tomatoes and lettuce leaves.

Mrs. G. William Miller

DAKOTA BEAN SALAD

Serves at least 30

1½ pounds pork or beef
  tenderloin
½ cup white corn, fresh or
  frozen
½ cup yellow corn, fresh or
  frozen
One 15-ounce can of each of
  the following seven kinds
  of beans:
    Pinto beans
    White beans
    Black beans
    Garbanzo beans
    Red kidney beans
    Pink kidney beans
    Fava beans

1 cup sliced celery hearts
1 red onion, cut into rings
1 large garlic clove, crushed
½ cup diced green pepper
½ cup diced yellow pepper
½ cup diced red pepper
½ cup sliced carrots
2 cups cooked brown rice
Italian, Caesar or vinaigrette
  dressing

Bake tenderloin to desired doneness. Chill completely. Cube into bite-sized pieces. • Blanch corn and drain. • Rinse and drain all beans well in a colander. In a large bowl, toss together beans, celery, onion, garlic, peppers, carrots, and corn. Fold in cooked rice and meat. Add dressing to taste. • Serve cold with your favorite bread.

Mrs. Larry Pressler
Wife of the Senator from South Dakota

COUSCOUS CHICKEN SALAD

Serves 4 to 6

1¼ cups chicken broth
1 tablespoon margarine
1 cup couscous
1 cup diced cooked chicken
4 large scallions, diced

Dressing:
¾ cup olive oil
3 tablespoons fresh lemon
  juice
1 teaspoon salt

1 large crisp apple, cored
  and diced
1 large stalk celery, diced
Lettuce, for serving
Parsley, for garnish

½ teaspoon ground coriander
½ teaspoon Dijon mustard
1 large clove garlic, minced
Freshly ground black pepper

Bring broth to a boil, add margarine and couscous, and bring to a boil again. Cover, remove from heat and let stand for 5 minutes. Uncover and fluff with a fork. • Combine chicken with scallions, apple and celery. • To prepare dressing, mix together olive oil, lemon juice, salt, coriander, mustard, garlic and pepper. • Combine the couscous with chicken mixture and add dressing. Mix, using a fork and spoon, to coat all ingredients well. Serve on a bed of lettuce. Garnish with parsley and sprinkle with freshly ground black pepper.

Goody L. Solomon, Executive Editor and Founder
Food Nutrition Health News Service

CRABMEAT AND RICE SALAD   Serves 6

Dressing:

½ cup olive oil	½ teaspoon Tabasco sauce
2 tablespoons vinegar	2 teaspoons Dijon mustard
2 tablespoons soy sauce	

Salad:

¾ cup rice	4 ounces pimentos, sliced
½ teaspoon salt	4 scallions, sliced with part
3 teaspoons olive oil	of green
1 package frozen snow peas	½ pound mushrooms, sliced
2 teaspoons sesame seeds	¾ pound crabmeat
¼ cup chopped green pepper	1 head of lettuce

Combine dressing ingredients in a bowl. • Cook rice according to package directions with salt and 2 teaspoons oil until fluffy. In a saucepan, pour boiling water over snow peas and return to boil. Cook for 1 minute and drain. Lightly brown sesame seeds in remaining 1 teaspoon of olive oil. Place rice, snow peas, sesame seeds, pepper, pimentos, scallions, mushrooms and crabmeat in a bowl. Mix well. Add dressing and toss. Line a serving bowl or platter with lettuce leaves and mound crabmeat mixture in the middle.

Mrs. Carl Swan Shultz

DOME BEAN RELISH   Serves 6 to 8

3 pounds canned dark red   1 tablespoon finely chopped
   kidney beans   white onion
¼ cup tangy Russian dressing   ½ cup mayonnaise
½ cup creamy French dressing   Minced garlic and salt to taste

Start by making Russian dressing. Recipe yields more than you need for
salad. • Place beans in a colander and wash the liquid away. Mix the Russian
and French dressings together with onion, mayonnaise, minced garlic and
salt. Add beans to sauce and stir to cover all of the beans. Adjust seasonings
and refrigerate. Keeps for 4–5 days.

Tangy Russian Dressing (Makes 2½ cups)
1 cup sweet relish   ½ cup chili sauce
½ cup mayonnaise   Dash of Tabasco sauce
½ cup ketchup

Chef Robert Traylor
The Dome Restaurant
Woods Hole, Cape Cod, MA

ENDIVE FARCIES AU CRABE   Serves 4 to 6

1 medium apple, peeled,   1 8-ounce package cream
   seeded and diced to ¼-inch   cheese, softened to room
   cubes   temperature
Lemon juice   Curry powder
½ red bell pepper, seeded   Worcestershire sauce
   and diced into ¼-inch cubes   Salt and pepper to taste
1 stalk celery, diced to ¼-inch ½ pound lump crabmeat
   cubes   4 heads of Belgian endive
                                 Chopped walnuts, for garnish

Sprinkle apple with a little lemon juice to prevent discoloration. Combine
with pepper and celery. Mix with cream cheese. Season with curry powder,
Worcestershire sauce, salt and pepper. Blend well. • Lightly clean crabmeat,
removing all bits of shell. Take care not to break up lumps of crab. Gently
fold into cream cheese mixture. • Separate endive leaves and discard solid
cores. Fill leaves with crabmeat and cream cheese mixture and reconstitute
each to shape of original endive. Wrap them tightly in plastic wrap and
refrigerate 2–3 hours, until firm. • Remove from refrigerator and slice into
rounds. Arrange on salad plates and garnish with walnuts.

Le Caprice Restaurant

GRANDMOTHER'S COOK'S COLE SLAW   Serves 6

½ teaspoon dry mustard
2 tablespoons cider vinegar
½ cup sour cream
2 eggs
4 teaspoons sugar

1 teaspoon butter
½ teaspoon salt (optional)
1 medium head cabbage,
    shredded

In the top of a double boiler, dissolve mustard in vinegar. Add sour cream, eggs, sugar and butter and cook, stirring constantly, until thickened. Do not boil. Cool and add up to ½ teaspoon salt, if desired. • Toss with cabbage 1 hour before serving.

NOTE: This dressing may be frozen.

Helen Rogers

HOT CHICKEN SALAD   Serves 6 to 8

4 whole chicken breasts,
    simmered in flavored broth,
    boned and diced
2½ cups diced celery
1 8½-ounce can water
    chestnuts, diced
6 scallions with tops, diced
1½–2 cups slivered, toasted
    almonds

1 cup mayonnaise
1 cup sour cream
4 tablespoons lemon juice
Salt and pepper to taste
½ cup grated cheese
1 cup toasted bread crumbs
Dash of cayenne pepper

Combine chicken, celery, water chestnuts, scallions and almonds. In a bowl, combine mayonnaise, sour cream and lemon juice and toss with chicken mixture. Place in a 13 x 9 inch ovenproof pan and season to taste, sprinkle with cheese and bread crumbs. Bake at 450° for 10 to 15 minutes, until bubbly.

NOTE: This may also be baked in a 1½-quart casserole for 25–30 minutes.

Sally Davidson

MARCH HARE SALAD   Serves 6

3 cups cottage cheese
2 tablespoons toasted sesame
  seeds
¼ cup toasted sunflower seeds
1 medium carrot, diced small
1 medium tomato, diced small
1 large scallion, diced small

1 stalk celery, diced small
1 small cucumber, diced small
½ cup watercress
1 cup alfalfa sprouts
Juice of ½ lemon
Salt and pepper to taste
Black olives for garnish

Combine all of the ingredients except olives and chill well. Decorate with
olives before serving.

Toni Walker

NINA'S GRILLED CHICKEN SALAD   Serves 6

"Especially nice in the fall when pomegranates are in season."

6 half chicken breasts
Blue cheese salad dressing
  (your own or bottled)
1 head Boston lettuce
1 head red oak lettuce
1 head radicchio
3 endive, sliced

1 bunch watercress or arugula
Blue cheese, crumbled
Chopped walnuts
⅓ cup chopped red onion
Red grapes
Pomegranate seeds (optional)
Lemon vinaigrette

Grill chicken breasts and slice. Mix with a small amount of blue cheese salad
dressing. • Layer in a bowl Boston lettuce, red oak lettuce, radicchio, endive,
watercress or arugula; arrange chicken on top. Sprinkle crumbled blue
cheese, walnuts, onion, grapes and pomegranate seeds on top. Pour lemon
vinaigrette over salad and serve with French bread.

Nina Pillsbury

SCANDANAVIAN CUCUMBERS   Serves 6

½ cup sour cream
1 tablespoon sugar
2 tablespoons chopped
  parsley
2 tablespoons tarragon
  vinegar

1 tablespoon chopped onion
¼ teaspoon dill
3 cups unpeeled cucumbers,
  sliced wafer-thin

Combine sour cream, sugar, parsley, vinegar, onion and dill. Mix with cucumbers. Cover and chill thoroughly.

Sarah T. Minikes

WATERCRESS, FENNEL AND ROMAINE SALAD WITH PERNOD-ORANGE DRESSING

Serves 8

2 bunches watercress, stems removed, and torn into pieces—do not cut
1 large head romaine, torn into small pieces—do not cut
1 head fennel, thinly sliced across the bulb
⅓ cup fresh orange juice
⅓ cup olive oil
Juice of ½ lemon or more to taste
1 tablespoon Pernod
Salt and pepper to taste
1–2 drops white wine vinegar (optional)

Wash greens and spin dry. Store in linen salad bag in refrigerator for 1–2 hours. • Whisk orange juice, olive oil, lemon juice, Pernod, salt and pepper together. If desired, add a drop or two of white wine vinegar. Toss with greens and serve.

Mrs. John C. Gore

ORIENTAL CHICKEN SALAD

Serves 6

1 large roasting chicken breast
3 bunches watercress, chopped
1 bunch scallions, sliced
1 8-ounce can sliced water chestnuts, drained
6 ounces bean sprouts (fresh, if possible)
3 stalks celery, sliced
¾ cup olive oil
¾ cup soy sauce (low sodium preferred)
6 radishes, cut into rosettes
Dash of cinnamon
1 head romaine lettuce, chopped
12 cucumber slices
6 ounces carrots, julienned
6 large mushrooms, sliced

Steam chicken breast until done. Cool, debone and shred using a fork or your fingers. • Combine watercress, scallions, water chestnuts, bean sprouts, celery and half of the chicken. • Mix olive oil, soy sauce and cinnamon to make dressing and pour ½ of dressing over chicken mixture. • Divide romaine lettuce among plates. Spoon chicken mixture onto lettuce and garnish each with 2 cucumber slices, 1 ounce carrots, 1 sliced mushroom, 1 radish and remaining chicken on top of salad plate. • Serve remaining dressing on the side.

Senator David Pryor
(Arkansas)

PAM'S BROCCOLI SALAD   Serves 6 to 8

1 pound bacon
3–4 cups raw broccoli florets,
   separated
2 large Red Delicious apples,
   unpeeled and cubed

½ cup raisins
1 cup mayonnaise
1 tablespoon red wine vinegar
1 tablespoon lemon juice
1 tablespoon sugar

Fry bacon until crisp. Drain on paper towels and crumble into bite-sized pieces. Place in airtight container and refrigerate. • Blanch broccoli for 1 minute in boiling water. • Place cubed apples, raisins and broccoli in a large bowl and mix. • Mix mayonnaise, vinegar, lemon juice and sugar together and toss with apple mixture. • Just before serving add bacon and combine gently.

Mrs. Jonathan W. Sloat

SALADE PROVENÇALE LE CAPRICE   Serves 4

1 head romaine lettuce
2 large vine-ripened tomatoes,
   peeled and sliced ¼-inch
   thick
8 ounces fresh goat cheese
1 red Holland pepper, sliced
   into rings

1 yellow Holland pepper,
   sliced into rings
12 niçoise olives
12 calamata olives
1 bunch fresh basil leaves
Freshly ground pepper

Vinaigrette:

12 ounces sweet Italian
   sausage, broken into small
   pieces

⅓ cup red wine vinegar
½ cup olive oil
Salt to taste

Wash and dry lettuce and arrange leaves to make beds on 4 large plates. Arrange tomato slices on lettuce, using 3–4 slices per plate. Slice goat cheese into 8 pieces and place 2 pieces in center of each plate on top of tomatoes. Place pepper rings of each color over cheese and sprinkle with olives. Save a few basil leaves for garnish; slice the rest in julienne strips and sprinkle over all. • Make vinaigrette by frying sausage in a hot skillet until nicely brown. Drain fat and deglaze pan with vinegar. Remove from heat and stir in olive oil. Add salt to taste, mix and pour over salad while hot, dividing sausage evenly among 4 plates. Garnish with whole basil leaves and pepper.

NOTE: This is also an excellent vinaigrette for spinach salad.

Leslie Blakey, Co-Owner, General Manager and Sommelier
Le Caprice Restaurant

RICE AND GREEN PEA SALAD   Serves 6

"Excellent summer salad. High in fiber. Low in calories!"

1 clove of garlic	1 tablespoon white wine vinegar
3 cups cold cooked rice	1 cup cold cooked peas
Salt and pepper	6 scallions, finely chopped
3 tablespoons olive oil	3 tablespoons minced parsley

Rub wooden salad bowl with a split clove of garlic. Place rice in bowl and season with salt and pepper. Mix oil and vinegar to make ¼ cup of French dressing and pour over rice. Toss in peas, scallions and parsley.

NOTE: The flavor improves if prepared a day in advance.

Mrs. Leonard P. Gollobin

SOUTH DAKOTA TACO SALAD   Serves 4 to 6

"This is a real tradition on the plains of South Dakota."

1 pound ground beef	1 15-ounce can red kidney
1 package taco seasoning mix	beans, drained
1 head iceberg lettuce,	2 cups shredded cheddar cheese
chopped or torn	1 8-ounce bottle Russian
2 medium tomatoes, cut	salad dressing
into wedges	8 taco shells or
1 green pepper, diced	1 bag taco-flavored chips
(optional)	

Brown meat according to taco mix directions. Add mix and cool. • In a large bowl, mix lettuce, tomatoes and green pepper with cooled beef, kidney beans and cheese. Carefully fold in Russian salad dressing. • When ready to serve, crush taco shells or chips and gently fold into salad for a nice, crunchy taste.

Senator Thomas Daschle
(South Dakota)

SPINACH SALAD   Serves 12

2 pounds fresh spinach, chopped

10 hard-boiled eggs, sliced or chopped

1 pound bacon, cooked and crumbled

1 medium head of lettuce, shredded

1 cup chopped scallions

1 10-ounce package frozen peas, thawed but not cooked

2½ cups mayonnaise

2½ cups sour cream

Lemon juice to taste

Salt and pepper

½ cup grated Swiss cheese

In a large glass salad bowl, place in order in layers the spinach, eggs, bacon, lettuce, scallions and peas. • Combine mayonnaise, sour cream, lemon juice, salt and pepper. Gently pour over the peas. Sprinkle cheese over all. • Cover and chill for 12 hours. Do not toss.

Marcia Coats
Wife of Senator Daniel R. Coats (Indiana)

SUMMER LUNCHEON SALAD   Serves 6 to 8

"Delicious at room temperature or chilled."

1 12¼-ounce can white albacore tuna in water

1 16-ounce box spinach rotini (spiral-shaped pasta), cooked

½ cup thinly sliced Bermuda onion

Oregano

Parmesan cheese

Cracked black pepper

Oil

Vinegar

2 tomatoes, cut into wedges

1 avocado, sliced

3–4 hard-boiled eggs, sliced

Toss tuna, pasta and onion with oregano, Parmesan, pepper, oil and vinegar. Place on a platter or in a large bowl. Arrange tomato wedges, avocado slices and egg slices alternately on top to make an attractive presentation. Sprinkle with additional pepper and Parmesan.

NOTE: Chef's choice as to amounts of oregano, Parmesan, pepper, oil and vinegar.

Jeffrey Weiss

SMOKED TROUT AND WATERCRESS SALAD   Serves 4

1 pound new red potatoes, unpeeled	2 cups fresh watercress
2 bay leaves	4 ounces smoked trout
1 cup fresh sliced asparagus (cut diagonally into 1-inch pieces)	2 tablespoons snipped chives
	1 teaspoon olive oil
	Juice of 1 lemon
	Pepper to taste

Cut potatoes into halves or quarters and combine with bay leaves and 2 tablespoons water in a glass or ceramic pan. Cover tightly and microwave at full power for 3 minutes. • While potatoes cook, cut asparagus into 1-inch

slices on the diagonal. Add to potatoes, cover again and microwave an additional 2–3 minutes, until potatoes are tender. Remove from microwave, loosen cover and allow to cool briefly. Remove bay leaves and drain well. • Clean watercress and remove stems. Cut trout into bite-sized pieces. Add watercress, trout and chives to potatoes and asparagus. • In a small bowl, combine oil, lemon juice and pepper and pour over potato mixture. Toss well and serve either at room temperature or somewhat chilled.

NOTE: If you prefer, place potato pieces in cold water to cover and bring to a boil. Simmer until tender for about 15 minutes. Asparagus may be steamed in ½ cup of salted water for about 12 minutes. Cool potatoes and asparagus before combining with watercress, trout and chives.

Elena Schupp Darden

VEGETABLE SALAD   Serves 8

"This salad is great for a large buffet dinner or a luncheon."

Vinaigrette Dressing:

¾ cup olive oil
¼ cup wine vinegar
Salt and pepper to taste

1 heaping teaspoon Dijon
  mustard
3 garlic cloves, crushed

Salad:

1 pound zucchini
1 pound yellow squash
4 scallions
¾ pound green beans
½ pound snow peas

2 stalks broccoli
8 radishes
¾ pound cherry tomatoes
1 head Boston lettuce

Combine all of the vinaigrette ingredients in a jar and shake well. Pour through a strainer to remove garlic. • Slice zucchini, squash and scallions in a food processor. Set aside. • Clean and cut green beans. Drop beans into boiling water and boil for 4 minutes, drain and plunge into cold water to stop further cooking. Marinate green beans in vinaigrette for 1 hour. • Clean and blanch snow peas for 1 minute. Cut broccoli into florets and blanch in boiling water for 1 minute. Clean and slice radishes. Place all vegetables, except tomatoes and green beans, in a large bowl and toss together. • Just before serving, add tomatoes and beans to other vegetables. Toss with vinaigrette dressing and place in a glass bowl lined with Boston lettuce.

Mrs. John E. Chapoton

WALNUT CHICKEN SALAD   Serves 4

1½ cups water
1 onion, quartered
6 black peppercorns
4 chicken breast halves,
  skinned and boned
2 tablespoons cider vinegar
1½ tablespoons vegetable oil
2 tablespoons honey

½ teaspoon dry mustard
½ teaspoon tarragon
½ teaspoon grated orange rind
2 oranges, peeled and sectioned
Boston lettuce leaves
2 tablespoons walnuts,
  chopped and toasted

Combine water, onion and peppercorns in a large skillet and bring to a boil. Reduce heat and simmer, covered, for 10 minutes. Add chicken breasts, cover and continue to simmer for 10 minutes until chicken is cooked. Remove chicken from skillet and cut into strips. Set aside. • Make dressing by whisking together vinegar, oil, honey, mustard, tarragon and orange rind. Add orange sections. • On each plate, place several leaves of lettuce. Remove orange sections from dressing and divide evenly among the plates. Place chicken strips in dressing and toss gently. Divide chicken strips evenly among the plates and drizzle remaining salad dressing over each plate. Sprinkle ½ tablespoon of walnuts over each salad.

Elena Schupp Darden

CYPRIOT SOUVLAKIA AND TALATTOURI SALAD

"Especially good to eat when the weather is nice and you can grill outside"

Lamb or pork, cubed	**Onions, chopped**
Salt to taste	**Cucumbers, chopped**
Pita bread, halved	**Tomatoes, chopped**
Lemon juice	**Parsley, chopped**

For each serving, place 4 or 5 pieces of meat on a skewer and grill. When cooked, remove meat from skewer, sprinkle with salt to taste, and place in half of a pita bread. Sprinkle meat with lemon juice (very important) and add onions, cucumbers, tomatoes and parsley in pita bread. Serve with talattouri.

Talattouri (Serves 4):

1 cup thinly sliced cucumbers	**3 cloves garlic, crushed**
Salt	**2 cups yogurt**
3 tablespoons olive oil	**Salt to taste**
1 tablespoon vinegar	**1 tablespoon dried mint**

Drain sliced cucumbers mixed with a little salt in a colander for about an hour. Slowly add oil, vinegar and garlic to yogurt. Add drained cucumber and combine gently. Add salt, if desired. Sprinkle with mint and refrigerate for 1 hour.

Mrs. Andrew Jacovides
Wife of the Ambassador of Cyprus

WEST COAST SALAD   Serves 12 to 16

"In both Sweden and Norway, West Coast Salad is served as a main course at elegant post-theater suppers. It is typically made with shellfish caught along the Atlantic west coast, fresh vegetables and a dill dressing. I like to arrange all of the components of the salad on a platter, but the Swedes quite often mix them all up in a bowl."

Salt

2 pounds medium-sized shrimp

2 lobster tails (about 1 pound each)

1 pound fresh cooked crabmeat

1 pound mussels (optional)

1 cup dry wine (if using mussels)

1 shallot, chopped (if using mussels)

Lettuce leaves (iceberg or romaine)

¾ pound small mushrooms, quartered

1 pound fresh asparagus, trimmed, blanched and chilled

1 cup fresh peas, or ½ pound snow peas, blanched and chilled

2 ripe tomatoes, peeled, seeded and diced

3 hard-boiled eggs, cut into wedges

1 cup caviar

Dill dressing:

½ cup salad oil

3 tablespoons white wine vinegar

6 tablespoons chopped fresh dill or 3 tablespoons dried dill

½ teaspoon salt

Dash of pepper

Garnish:

2 lemons, cut into wedges

Fresh dill

Bring a large pot of water to a boil, adding 1 tablespoon of salt for each quart water. Add the shrimp and cook for 3 minutes, or until just pink. Remove with slotted spoon (saving water), cool and refrigerate. • Bring the water to a boil again and add the lobster tails. Cook for 8 minutes, or until just pink. Drain, cool and refrigerate. • Pick over the crabmeat to remove any shells and refrigerate. • If using mussels, scrub them and remove the beards. In a saucepan, heat the wine and shallots until boiling. Add the mussels and cook for 2 minutes, uncovered, until they open. Discard those that don't open. Drain and chill. • Shell and devein the shrimp. Crack the lobster tails and remove the flesh, then cut into slices. Remove the mussels from their shells. Arrange lettuce leaves on a large platter and place the caviar in the center. Then arrange separately the shrimp, lobster, crabmeat, mussels (if using), mushrooms, asparagus, peas, tomatoes and eggs. • Whisk together all dressing ingredients in a small bowl and drizzle over the salad. Surround with the lemon wedges and garnish with fresh dill.

Mrs. Jukka Valtasaari
Wife of the Ambassador of Finland

ARTICHOKES STUFFED WITH SHRIMP   Serves 6

6 artichokes
8 tablespoons lemon juice
4¾ teaspoons salt
1½ pounds raw small shrimp
   or 14 ounces frozen cooked
   shrimp

½ teaspoon tarragon
¼ teaspoon ground black
   pepper
1 cup mayonnaise

Prepare the artichokes by removing stems, cutting half an inch off the tops and snipping off the sharp tips of each leaf. Cook, tightly covered, in plenty of boiling water with 2 tablespoons lemon juice and 2 teaspoons salt, until the base can be pierced with a fork, about 30–40 minutes. Drain well. • Bring 1 quart of water to boil. Add shrimp, 1 tablespoon lemon juice and 2 teaspoons salt. Cook, covered, 3–5 minutes. Reserve ½ cup of cooking liquid. Drain, peel and clean the shrimp. • Reserve 18 shrimp for garnish (see note). Place remaining shrimp in a food processor fitted with a steel blade. Add reserved liquid, remaining ¾ teaspoon salt and 5 tablespoons lemon juice, tarragon, pepper and mayonnaise. Blend until shrimp are coarsely chopped. Chill. • When artichokes have cooled, spread leaves and carefully remove chokes by pulling out innermost thorny leaves and scraping out fuzzy choke. • When ready to serve, fill center of each artichoke with the shrimp mixture and garnish with reserved whole shrimp.

NOTE: If frozen cooked shrimp are used, thaw according to package directions. Use ½ cup chicken broth in place of ½ cup shrimp cooking liquid.

Antonia Gore

POACHED CHICKEN BREAST   Serves 6
WITH THAI PEANUT SAUCE AND NOODLES

"Simple, elegant and delicious."

⅔ cups chunky peanut butter
1½ cups coconut milk
  (see note)
2 tablespoons soy sauce
¼ cup freshly squeezed lemon
  juice
2 teaspoons brown sugar
4 cloves garlic, crushed or
  minced
Salt
Cayenne pepper
¼ cup chicken broth
¼ cup heavy cream
1 pound mein (Chinese
  noodles) or other thin pasta

2 tablespoons peanut oil
6–8 scallions, thinly sliced
3 whole chicken breasts,
  skinned, boned, halved and
  poached
1 pound snow peas, trimmed,
  cut into very thin julienne
  strips, blanched until
  crisp-tender, then cooled in
  ice water and drained
Unsalted dry-roasted peanuts,
  chopped
Lightly toasted sesame
  seeds (see note)
Fresh cilantro sprigs

Combine peanut butter, coconut milk, soy sauce, lemon juice, brown sugar, garlic, salt and cayenne to taste in a small saucepan over low heat. Stirring constantly, cook until smooth and thickened. Place mixture in a blender or food processor and purée briefly. Add chicken broth and cream. Blend until smooth. Pour into a bowl, cover and set aside. (This can be made several hours ahead and refrigerated.) • Cook noodles in 4 quarts of boiling water until al dente. Drain and rinse in cold water, then drain again. Place in a large bowl, toss with peanut oil and cool to room temperature, occasionally stirring the pasta to coat thoroughly. • Just before serving, place pasta on individual plates. Spoon peanut sauce over pasta and sprinkle with scallions. Slice poached chicken breast halves on the diagonal and reassemble, one on top of each pasta serving. Surround pasta with snow peas to resemble a nest. Sprinkle pasta with peanuts and sesame seeds. Garnish with cilantro sprigs.

NOTES: To make your own coconut milk, grate fresh coconut into a bowl and cover with boiling water. Let stand for 30 minutes before straining through a cheesecloth; squeeze cloth to extract all the milk. Canned coconut milk is available, or you can make a reasonable substitute by dissolving ⅓ cup of readily available canned cream of coconut in 1¼ cups hot water. To toast sesame seeds, place in a small heavy frying pan over moderate heat. Stir until seeds are golden. Remove from heat and pour onto a plate to cool.

Barbara Kilcarr

SPINACH, BACON AND APPLE SALAD   Serves 6

¼ cup olive oil
3 tablespoons wine vinegar
1 teaspoon sugar
½ teaspoon prepared mustard
Salt and pepper to taste
5 slices bacon, cooked until
    crisp and crumbled

⅓ cup sliced almonds
1 pound fresh spinach
1 red apple, cored and
    chopped (unpeeled)
3 scallions, thinly sliced

Combine olive oil, vinegar, sugar, mustard, salt and pepper in a jar and shake well. Refrigerate until ready to use. • In a large skillet, cook bacon, drain on paper towel and set aside. Discard all but 1 tablespoon bacon fat from skillet. Add almonds and, over medium high heat, shake until nuts are lightly toasted. Remove from heat. • Combine washed spinach with bacon crumbs, almonds, apple and scallions. Toss lightly. Shake dressing and pour over salad. Toss again.

Karin G. Weber

POTATO SALAD WITH DILL   Serves 6–8
AND SCALLIONS

"Delicious. A good dish to make ahead."

8 medium red potatoes,
    unpeeled
1½ cups mayonnaise
1 cup sour cream
1 teaspoon horseradish

1 teaspoon celery seed
½ to 1 teaspoon salt
1 cup minced fresh dill
1 bunch scallions, chopped
    (white and some green)

Boil potatoes until cooked, about 20 minutes. When cooled, slice to ¼ inch thickness. • Stir together the mayonnaise, sour cream, horseradish, celery seed, salt and pepper and set aside. • In a separate bowl, mix dill and scallions and set aside. • In a large glass bowl place a layer of potatoes. Top with some of mayonnaise mixture, then scallion and dill mixture. Repeat until bowl is full, ending with scallion and dill mixture. • Refrigerate for at least 8 hours before serving. Do not stir.

Mrs. Ben F. Dixon IV

DIET SALAD DRESSING   Makes 2 cups

"Thirty calories per tablespoon!"

1 cup chicken broth
½ cup balsamic vinegar
½ cup safflower oil
2 cloves of garlic
½ teaspoon pepper

½ teaspoon salt
¾ packet Equal
Pinch dry mustard
Finely grated Jarlsberg cheese
   (optional)

Mix all of the above ingredients, except the cheese. Refrigerate for several hours so that the garlic will permeate dressing. Remove garlic cloves if dressing is kept for more than 24 hours. Dressing will keep at least one week in refrigerator. Serve over greens on individual plates with a sprinkling of grated cheese, if desired.

Chris Hunter

GEORGIA PEANUT SALAD DRESSING   Makes 2 cups

½ teaspoon salt
1 teaspoon garlic, mashed
1 tablespoon chopped fresh tarragon
1 tablespoon chopped fresh chives

1 tablespoon chopped parsley
1 teaspoon ground black pepper
2 tablespoons brown sugar
⅔ cup malt vinegar
1¼ cups peanut oil

Combine all ingredients and mix well. Allow to age for 24 hours.

Chef Michael Patton
1789 Restaurant

LEMON HONEY VINAIGRETTE   Makes 1½ cups

1 bunch of scallions
⅓ cup cider vinegar
1 cup vegetable oil

Juice of 1 lemon
1 tablespoon honey

Mince the white part of scallions and add to other ingredients. Mix well and refrigerate until ready to serve. Pour over salad greens.

Fearrington House
Chapel Hill, North Carolina

CREAMY ROASTED GARLIC DRESSING   Makes 1 cup

1 garlic bulb, soaked in olive oil
2 teaspoons olive oil
½ cup sour cream
¼ cup mayonnaise
2 scallions, thinly sliced

1 tablespoon champagne vinegar
¾ teaspoon freshly cracked black pepper
½ teaspoon salt

Preheat oven to 300°. • Place garlic on a cookie sheet brushed with olive oil and roast slowly for 45 minutes, until soft. Remove from oven and allow to cool. • Put sour cream and mayonnaise in a mixing bowl. Squeeze in roasted garlic. Use a rubber spatula to mash garlic into mixture. Stir in scallions, vinegar, pepper, and salt. This dressing may be made up to two days in advance.

Chef Michael Patton
Assistant Chef Tom Blundell
1789 Restaurant

LOW CALORIE SALAD DRESSING   Makes ½ cup

½ cup white wine vinegar
4 sage leaves, crushed
¼ teaspoon tarragon
1 pinch of savory
1 tablespoon fresh parsley,
  minced or 1 teaspoon dried
  parsley flakes

½ clove garlic, crushed
¼ teaspoon dried dill weed
Salt, if desired
Pepper to taste

Combine all of the above ingredients in a jar and shake well.

Committee

ROQUEFORT CHEESE SALAD DRESSING   Makes 1¾ cups

"My most copied recipe!"

½ cup crumbled Roquefort
  cheese
1¼ cups mayonnaise
2 tablespoons light cream

1 teaspoon Worcestershire
  sauce
¼ teaspoon salt
Pinch of garlic powder
Pinch of white pepper

Mix all ingredients well. Let stand, covered, at least 4 hours before using. This will keep up to 2 weeks in refrigerator.

Mary Beth Gosende

CREAMY VINAIGRETTE   Makes 1¼ cups

"Excellent on artichokes and salads."

⅔ cup plain, low-fat yogurt
⅓ cup apple cider vinegar
2 tablespoons olive oil
1 tablespoon Dijon mustard

1 tablespoon fresh lemon juice
1 very large clove garlic,
  crushed
¼ teaspoon dried dill

Combine ingredients in a jar. Shake or whisk well. Refrigerate. Keeps almost forever.

Jane Brody

Accompaniments

SUGARED BACON

½ pound bacon, sliced
(not thick)
½ cup packed light brown
sugar

1 tablespoon Dijon mustard
2 tablespoons red wine

Preheat oven to 325°. • In a flat large pan, bake bacon until crisp (about 10–15 minutes). Drain off the fat. • Mix the remaining ingredients together and pour over both sides of bacon. Bake again at 350° for about 10 minutes or until bubbles appear on bacon. Remove from pan onto foil. Keep at room temperature until served. Will be crunchy.

Mrs. Eugene B. Casey

CRANBERRY ORANGE RELISH

"No turkey should be without this!"

1 orange
1 pound fresh cranberries

2 pippin apples, cored
and peeled
1 cup sugar

Peel the orange, saving the peel. Remove the white membrane and cut the orange into 1-inch cubes. Remove white membrane from the orange peel and cut into 1-inch pieces. • Cut apples into 1-inch pieces. • Place cranberries, apples, orange and orange peel in food processor and pulse until coarsely chopped. Stir in sugar. • This relish should be made 3–4 days ahead. Keeps beautifully in refrigerator for 3–4 weeks.

Sally Davidson

FRESH CRANBERRY SAUCE

1 package fresh cranberries
1½ cups sugar
1 12-ounce can chunk
pineapple

1½ teaspoons cinnamon
1 teaspoon nutmeg
½ teaspoon ground cloves
1 orange, cut in slices

Place cranberries and sugar in saucepan. Add liquid from pineapple. Simmer for 15 minutes, or until cranberries start popping. Add cinnamon, nutmeg and cloves. Remove from heat. When mixture is cool, add pineapple chunks and orange slices.

Terry Stone

HURRY CURRY SAUCE

3 egg yolks
2 tablespoons light cream
   or milk
1–2 tablespoons freshly
   squeezed lemon juice

½ teaspoon curry powder
Salt to taste
½ cup melted butter

In an electric blender, combine egg yolks, cream or milk, lemon juice, curry powder and salt. Process for 10 seconds, until smooth. With blender on high speed, very gradually add melted butter while bubbly and hot. Process until sauce is smooth and slightly thickened. • Serve over vegetables such as asparagus, broccoli and cauliflower or over poached eggs.

Senator Dale Bumpers
(Arkansas)

MAMA TRAMONTE'S PESTO   Makes 8 cups

10 ounces Locatelli Romano
   cheese
10 ounces Parmigiano-
   Reggiano cheese
8 large cloves garlic, peeled
9 ounces Gitterio pancetta,
   diced

4 cups extra virgin olive oil
1 10-ounce package frozen
   spinach, defrosted
6–7 cups fresh basil leaves
½ cup pine nuts
Salt and pepper to taste

Cut both Romano and Parmigiano cheeses into 1-inch cubes and blend in a food processor. Add garlic cloves, pancetta and half of olive oil and blend. Add spinach and blend. Add basil leaves gradually and more oil as necessary. Add pine nuts, salt and pepper and blend.

The Italian Store
Arlington and Falls Church, VA

PEPERONATA PASTA SAUCE   Serves 4 to 6

2 red peppers	2 onions
1 orange pepper	6 mushrooms, sliced
2 green peppers	Olive oil
1 yellow pepper or	1 teaspoon minced garlic
any combination of the	1½ cups beer
above	Flour or cornstarch (optional)

Chop peppers and onions. Slice mushrooms. In a large skillet, sauté peppers, onions and mushrooms in olive oil until tender. Add garlic and beer and cover. Simmer for 20–30 minutes. If desired, thicken sauce with flour or cornstarch. • Serve over freshly cooked pasta.

Richard S. Morehouse

MARINADE FOR STEAK

"Great on all meats."

3 tablespoons butter	1 teaspoon Worcestershire
1 teaspoon mustard	sauce
1 teaspoon soy sauce	

To make marinade, melt butter and combine with mustard, soy sauce and Worcestershire sauce. Increase amounts proportionally depending on amount of meat and whether you wish additional marinade for sauce. • Try with beef tenderloin or flank steak, rubbed all over with Lawry's salt. Marinate meat for an hour or two before grilling or broiling.

Mary Doremus

MUSTARD SAUCE   Makes 1 quart

"Terrific! A great gift! Keeps indefinitely in refrigerator."

½ cup Coleman's dry mustard	1 can Campbell's beef
2 tablespoons flour	consommé
1 cup dark brown sugar	1 cup cider vinegar
	3 eggs, beaten

Blend dry ingredients in the top of a double boiler. Add liquids and cook, stirring with a wire whisk, until thickened. Cool and pour into jars with pretty covers. Good with ham, on sandwiches, or whenever else you use mustard.

Sarah T. Minikes

MY SISTER'S MOTHER-IN-LAW'S BARBECUE SAUCE

"This is great on pork chops, country spare ribs and chicken."

1 small bottle ketchup
1 cup water
2 beef bouillon cubes
⅓ cup vinegar
Juice of 1 lemon
1 clove garlic
2 onions, chopped

1 teaspoon Worcestershire
sauce
1 tablespoon chili powder
1 tablespoon mustard
1 tablespoon H & P Sauce
Dash Tabasco sauce

Simmer all ingredients for 10 minutes. Pour over meat and marinate for approximately 1 hour before cooking. Baste meat frequently while cooking. Can be used when broiling in oven or grilling out-of-doors. Serve meat with remaining warm sauce.

Dotty Wexler

APPLE AND SAUSAGE DRESSING   Serves 6
TO SERVE WITH TURKEY

1 pound sweet Italian sausage
2 tablespoons butter
1 onion, chopped
3 celery stalks, diced
2 cups peeled and chopped
Granny Smith apples

1 pound stale French bread,
cubed
1 teaspoon sage
1 teaspoon thyme
Salt and pepper to taste
2 eggs, beaten
2 cups chicken broth

Preheat oven to 375°. • Cut sausage into small pieces and place in ovenproof dish. Cook sausage in oven for about 15 minutes, until cooked through. Remove sausage with slotted spoon and drain on paper towels. • While sausage is cooking, melt butter in a large skillet and sauté onion and celery until onion is translucent. Remove from heat and allow to cool. • Mix sausage with onion, celery, apples, bread cubes, sage, thyme, salt and pepper. Slowly add the eggs and chicken broth. Mix gently. • Pour into a greased casserole dish, cover and bake for 40 minutes. Remove cover and continue cooking for 20 minutes until slightly brown.

Elena Schupp Darden

BULGARIAN TARATOR

3–4 cloves garlic, minced
2 tablespoons olive oil
Salt to taste
¼ cup finely chopped walnuts
2 cups yogurt

2 small cucumbers, finely
   chopped (approximately
   ⅔ pound)
Dill to taste

Crush garlic, olive oil, salt and walnuts together. Stir in yogurt and finally add the cucumber and dill. The mixture obtained is diluted with water to taste.

Embassy of Republic of Bulgaria

TURKISH TARATOR   Serves 6

*"Excellent accompaniment for almost any vegetable,
but especially beans or eggplant."*

1 cup pine nuts
2–3 cloves garlic, crushed
   with a pinch of sea salt
⅓ cup water, plus a few
   tablespoons water as
   needed

2 cups cubed stale bread,
   crusts removed, soaked
   in water and squeezed dry
3 tablespoons lemon juice
   or white wine vinegar
Salt to taste
2–3 tablespoons olive oil

Place pine nuts in very low-temperature oven until slightly brown (5–10 minutes). Shake every minute or 2. Watch carefully to ensure they do not burn. • Put nuts in blender or food processor along with garlic and water. When mixture is smooth, add bread, lemon juice, salt and olive oil and continue to blend. Add a little water as needed. • Let sit at room temperature for 2–3 hours before serving.

Paula Jeffries

SAUCE MOUTARDE

⅓ cup Dijon mustard
2 eggs
1 cup heavy cream

1 tablespoon vinegar
¼ teaspoon tarragon or
  dill weed (optional)

Heat all ingredients over low heat, stirring constantly, until mixture thickens. Wonderful on fish, hot or cold.

Mrs. Robert H. Craft, Jr.

CHOCOLATE SAUCE

1 5-ounce can of evaporated
  milk
1 cup sugar
Dash of salt

2 squares semi-sweet chocolate
1 tablespoon butter or
  margarine
1 teaspoon vanilla

Place evaporated milk, sugar and salt in a saucepan and heat to boiling over very low heat, stirring occasionally. Add chocolate, butter or margarine and vanilla and stir continuously until mixture thickens. The sauce may be stored, covered, in refrigerator and reheated when needed.

Linda Terry-Choyke

SINFUL SAUCE

5 ounces unsweetened
  chocolate
1 cup heavy cream
1½ cups sugar

¼ cup corn syrup
¼ teaspoon salt
2 tablespoons butter

Heat chocolate with cream over low heat until it melts, stirring occasionally. Add sugar, corn syrup and salt and continue stirring until smooth (being careful not to burn). Add butter and stir well. Cool and refrigerate. Sauce keeps indefinitely.

Mrs. Elizabeth Beach Rea

TEMPURA BATTER FOR SHRIMP OR CHICKEN
Makes enough batter for 3 pounds shrimp or chicken

2 eggs
1 cup milk
⅛ cup flour

½ teaspoon salt
Dash of Tabasco sauce
2 teaspoons baking powder

Beat eggs in small mixing bowl and stir in milk. Add flour, salt and Tabasco sauce. Beat until thoroughly blended. Add baking powder and mix well. Dip either shrimp or chicken in batter and fry in hot oil.

William H. Darden

WATERCRESS MAYONNAISE EILEEN FORD

1 cup Hellman's regular
   or light mayonnaise

1 bunch watercress, including
   ½ of the stems
Pinch of salt

Chop watercress as finely as possible and mix with mayonnaise. Salt to taste. This tastes better when made a day ahead. Serve with cold fish or lobster.

Mrs. Robert H. Craft, Jr.

ZUCCHINI PICKLES
Makes enough for 6 half pint jars

8 cups zucchini, thinly sliced
2 medium onions, thinly
   sliced
¼ cup kosher salt
2 cups vinegar

2 cups sugar
1 teaspoon celery seed
2 teaspoons mustard seed
1 teaspoon turmeric
½ teaspoon dry mustard

Combine zucchini, onions and salt. Cover with water and let sit for 2 hours. Drain, rinse, and drain again. • Boil together vinegar, sugar and spices for 2 minutes. Add zucchini and onion and bring to a simmer. Put in jars and seal while hot.

Paula Jeffries

Breads

ALAND PANCAKE WITH PRUNE SAUCE   Serves 4

A Finnish favorite.

Pancake:

⅓ cup rice
⅔ cup milk plus 2½ cups milk
⅓ cup water
⅕ teaspoon plus ½ teaspoon salt

½ cup wheat flour
1 teaspoon ground cardamom
3 eggs
¼ cup sugar
1 tablespoon butter

Prune Sauce:

8 ounces pitted prunes
1⅔ cups water
3 tablespoons sugar

1 cinnamon stick
¾ teaspoon potato flour
3 tablespoons red wine

Preheat oven to 400°. To make pancakes, make a porridge from the rice, ⅔ cup milk, water and ⅕ teaspoon salt. Let the ingredients cook gently, uncovered, for about 10 minutes and then cover and let simmer on low heat for about 15 minutes, or until the rice has swollen. • Pour the warm, not completely cooked, rice porridge into the remaining 2½ cups milk. Stir and fold in the wheat flour, then add ½ teaspoon salt and the cardamom. • In another bowl, whip the eggs with the sugar until the mixture is fluffy and light yellow, then fold into rice mixture. • Butter an oven-safe baking pan (e.g., cast iron, 12-inch frying pan), pour in the batter and bake the pancake on the middle rack of the oven for 20 minutes. Then, move the pancake to the bottom rack for 15 minutes. Test with a knife to see when pancake is baked. • To make prune sauce: soak prunes in the water with sugar and cinnamon stick for about an hour, then gently simmer on low heat. • When the prunes have softened, but not cooked to pieces, remove them with a slotted spoon and place them in a serving bowl, discarding the cinnamon stick. Add the potato flour, which has been softened with a little water, to the prune water and bring to a boil, adding red wine to taste. Allow the sauce to simmer for a few minutes, then pour it over the prunes and chill until the Alard pancake is to be served, suitably warm. Serve pancake with lightly whipped cream and the prune sauce.

Ingmar Byorksten,
Cultural Counselor, Embassy of Sweden

BANANA BRAN MUFFINS

Makes 12 large
or 24 mini-muffins

1 very ripe banana, mashed
1 egg
¾ cup 2% milk
2 tablespoons butter, melted
1 cup bran

1 cup flour
3 teaspoons baking powder
¼ cup sugar
¼ teaspoon salt

Preheat oven to 400°. • In a bowl, mix banana, egg, milk, butter and bran. Allow to stand 10–15 minutes. • In another bowl, mix flour, baking powder, sugar and salt. Combine flour and bran mixtures. Do not overmix. Spoon into non-stick muffin tins. Bake for 25 minutes for 12 regular-sized muffins, or 12 minutes for 24 mini-muffins. These may be frozen and reheated in microwave.

Mrs. Porter K. Wheeler

BASIL BISCUITS

Makes 18 biscuits

1 cup flour
1½ teaspoons baking powder
¼ teaspoon salt
3 tablespoons cold, unsalted
   butter cut into small pieces

2 tablespoons chopped
   fresh basil
1½ teaspoons minced shallots
⅓ cup milk

Preheat oven to 450°. • Combine flour, baking powder and salt. Cut in the butter until mixture resembles coarse meal. Stir in basil and shallots. Add milk and stir quickly to combine. • Quickly roll out dough on a lightly floured surface to 1-inch thickness. • Cut out biscuits using a 2-inch round cutter. • Bake on an ungreased baking sheet for 12–15 minutes or until golden on top.

Katie Hunnicutt

BEER BREAD

Makes 1 loaf

"A fun way to use that stale beer."

3 cups self-rising flour
1½ cups stale beer
3 tablespoons sugar

Mix all ingredients and pour into a greased loaf pan. Do not let rise. Bake at 375° for 45 minutes. Serve warm.

Freddie Williams

BLUEBERRY APPLE COFFEE CAKE

½ cup butter, softened
1 cup sugar
3 eggs, lightly beaten
1 teaspoon baking powder
¼ teaspoon salt
1 teaspoon baking soda
2¼ cups unbleached flour
1 cup sour cream

2 cups blueberries (fresh or
  frozen)
1 Granny Smith apple,
  peeled, cored and chopped
1 cup brown sugar
¼ cup butter
½ teaspoon cinnamon

Preheat oven to 350°. • Cream butter and sugar. Add eggs, baking powder, salt and baking soda. Alternating, add 2 cups flour and sour cream. Mix well (this can be done in a food processor). • Fold in blueberries and apple. Place in a well-buttered 9 x 13 x 2 inch cake pan. • Using your fingers, mix brown sugar and butter. Add remaining ¼ cup flour and cinnamon, crumble until thoroughly blended and sprinkle over top of batter by hand. • Bake for 40 minutes.

Mrs. Ben F. Dixon, IV

BLUEBERRY PANCAKES

2 cups flour
3 tablespoons sugar
1 tablespoon baking powder
Pinch of salt
1½ cups milk

1 egg
¼ cup oil or bacon drippings
1 cup blueberries
¼ cup wheat germ, toasted

Mix flour, sugar, baking powder and salt until well blended. • Combine milk, egg and oil and add to flour mixture. Gently fold in blueberries. Pour batter onto greased griddle and fry until lightly browned. Sprinkle with wheat germ before turning. Brown second side. Serve immediately.

Alice K. Dawkins

BRIOCHE LOAF

½ cup lukewarm milk
¼ cup sugar
1 teaspoon salt
¼ cup soft butter
1 cake compressed yeast
  or 1 package dry yeast

1 egg
1 egg yolk
2½–2¾ cups unbleached flour
Melted butter

Combine milk, sugar, salt and butter. Crumble yeast into mixture and stir until yeast is dissolved. Stir in egg and egg yolk. Add flour and mix well. • Turn dough onto a lightly floured board. Cover and let stand for 10 minutes. Knead until smooth and elastic. • Divide dough into 3 ropes, each 12 inches long. Make a braid of the ropes, pressing ends to seal them. Place in a greased 9 x 5 x 3 inch or 8 x 4 x 3 inch bread pan. Cover and let rise at room temperature until doubled in size, about 2 hours. Top of loaf should be about level with the top of the pan. • Brush with melted butter. Bake at 375° for 30 minutes.

Paula Jeffries

CHEDDAR CORNMEAL CRACKERS   Yields 80

2 cups coarsely shredded   **½ cup cornmeal**
   sharp cheddar cheese   **½ teaspoon ground cumin**
   (white or yellow)   **¼ teaspoon cayenne pepper**
6 tablespoons unsalted butter   **¼ teaspoon salt**
¾ cup flour

Have all ingredients at room temperature. In a food processor, combine cheese and butter. • Mix dry ingredients and add to cheese mixture. Process until dough forms a ball. Divide dough in half and roll each half into a 1½-inch cylinder. Wrap in plastic and refrigerate until completely chilled for several hours or overnight. You may also freeze dough for future use. • To bake, cut dough into ⅛ inch thick rounds, arrange on a cookie sheet 1 inch apart and bake for 10 minutes at 350°, until lightly brown around edges. • Remove immediately from cookie sheet and cool on wire racks. Store in air-tight containers.

Loni Landfield

AUNT EVELYN'S JOHNNY CAKES

1½ cups cornmeal   **1½ teaspoons baking powder**
½ cup flour   **1 egg, beaten**
¼ cup sugar   **1¼ cups sour milk (buttermilk**
1 teaspoon salt   **may be substituted)**
¾ teaspoon baking soda   **3 tablespoons butter, melted**

Preheat oven to 425°. • Sift cornmeal, flour, sugar, salt, baking soda and baking powder together. Combine egg, sour milk and butter and add to dry mixture. Stir lightly and pour into greased 9 x 9 inch pan or muffin tins. Bake for 25 minutes.

Senator John H. Chafee
(Rhode Island)

BIRCHERMUESLI

Makes 15 10-ounce servings

42 ounces Quick Quaker
   Oats (2⅓ 18-ounce boxes)
6 cups skim milk
1½ cups orange juice
1 cup sugar
⅔ cup plain yogurt
2 pears

2 apples
1 canteloupe
1 banana
2 cups seedless grapes
15 strawberries
Whipped cream, for garnish
   (optional)

In a large mixing bowl, mix together oats, skim milk, orange juice, sugar and yogurt. Peel and dice pears, apples, canteloupe and banana and add to oat mixture. Add grapes and allow to sit for 15 minutes before serving. Garnish with a strawberry and whipped cream, if desired. Serve as a dessert, snack, or breakfast. Keeps refrigerated for 2–3 days.

Lou McDuffee, General Manager
Bread & Chocolate

COFFEE COFFEE CAKE
WITH COFFEE GLAZE

Cake:
½ cup unsalted butter,
   softened
1¼ cups sugar
2 eggs
1 tablespoon espresso coffee
½ teaspoon vanilla extract
2 cups sifted flour
1 teaspoon baking powder
1 teaspoon baking soda

⅛ teaspoon salt
1¼ cups sour cream
¼ cup currants
½ cup packed dark brown
   sugar
⅓ cup finely chopped pecans
2 teaspoons cinnamon
2 teaspoons instant coffee
   powder

Coffee glaze:
1 cup powdered sugar
3 tablespoons strong coffee

½ teaspoon half and half
¼ teaspoon vanilla extract

Heat oven to 375°. • Cream butter and sugar. Add eggs one at a time, beating well after each addition. Stir in coffee and vanilla. • Mix flour, baking powder, baking soda and salt. Add to butter mixture, alternating with sour cream, beating well after each addition. • Soak currants in hot water to cover for 8–10 minutes. Combine drained currants, brown sugar, pecans, cinnamon and coffee powder. • Spread ¼ of batter in a well-buttered 12-cup Bundt or 10-inch tube pan. Sprinkle with ⅓ of currant mixture. Repeat layering twice, ending with batter. • Bake for 55–60 minutes, until a toothpick inserted in center comes out clean. • Cool on a wire rack for 20 minutes. Remove from pan. Cool completely. • To make glaze, mix all ingredients until smooth and pour over cooled cake.

Mrs. John Hunnicutt

CRANBERRY BREAD   Serves 8

¼ cup butter or margarine,
   softened
1 cup sugar
2 eggs
1 cup chopped Massachusetts
   cranberries
½ cup water

1¾ cups flour
½ teaspoon baking soda
1½ teaspoons baking powder
1 teaspoon salt
½ teaspoon cinnamon
½ cup chopped nuts

Preheat oven to 350°. • In an electric mixer, cream butter and sugar. Add eggs and beat. Stir in cranberries and water. • Sift together flour, baking soda, baking powder, salt and cinnamon. Stir into butter mixture. Add nuts and stir. • Pour into a loaf pan and bake for 55 minutes.

Senator John F. Kerry
(Massachusetts)

CORNBREAD OLÉ   Yields 16 to 18 pieces

2 10-ounce packages
   cornbread mix
1 teaspoon salt
1 cup chopped scallions
½ cup chopped fresh cilantro
3 tablespoons chopped fresh
   jalapeño or drained pickled
   jalapeño peppers
1 cup sour cream
1 cup cottage cheese

¾ cup margarine or butter,
   melted
4 eggs
1 16-ounce package frozen
   corn, red and green peppers,
   thawed, or
   canned corn with peppers,
   drained
1 cup shredded sharp Cheddar
   cheese (4 ounces)

Heat oven to 400°. • Grease a 13 x 9 inch baking pan. Combine all ingredients and mix well. Spread in greased pan and bake for 34–42 minutes until deep golden brown and a toothpick inserted in center comes out clean. • Cool for 10 minutes and cut into squares. Olé!

Nina Pillsbury

EASY ENGLISH MUFFIN BREAD

6 cups flour
2 packages dry active yeast
1 tablespoon sugar
1½ teaspoons salt

¼ teaspoon baking soda
2 cups lowfat milk (2%)
½ cup water
Cornmeal

Preheat oven to 400°. • Combine 3 cups of flour, yeast, sugar, salt and baking soda in a large bowl and set aside. • Heat milk and water in a small saucepan to 120°. Slowly add the milk mixture to dry ingredients, mixing with an electric beater on low speed for 2 minutes. • Add enough of the remaining 3 cups of flour to make a soft dough. (This can vary due to type of flour, humidity, etc.) Divide dough in half and shape into loaves. Grease two 8½ x 4½ x 3 inch loaf pans and sprinkle bottoms and sides with cornmeal. Place dough in pans and sprinkle tops with cornmeal. Cover with clean, dry towels and allow dough to rise in a warm place until double in size, about 45 minutes. • Bake for 25 minutes.

Mrs. Porter K. Wheeler

ENGLISH MUFFINS   Makes 12 to 15

2 tablespoons sugar
1 teaspoon salt
1 package yeast
5 cups flour
1½ cups milk

¼ cup butter
1 egg
2 tablespoons yellow cornmeal
Vegetable oil

Combine sugar, salt, yeast and 1½ cups flour. • Heat milk and butter until warm and butter is melted. Beat liquid into dry ingredients for 2 minutes. Gradually beat in egg and 1 additional cup flour. Add remaining 2½ cups flour. Knead for 2 minutes. • Shape into a ball and let rise until double in size, about 2½ hours. • Punch dough down and allow to rest for 15 minutes. • Place cornmeal on a pie plate. • Roll out dough to ⅜ inch thickness, cut into 3-inch rounds, dip in cornmeal and place 1 inch apart on cookie sheets. Cover and let rise for 45 minutes. Fry in oiled skillet 8 minutes per side.

Mrs. Richard S. Morehouse

FLAT ONION BREAD   Makes 16 rounds

6 tablespoons butter
1½ cups finely chopped
  onions

¾ cup lukewarm water
1 teaspoon salt
2½–3 cups flour

Melt 1 tablespoon of butter in a heavy 10–12 inch skillet over high heat. Add

onions, reduce heat to low and cook 3–5 minutes, stirring occasionally, until onions are soft but not brown. Transfer to a bowl and cool to room temperature. • Melt remaining 5 tablespoons butter in the skillet and pour into a large mixing bowl. Add lukewarm water and stir in chopped onions. Add salt and 2½ cups of flour, half a cup at a time. If necessary, add up to another ½ cup of flour as needed to make a dough that does not stick to your fingers. • Gather the dough into a large, compact ball and divide into 16 pieces. With the palms of your hands, shape each piece into a 1½ to 2-inch ball. With a lightly floured rolling pin, roll out each ball, one at a time, into a circle about 8 inches in diameter. Set the rounds of dough aside. • Place heavy, ungreased 10–12 inch skillet over high heat. When a drop of water flicked across the surface of the skillet evaporates instantly, place one round of dough in the center. Brown for 3–4 minutes on each side. (Do not be concerned if dough does not brown evenly.) • Transfer to a rack to dry and continue with dough until all 16 rounds have been cooked.

Mrs. G. William Miller

FRENCH BREAD I   Makes 4 loaves

5 cups flour
2 packages dry yeast
2 cups warm water

1 tablespoon sugar
Salt to taste

Place flour in a large bowl or food processor. Mix yeast, warm water and sugar in another bowl to proof. Pour yeast mixture into flour and mix until well blended. Place in a bowl, cover and let double in size in a warm place. • Punch down and divide into 4 balls. Shape into long loaves, place in French bread pans and let rise. Bake at 400° for 30–35 minutes.

Paula Jeffries

FRENCH BREAD II

Makes 2 loaves

1 package yeast
¼ cup warm water
½ cup milk, scalded
1 cup boiling water
1½ tablespoons vegetable oil
1½ tablespoons sugar

4 cups enriched white flour
2 teaspoons salt
1 egg white combined with
    1 tablespoon cold water
    for egg wash

Dissolve yeast in warm water. Set aside. • Combine scalded milk, boiling water, vegetable oil and 1 tablespoon sugar. Cool to lukewarm. • Combine flour, salt and remaining ½ tablespoon sugar in a bowl. • Add yeast to cooled milk mixture and stir until well blended. Gradually add liquids to flour mixture and stir well. Add more flour to form dough that is firm and elastic but not sticky. Do not knead. • Cover with wax paper and set in a warm place to rise until it doubles in bulk, about 1 hour or more. (I put it in an unheated oven with a cake pan filled with boiling water on the lower rack.) • When dough has risen, punch down and divide into two equal parts. • On a floured surface shape the dough into two long, symmetrical rolls and place into a buttered double French bread pan (most are 18 inches long). With sharp scissors, cut at least 3 diagonal slits into each loaf. • Set in a warm place to rise until double in bulk. • Preheat oven to 400° and place a cake pan filled with boiling water on lower rack. Bake bread on middle rack for 15 minutes. Lower heat to 350° and continue cooking for 25 minutes. • Brush loaves with egg wash and bake another 5 minutes at 350°.

Toni Gore

THE GRASSLEY FAMILY'S FAVORITE CORNBREAD

½ cup butter, softened
1 cup sugar
2 eggs
1 cup cornmeal

1½ cups flour
2 teaspoons baking powder
¼ teaspoon salt
1½ cups milk

Preheat oven to 375°. • Cream butter and sugar. Mix in eggs and cornmeal. Sift together flour, baking powder and salt. Add flour mixture to butter mixture alternately with milk, beating after each addition. Do not overbeat. • Place in a greased 8-inch square or 9 x 13 inch pan. Bake for 35 minutes (less for larger pan) until done.

Senator Charles E. Grassley
(Iowa)

HUNGARIAN DINNER CRESCENTS   Makes 24 to 32

1 package active dry yeast	1 teaspoon salt
¼ cup warm water (110°)	3½ cups all-purpose flour
1 cup milk	1 egg
¼ cup sugar	1 egg yolk mixed with a
4 tablespoons butter	little milk for egg wash

Soften yeast in warm water and set aside. • Combine milk, sugar, butter and salt. • Heat over low heat to melt butter and set aside to cool. • Place all of the flour in a mixing bowl. Gradually add the milk mixture. Add the yeast and the egg. The dough should be sticky but not overly soft. • Beat dough until smooth ball forms. Place in a greased bowl to rise, about 1½–2 hours. • Turn dough onto lightly floured surface. Working with half the dough, roll into a circle and cut into 12–16 equal triangular pieces (like a slice of pie). Roll wide end of each triangle toward point to form a crescent. Place crescents on a greased cookie sheet, well separated, and brush tops with egg wash. Follow the same procedure with second half of dough. Allow to rise before baking (about 25 minutes). • Bake in a 400° oven for 12–15 minutes, until rosy. • If prepared ahead, place rolls in 350° oven for a few seconds to crisp just before serving.

Mrs. Richard Landfield

JALAPEÑO CHEESE CORNBREAD

1½ cups cornbread mix	¼ cup canned chopped
¾ cup milk	jalapeño peppers
1 egg	¾ cup grated cheddar or
½ cup creamed corn	Monterey Jack cheese
½ scallion, chopped	1 tablespoon sugar
	2 tablespoons oil

Preheat oven to 425°. • Combine all ingredients in a bowl and mix well. • Pour into a rectangular, buttered baking dish and bake for 25 minutes or until done. Cool in the pan and cut into squares to serve. • Corn bread may be varied to suit your taste by adding bacon bits, chopped pimento, chopped garlic or chopped, grilled onion.

Governor Ann Richards
(Texas)

KNÄCKEBRÖD
(SWEDISH HARDTACK)

2 cups buttermilk
1½ cups sugar
½ cup butter, melted

1 teaspoon salt
1 teaspoon baking soda
2 cups coarse rye flour, more if
　　needed

Preheat oven to 425°. Combine all ingredients to make a thick dough. Form into 1-inch balls. Roll balls in additional flour and, with a pegged rolling pin, roll out dough into thin circles. (If you use a smooth rolling pin, dough must be scored and pricked.) • Bake on a cookie sheet until lightly browned. Serve with soup, salad or as a cocktail snack.

Mrs. Charles J. DiBona

MRS. BAILEY'S LEMON BREAD

½ cup shortening
1 cup sugar
2 eggs
1½ cups cake flour
½ teaspoon salt

½ teaspoon baking powder
½ cup milk
1 teaspoon lemon extract
Grated rind of 1 lemon

Topping:
Juice of 1 lemon

½ cup sugar

Preheat oven to 350°. • Do all mixing by hand. Cream together shortening and sugar. Add eggs and beat until smooth. Sift together dry ingredients and add to creamed mixture alternately with milk. Add lemon extract and rind. Pour batter into a 12 x 4 inch loaf pan and bake for 40–45 minutes. To make topping, mix lemon juice and sugar and let stand until bread is done. With a brush or spoon, spread juice mixture over top of bread. Cool in baking pan.

Meredith A. Gonyea

SWEDISH PANCAKES

**Makes 1 large pancake
or 8 to 10 small ones**

1½ cups flour
1 scant teaspoon salt
3 teaspoons sugar

3 large eggs or 4 smaller ones
2 cups milk
1 tablespoon butter, melted

Combine flour, salt and sugar in a bowl. Whisk the eggs and milk together and slowly blend into flour mixture. Add melted butter and stir. • For one large pancake, preheat oven to 350°. Pour batter into a greased 12-inch cast iron skillet and bake until brown. • For individual pancakes, use a scant half-cup of batter per pancake and fry in a greased skillet. These will be very thin and may be rolled. • Prepared either way, they can be served sprinkled with lemon juice, powdered sugar and fresh fruit, such as strawberries.

Senator Patty Murray
(Washington)

OVEN-COOKED PANCAKE

2–4 tablespoons butter	½ cup milk
½ cup flour	Pinch of nutmeg
2 eggs	

Accompaniments:

Juice of half a lemon	Stewed apples, baked plums,
2 tablespoons sugar	stewed cranberries, honey, maple syrup or any fruit preserve

Preheat oven to 425°. • Melt butter in a shallow baking dish. Combine flour, eggs, milk and nutmeg, beating lightly. Pour into dish with melted butter and bake for 15–20 minutes, until mixture rises to consistency of a fluffy soufflé. • Serve sprinkled with lemon juice and sugar or any of the other suggested accompaniments.

Sylvia Jukes Morris

SAUSAGE UPSIDE-DOWN CORNBREAD

1 pound bulk pork sausage, medium or hot	Dash of salt
1 onion, chopped	1 teaspoon chili powder
½ green bell pepper, chopped	⅛ teaspoon pepper
2 tablespoons flour	4 ounces sharp cheddar cheese, cubed
1 8-ounce can tomato sauce or ¾ cup salsa	½ cup sliced black olives
	1 10-ounce package cornbread mix

Preheat oven to 400°. • In a skillet, sauté sausage, onion and green pepper until sausage is brown and crumbly. Drain fat and stir in flour, tomato sauce or salsa, salt, chili powder and pepper. Remove from heat and add cheese and olives. Spread evenly in a 9-inch pan. • Prepare cornbread in accordance with package instructions and spread over sausage mix. Bake for 30–35 minutes. Remove from oven and allow to stand for 5 minutes. Loosen edges and invert on serving plate. Serve immediately.

Virginia Wile

SPOON BREAD   Serves 4

½ cup water-ground cornmeal   1 tablespoon butter
½ teaspoon salt   2 eggs, beaten (see note)
2 cups milk

Place cornmeal and salt in a saucepan. Gradually stir in milk. Cook over
medium heat until mixture thickens. Add butter and, when thoroughly melted, add eggs. Mix well. • Pour batter into buttered soufflé dish. Bake at 375°
for 40 minutes. • This recipe can be halved, shortening cooking time to 35
minutes. Or it may be doubled, increasing cooking time to 1 hour.

NOTE: For a puffier dish, egg whites can be separated, whipped and folded
in after adding egg yolks.

Mrs. William B. Garrison, Jr.

SEMLA   Makes 12 buns
(SHROVE TUESDAY BUNS)

Dough:
1 package active dry yeast   3 cups flour
¼ cup warm water   ½ cup sugar
½ cup butter   ¼ teaspoon salt
½ cup milk   1 egg white, slightly beaten

Filling and garnish:
½ cup ground blanched   1 egg white, slightly beaten
   almonds   1 cup heavy cream, whipped
½ teaspoon almond extract   Powdered sugar
1 cup powdered sugar

Dissolve yeast in warm water. Melt butter in saucepan, add milk and heat over
low heat until lukewarm. Mix 1 cup of flour with sugar and salt and add to
milk, beating with a wooden spoon until smooth. Gradually add remaining 2
cups of flour and continue beating until dough is smooth and firm. Cover and
let rise in a warm place until double in size, about 1 hour. • Punch dough down,
turn onto a floured baking board and work until smooth. Shape dough into 12
buns and place on a greased cookie sheet. Cover with towel and let rise to double in size. Brush buns with egg white and bake at 425° for 10–12 minutes,
until golden brown. Cool, covered, on a rack. • Prepare filling by mixing
almonds, almond extract, sugar and egg white. Work until smooth. If needed,
add a small amount of water. Cut off top of buns. Fill with almond paste and
garnish with whipped cream. Replace tops. Dust with powdered sugar. • Serve
in deep individual dishes with hot milk or as a pastry with coffee.

Mrs. Charles J. DiBona

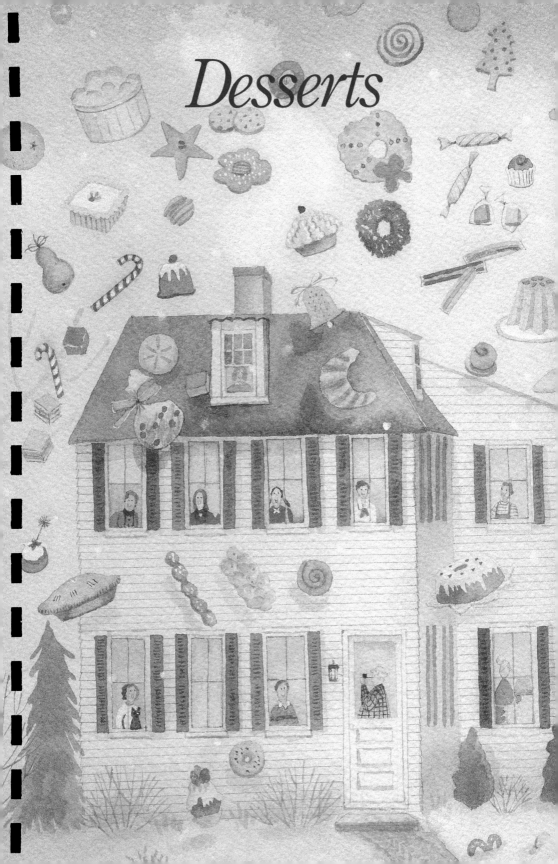

Desserts

FRUIT COBBLER   Serves 4 to 6

2 cups blueberries, other   1½ cups sugar
   berries or mixed fruit   1 cup flour
Juice of ½ lemon   1 teaspoon baking powder
½ teaspoon cinnamon   Dash of salt
1 tablespoon butter   1 tablespoon cornstarch
½ cup milk   1 cup boiling water

Preheat oven to 375°. • Place berries or mixed fruit in a greased 8-inch baking pan. Mix lemon juice and cinnamon and sprinkle on berries. • Cream butter, milk and ½ cup sugar. In a bowl, mix flour, baking powder and salt.
Combine flour mixture with butter mixture, making a batter. Spread batter
over berries in pan. • Mix remaining cup of sugar and cornstarch and sprinkle over batter. Pour boiling water over all. Do not stir. Bake for 1 hour.

Mrs. Richard Morehouse

RAY HUTCHINSON'S HOMEMADE   Makes 1 gallon
VANILLA ICE CREAM

4 eggs   1 can Eagle Brand condensed
4 cups sugar   milk
2 cups half and half   2 teaspoons vanilla extract
2 cups heavy cream   Whole milk to fill
1 box vanilla junket

In an electric mixer, blend eggs and sugar. Add half and half and heavy
cream and mix until sugar dissolves. Dissolve junket in a small amount of
milk. Blend into egg mixture. Add condensed milk and vanilla, stirring until
smooth. Pour into freezer container (see note) and fill to capacity with milk.
Freeze according to freezer directions.

NOTE: These amounts are for a 1-gallon freezer. Adjust proportionately if
you have a ½- or 1½-gallon freezer.

Senator Kay Bailey Hutchison
(Texas)

SALZBURGER NOCKERL   Serves 8

½ cup butter   10 egg whites, stiffly beaten
1 cup sugar   ¼ cup hot milk
10 egg yolks   2 tablespoons sugar
1 tablespoon flour

Preheat oven to 350°. • In an electric mixer, beat butter, sugar and egg yolks until fluffy. Add flour. Fold in egg whites. Cover the bottom of an ovenproof dish with hot milk. Pour batter over milk. • Bake for 10 minutes, until slightly yellow on top. Remove in big spoonfuls to a platter. Sugar lavishly. Serve at once.

Mrs. Helmut Tuerk
Wife of the Ambassador of Austria

KOLACHES
(Apple Turnovers)

Makes 16 turnovers

2 3-ounce packages cream
   cheese, softened
1 cup butter
2 cups flour
4 cups sliced apples
Cinnamon to taste

Sugar to taste
1 cup powdered sugar
½ teaspoon vanilla extract
½ teaspoon lemon extract
Few drops of water

Whip cream cheese with a fork. Combine cheese with butter and add flour one cup at a time. Mix well and knead into a ball. Refrigerate for 3–4 hours. • Slice apples and coat with a mixture of cinnamon and sugar. • Remove dough from refrigerator and divide into four parts. Roll out each part and divide into four squares. Place some apples in the middle of each square and fold up closing edges. Preheat oven to 400°. • Place kolaches on an ungreased cookie sheet and bake for 20–25 minutes, until golden. Remove from oven. Combine powdered sugar, vanilla, lemon extract and a few drops of water to make a glaze. Brush each kolach with glaze and allow to cool slightly before serving.

Senator Don Nickles
(Oklahoma)

BERRIES AND AMARETTO CREAM

4 ounces cream cheese,
   (can be light)
2 tablespoons Amaretto
½ cup sugar

½ cup heavy cream
1½–2 cups raspberries or
   blueberries
4 sprigs fresh mint (optional)

In a food processor, blend cream cheese, Amaretto and sugar. Slowly add heavy cream. • Distribute half of berries among 4 wine glasses and top with Amaretto cream. Distribute remaining berries over top and decorate with mint sprigs.

Sarah T. Minikes

RICHARD'S LEMON ICE   Serves 6

2 tablespoons grated
   lemon peel
1½ cups sugar
2 cups water

½ cup fresh orange juice,
   seeded but not strained
¾ cup fresh lemon juice,
   seeded but not strained
1 honeydew melon

Grate lemon peel with care so as to avoid getting any of white part. Combine peel with sugar and water. Cover and allow to stand for at least 4 hours. • Stir sugar mixture and strain through a wire strainer. Discard lemon peel. Add orange juice and lemon juice. Mix well and pour into a shallow metal pan. Place in freezer at 0° or colder. Freeze until firm. • Remove from freezer and allow to warm until ice breaks into chunks. Beat slowly with an electric mixer. Increase speed of mixer gradually to high as ice turns to slush. Pour back into pan (or lemon shells) and return to freezer. (The ice can be stored up to 2 months in an airtight container.) Serve over wedges of honeydew melon.

Meredith Gonyea

PLUM COBBLER WITH CINNAMON ICE CREAM   Serves 6

"Gourmet cobbler with summer ripe plums!"

Crust:

¾ cup cold butter cut
   in small chunks

2 cups flour
⅓–½ cup ice water

Filling:

12 fresh plums, pitted and
   cut into 6 slices
¼ cup flour
½ cup sugar
1 teaspoon cinnamon

1 tablespoon freshly grated
   nutmeg
½ teaspoon ginger
½ teaspoon allspice

Topping:

6 tablespoons cold butter
   cut in small chunks
½ cup flour

⅔ cup sugar
1 teaspoon cinnamon

To make crust, cut butter into flour with pastry blender until the size of small peas. Add water and mix until mixture forms a dough. Place on sheet pan and refrigerate for 30 minutes. • Roll out on lightly floured board to thickness of ⅛ inch. Cut into 6 4-inch circles. • Spray 6 3-inch tart molds with non-stick coating and line with dough. (Dough should come ¼ inch above the rim.) Return to refrigerator. • To make filling, combine all ingredients in a bowl and mix well. Save slices from 2 of the cut-up plums for garnish. Divide filling evenly among the 6 pastry cups. • To make topping, mix all ingredients with hands until coarse. Place on the tops of the plum cobblers. • Place cobblers in preheated oven at 350° for 30–35 minutes or until sides are golden brown. Remove and cool for 20 minutes. Remove from molds and place on individual plates. • Garnish with reserved plum slices. Serve warm with cinnamon-flavored ice cream.

Todd Philbrook, Pastry Chef
Restaurant Associates, Kennedy Center

PASKHA   Serves 14 to 16
(RUSSIAN EASTER DESSERT)

"A delectable adventure."

4 8-ounce packages cream cheese, softened	3 teaspoons vanilla
½ cup unsalted butter, softened	Pinch of salt
	Grated rind of 1 lemon
2 cups sifted powdered sugar	¾ cup ground almonds
3 egg yolks	Strawberries, raspberries or other fruit in season, cut-up

Place the cheese and butter, cut up, in the bowl of an electric mixer. Beat at medium speed until combined, then increase the speed and continue beating until thoroughly mixed. Gradually add the sugar, beating constantly. When all the sugar is in, add the egg yolks, one at a time, beating after each addition. With a wooden spatula, stir in the vanilla, salt, lemon rind and almonds. • To mold, use any shape mold and line it carefully with a damp double-thickness cheesecloth. Leave a generous fringe of cheesecloth all around. Spoon the mixture into the mold, tapping it down so it will be compact and shapely. Fold the loose fringe on top, cover with plastic wrap and refrigerate overnight. • To unmold, pull the cheesecloth, very gently, all around to loosen paskha. Then place a platter or a cake stand over the mold and invert quickly. Lift off the mold and gently remove the cheesecloth. • Surround with strawberries or raspberries, or both, or with any cut-up fruit in season.

Mrs. G. William Miller

SMITH FAMILY GINGERBREAD   Makes 16 pieces

1 cup vegetable shortening
  or margarine
1 cup dark molasses
1 cup sugar
1 cup sour milk (milk with
  1 tablespoon lemon juice
  or vinegar)

1 egg, well beaten
1 teaspoon baking soda,
  dissolved in 2 teaspoons
  boiling water
Pinch of salt
2¼ cups flour
2 teaspoons ginger

Preheat oven to 325°. • Bring shortening, molasses and sugar to a boil and set aside. Mix sour milk, egg, baking soda dissolved in water and salt and add to molasses mixture. Sift flour and ginger together and add to mixture. • Bake in an 8 x 8 x 2 inch pan for 45–60 minutes.

Mary Jo Smith
Wife of Senator Bob Smith (New Hampshire)

POIRE WILLIAM SORBET   Serves 6 to 8

"For a truly elegant dessert, try serving this intensely flavored sorbet over a fan of poached pears. It is a non-fat, delectable treat for all seasons."

⅔ cup water
⅔ cup sugar
3 pounds fresh ripe pears,
  peeled, quartered and
  seeded

6 tablespoons fresh lemon
  juice
½ cup Poire William or pear
  schnapps

Make syrup by combining the water and sugar in a non-reactive saucepan and bring to a boil. Simmer for 5 minutes. Remove from the heat and cool. • Purée the pears in a food processor or blender (if pears are not ripe and soft, slice and simmer them in the syrup mixture until soft enough to purée). Strain the purée through a fine sieve and add the sugar syrup, lemon juice and Poire William.

To freeze:

Use an ice cream maker or proceed as follows: Pour the sorbet mixture into a freezer container, cover and freeze until the mixture forms a 1- to 2-inch frame of ice around the inside of the pan (1½–2 hours). • Remove sorbet from freezer, scrape ice from the sides of the container and stir with a whisk. (Alternatively, pour into a mixer bowl and, with electric mixer, break up the ice crystals, incorporating air into the mixture.) • Return to the freezer for 30–50 minutes and repeat the process. You may have to repeat the process 1 or 2 more times, depending on the temperature of your freezer and the desired smoothness of the sorbet. The sorbet is finished when you are able to form it or scoop it into shape. • If you intend to serve the sorbet several hours later, repeat the stirring process every couple of hours to keep it from hardening.

Jon Jividen, Executive Chef
Ridgewell's

CRÈME CARAMEL   Serves 6

1 cup sugar
½ cup hot water
4 eggs
4 egg yolks

Pinch of salt
1 cup heavy cream
2½ cups milk
½ teaspoon vanilla extract

Preheat oven to 325°. • In a saucepan, heat ⅔ cup sugar over low flame until melted and caramel colored. Remove from heat and add hot water. Return to low heat and stir until caramel is dissolved and mixture thickens slightly. Pour into a 1½-quart soufflé dish or ring mold. Rotate to coat all sides and place in a bowl of cold water to harden caramel. • Beat eggs and egg yolks. Beat in remaining ⅓ cup sugar and salt. Scald cream and milk and add to egg mixture. Beat thoroughly. Add vanilla and strain into caramel-lined dish. Place dish in a shallow baking pan with 1 inch of water on the bottom. Bake for 45–50 minutes, or until a knife comes out clean. Set in cold water to cool. Chill. Unmold onto a serving plate.

Mrs. Jerold J. Principato

ORANGE MOUSSE   Serves 6

5 eggs
½ cup sugar
1½ envelopes gelatin
Juice of 3 oranges

Juice of 1 lemon
Zest of 1 orange
¼ cup Grand Marnier
1 cup heavy cream

Separate the eggs. Beat the yolks with sugar over warm (not boiling) water. Stop when mixture becomes creamy. Pour into a large container. • Dissolve gelatin in ½ cup of orange juice. Heat briefly to make sure all granules dissolve. Add to the egg yolk mixture. Stir in remaining orange juice, lemon juice, orange zest and Grand Marnier. • Beat egg whites until stiff but not dry. Fold into orange cream. Do not overblend. Beat heavy cream until stiff and fold into mixture. Pour into a mold or serving bowl. • Refrigerate for 24 hours before serving.

Mme. Raoul Calvignac
Embassy of France

NORA'S APPLE WALNUT RAISIN STRUDEL   Serves 4

4 sheets Greek phyllo
    pastry or
    2 sheets strudel pastry,
    defrosted
2 tablespoons melted,
    unsalted butter
1 tablespoon fine breadcrumbs
1 tablespoon sugar

1 pound tart apples (like
    Granny Smith), cored,
    quartered and thinly sliced
¼ cup raisins, plumped in
    hot water for 2 minutes
¼ cup walnuts, coarsely
    chopped
Powdered sugar for garnish
Light whipped cream
Mint leaves for garnish

Preheat oven to 375°. • Moisten a kitchen towel under cold running water and wring out until nearly dry. Spread towel with long side along the counter over work surface. Place 1 sheet of pastry on wet towel. Cover remaining pastry with another wet towel so it does not dry out while you work. With a pastry brush, spread some melted butter over pastry sheet. Sprinkle with some breadcrumbs and sugar. Place next pastry sheet on top of first and repeat procedure. Continue until all pastry sheets have been layered on top of each other. • Spread apple slices over prepared pastry, leaving a 3-inch border on the long side away from you and narrow borders on the other sides. Sprinkle with raisins and walnuts and any leftover breadcrumbs and sugar. Pick up the edge of towel closest to you and use it to shape strudel into a jelly roll, lifting and rolling away from you toward back edge of dough. Use the towel to pick up and transfer strudel onto a baking sheet. Remove towel and tuck strudel ends under. Brush with remaining butter. Score the top layer of strudel into 4 portions with a sharp knife to prevent excessive flaking. • Bake for 40 minutes, until apples are cooked and juicy and strudel is golden brown. To serve, cut strudel into 4 servings along scored lines and arrange each on a plate. Dust with powdered sugar. Add a dollop of whipped cream and garnish with mint leaves.

Nora Pouillon
Nora's Restaurant

STRAWBERRY SORBET   Serves 8

2 cups superfine sugar
2 cups water
4 cups fresh ripe strawberries,
    hulled and washed

Juice of ½ orange
¼ cup Grand Marnier
Fresh strawberries and
    mint leaves for garnish

Make a syrup by combining the sugar with water. Bring to a boil and reduce heat to simmer for 10 minutes. Cool. • Make sorbet in two batches. For each batch, put half of the syrup, strawberries, orange juice and Grand Marnier in a food processor. Process with steel blade and place in ice trays, cover and freeze to slush. Process in food processor once again, return to container and freeze fully. (Can also be made in an ice cream maker, using directions for sorbet.) Serve, garnished with fresh strawberries and mint leaves.

Mariana M. Grove

POACHED PEARS WITH RASPBERRY SAUCE   Serves 6

6 firm Bosc pears
2 tablespoons fresh lemon
  juice
4 cups water
2 cups sugar

1 teaspoon grated lemon rind
1 stick cinnamon
3 whole cloves
Sprigs of mint

Sauce:
1 10-ounce package frozen
  raspberries
2 tablespoons sugar

1 tablespoon orange liqueur
1 teaspoon fresh lemon juice

Peel pears, leaving stems on. Drop into cold water to which has been added 1 tablespoon lemon juice. Set aside. • Bring water, sugar, remaining tablespoon lemon juice and lemon rind to boil. Add cinnamon, cloves and pears. Cover and keep at a rolling boil for 30 minutes, or until pears are tender. Pears should be slightly translucent and easily pierced with a fork at the base. • Remove pears, trim bottoms so they will stand, and transfer to a shallow, flat-bottomed dish. Spoon a little poaching syrup over each pear, cover with plastic wrap and chill. • To make sauce, purée the raspberries with sugar until slightly frothy in a food processor fitted with steel blade. Strain to remove the seeds. Stir in liqueur and lemon juice. Cover and chill. • When ready to serve, spoon a pool of sauce on each dessert plate, stand a pear in the center and garnish with a sprig of mint.

NOTE: Poaching syrup may be bottled tightly and refrigerated to be used to poach pears again. Add more ingredients as needed to get the proper amount to cover pears. • All except assembly may be done ahead of time. The sauce can even be done several days ahead of time. Pears may be served in a pool of chocolate sauce flavored with rum — or with a créme anglaise. I serve the pears with raspberry sauce with chocolate iced cookies.

Mrs. John C. Gore

ROULADE   Serves 6 to 8

4 eggs, separated   Vanilla extract
½ cup sugar, plus a little   Generous ½ cup flour
   extra for sprinkling   Parchment paper

Preheat oven to 375°. • Beat egg whites until frothy. Add about ⅓ of the
sugar and continue beating until stiff. • Beat egg yolks with remaining sugar
until light yellow and thick. Add vanilla. Sift flour over the egg yolk mixture
and stir well. • Stir ⅓ of the egg white mixture into the yolks. Fold in the
remaining egg whites and blend well. • Grease a sheet pan and line with
parchment paper. Spread mixture on sheet pan and bake for 9 -10 minutes,
until top springs back to touch. • Loosen edges and turn out onto counter.
Peel off parchment paper. Sprinkle paper with a little granulated sugar.
Place cake on paper and roll up. Allow to cool.

Lemon curd filling:
Juice of 4 lemons   1¼ cups sugar
Zest of 4 lemon rinds   1 cup (½ pound) butter, cubed
4 eggs

In a medium size saucepan, place juice from 4 lemons and zest of the rind.
Beat in eggs with a whisk. Beat in sugar. Blend well. Add butter and mix. •
Bring to a full boil over medium heat, scraping the bottom and sides of pan
carefully with the whisk to avoid scorching. Strain through a fine sieve. Cool
and refrigerate. • Unroll the cooled cake and fill with lemon mixture. Reroll
without the parchment paper. Decorate and serve.

Michele Small
L'Académie de Cuisine

APPLE CRUMBLE   Serves 6

"This is our family's favorite dessert and comes from England."

1½ pounds cooking apples   ½ cup butter
3–4 tablespoons sugar, plus   2 cups flour
  ½ cup sugar   ¼ teaspoon ground ginger
Juice of ½ a lemon   Heavy cream
¼ teaspoon cinnamon

Preheat oven to 350° . • Peel and core apples and cut into eighths. In a 1-quart
glass baking dish, mix apples with 3–4 tablespoons sugar, lemon juice and
cinnamon. • In a mixing bowl, combine butter and flour. Rub butter into flour
until mixture is the consistency of fine breadcrumbs. Add ½ cup sugar and
ginger and mix well. Sprinkle butter and flour crumble over apples and press
down lightly. • Bake for 30–40 minutes, until apples are cooked and top is

golden brown. Serve with a small jug of cream.

NOTE: Other fruits (blueberries, peaches, etc.) may be substituted for apples.

Mrs. Paul S. Sarbanes
Wife of the Senator from Maryland

TIRAMISU   Serves 4 to 6

Cream:

1 egg white

3 egg yolks

6 tablespoons sugar

5 ounces mascarpone cheese

3 tablespoons any desired liqueur

Ladyfingers:

1 cup freshly made espresso coffee, slightly sweetened

3 tablespoons liqueur (use same kind as above)

1 package ladyfingers

Bitter cocoa

To make cream, beat egg white until stiff. • Beat egg yolks with sugar until creamy. Add mascarpone to egg yolks, beating well, then, mixing delicately,

add egg white and, at the end, the liqueur. • To prepare the ladyfingers, warm sweetened espresso with liqueur. Quickly dip ladyfingers in the coffee and arrange in one layer in serving dish. Cover with cream. Repeat with another layer of ladyfingers and another layer of cream and sprinkle bitter cocoa over the top.

Silvia Ottone
Embassy of Italy

CHARLOTTE "LA COLLINE"   Serves 8 to 10

"This charlotte is made from 3 distinct recipes: ladyfingers, strawberry bavaroise and chocolate mousse"

Ladyfingers:

3 eggs, separated	**½ cup flour, sifted**
½ cup sugar	**Powdered sugar**

Preheat oven to 375°. • Whisk eggs yolks and all but 3 tablespoons of sugar in an electric mixer until very pale in color. Fold in flour. • Beat egg whites to soft peaks and gradually add remaining sugar until stiff peaks form. Fold into egg yolk mixture. • Using a pastry bag with plain tip, pipe out 16 fingers onto a greased cookie sheet. Dust with powdered sugar. • Bake for 10–15 minutes, until light brown. When ladyfingers are cool, use them to line a round 9-inch mold.

Strawberry bavaroise:

2 cups fresh or drained	**¼ cup water**
frozen strawberries	**1½ tablespoons gelatin**
1 cup heavy cream	**¼ cup plus 2 tablespoons sugar**
¼ cup kirsch	

Purée strawberries in food processor or blender. • Whip cream into soft peaks and refrigerate. • In a stainless steel bowl, mix kirsch, water, gelatin and sugar over low heat, stirring constantly, until dissolved. Whisk hot gelatin mixture into strawberry purée and allow to cool until almost set. Fold in cream. • Fill the bottom half of ladyfinger mold with strawberry bavaroise. Chill in refrigerator for 3 hours.

Chocolate mousse:

4 ounces bittersweet	**2 cups heavy cream**
chocolate	**Chocolate shavings**
2 egg whites	**Powdered sugar**
½ cup sugar	

In a double boiler, melt chocolate. Cool. • Whisk egg whites and sugar together over hot water until warm. Beat egg mixture until cool and glossy. • Whip cream into stiff peaks. • Fold chocolate into egg whites. Fold cream into chocolate mixture. Refrigerate. • When chocolate mousse is cold, transfer to ladyfinger mold. Decorate the top with chocolate shavings and lightly dust with powdered sugar.

Robert Greault, Chef
La Colline Restaurant

ALMOND SOUFFLÉ WITH TANGERINE SAUCE

Serves 6 to 8

Butter
Sugar
2 tablespoons cornstarch
2 cups cold milk
8 eggs, separated

1 cup sugar
¼ teaspoon salt
1 teaspoon almond extract
1 teaspoon vanilla extract
¼ cup ground almonds

Preheat oven to 325°. • Butter a 2-quart soufflé dish and dust with sugar. • Put cornstarch in a saucepan and slowly add milk, stirring until smooth. Bring to a boil over medium heat, stirring frequently, and boil for 1 minute. • Combine egg yolks, ½ cup sugar and salt and beat until thick and light. Slowly pour in milk mixture, stirring briskly. Cool for 10–15 minutes. Add almond and vanilla extracts. • With an electric mixer, beat egg whites until they form soft peaks. Gradually add remaining sugar and continue beating until stiff, glossy peaks form. Fold gently and thoroughly into egg yolk mixture. Pour into prepared soufflé dish and set into a shallow pan filled with 1 inch of hot water. Sprinkle top of soufflé with ground almonds. Bake for 60–65 minutes.

Tangerine sauce (Makes about 1½ cups):

1 tablespoon butter or
   margarine
1 tablespoon cornstarch
½ cup sugar
¼ teaspoon salt
1½ cups tangerine juice

2 tablespoons grated
   tangerine zest
2 tangerines, peeled and
   sectioned, all membranes
   removed
2 tablespoons apricot brandy

Melt butter in a heavy saucepan. Stir in cornstarch, sugar and salt. Slowly add tangerine juice and stir until smooth. Cook, stirring, over medium heat until sauce boils and is thick and clear. Add tangerine zest, tangerine sections and apricot brandy and stir until blended. Serve warm.

Mrs. E. Edward Bruce

CHOCOLATE MOUSSE IMPERIAL   Serves 12 to 18

12 eggs, separated
1 cup sugar
2 12-ounce packages
    semi-sweet chocolate chips
1 teaspoon vanilla

3 tablespoons dark rum or
    Armagnac
½ cup unsalted butter or
    margarine, softened
1 cup chopped walnuts

Topping:
2 cups heavy cream
¼ cup sugar
1 teaspoon vanilla extract

Dark chocolate shavings
Candied violets

To make mousse, beat yolks with sugar until very light and thick. • Soften chocolate chips in double boiler or in microwave oven at lowest setting. Chocolate should not be hot. • Beat egg whites until stiff. • Combine egg yolks chocolate, vanilla and rum. Beat mixture until smooth, adding butter a little at a time. Using a spatula, gently fold in egg whites and walnuts. • Pour mousse into a serving dish and refrigerate 4–5 hours before serving. • To make topping whip cream with sugar and vanilla until stiff. Decorate mousse with some of whipped cream, chocolate shavings and candied violets. Serve remaining whipped cream separately.

Mrs. Wilfried Platzer

FRAN'S BLUEBERRY CRISP   Serves 8 -10

"Very easy and amounts are flexible to taste."

4–6 cups blueberries, fresh
    (1–1½ quarts) or frozen
¼ cup sugar
2–3 tablespoons lemon juice
2–3 tablespoons plus ⅔ cup
    flour

⅔ cup brown sugar
⅔ cup Quaker Oats
    (old-fashioned style)
⅓ cup butter or margarine,
    softened
1½–2 tablespoons cinnamon

Preheat oven to 350°. • Toss berries with sugar, 2–3 tablespoons flour and lemon juice in a 2-quart baking dish. • Mix brown sugar, ⅔ cup flour, oats, butter and cinnamon in a bowl with your fingers until crumbly and sticky. Spread oat mixture over berries, pressing down slightly to make a thick crust. • Bake for 25–35 minutes, until top is slightly brown. Serve warm with whipped cream or ice cream.

NOTE: This recipe can be made with fresh, tart apples instead of blueberries, if desired.

Mrs. Elliot Richardson

CHARLOTTE RUSSE   Serves 8 to 10

1½ envelopes plain gelatin
½ cup milk
4 eggs, separated
1 cup sifted powdered
  sugar, plus 2 tablespoons

1 teaspoon vanilla extract
2 cups heavy cream
12 ladyfingers
Maraschino cherries

Dissolve gelatin in 2 tablespoons cold water. Heat milk (do not boil), add gelatin and cool. • Beat egg yolks and add 1 cup sugar and vanilla. Mix well. • Beat egg whites until stiff and fold into egg yolks. Fold in gelatin mixture. • Whip half of the heavy cream and fold into egg mixture. Allow to stand for a few minutes. Fold and let stand again twice more. • Split the ladyfingers and line the sides of a two-quart bowl, flat side against bowl. Pour in custard and refrigerate. • One hour before serving, whip remaining cream with remaining 2 tablespoons powdered sugar. Decorate top with whipped cream and maraschino cherries and refrigerate.

Helen Tetzel

LIME MOUSSE   Serves 8

4 eggs, separated
1½ cups sugar
1 package unflavored gelatin
¼ cup cold water
1 teaspoon cornstarch
½ cup fresh lime juice

2 tablespoons grated lime zest
4 tablespoons rum (optional)
1½ cups heavy cream
3 tablespoons powdered sugar
Fresh berries or shaved
  chocolate

Beat egg yolks and sugar. • Soften gelatin in cold water. • Combine cornstarch and 3 tablespoons lime juice. Stir well and add remaining lime juice, lime zest and gelatin. Add this mixture to the egg yolks and place in top of double boiler. Stir while heating over medium-low heat until it thickens, about 20 minutes. (Add 2 tablespoons rum, if desired, and continue cooking for 1 minute.) Pour into a large bowl and refrigerate, covered, until the custard begins to set. • Whip cream with powdered sugar (and 2 tablespoons rum) until stiff. Beat egg whites until stiff. Fold egg whites and cream into custard. Blend well and refrigerate until stiff. Garnish with fresh berries or chocolate shavings.

Elizabeth Beach Rea

AUSTRALIAN PAVLOVA   Serves 6

*"This well-known Australian dessert was named
after the ballet dancer, due to its lightness."*

6 egg whites, at room
   temperature
1½ cups sugar
½ teaspoon vanilla extract
1½ teaspoons white vinegar
1 tablespoon cornstarch

2 cups heavy cream
3 tablespoons powdered sugar
2 kiwi fruit
1 pint strawberries
1 passion fruit (optional)

Preheat oven to 250° and line a baking sheet with greaseproof (parchment) paper which has been buttered lightly and dusted with cornstarch. Mark a 9-inch circle. • Beat egg whites at high speed until they form soft peaks. Pour in ½ cup of sugar and continue beating for 10 minutes, gradually adding the remaining sugar. Beat another 2 minutes. Finally, fold in the vanilla, vinegar and cornstarch. The mixture should be white and very thick. Spoon meringue mixture into circle, spreading out to the edge. It should be approximately 2 inches high. Bake for 1½ hours. • Turn off oven and leave meringue to cool and dry out for about 2 hours. (Meringue may be made 2–3 days ahead and wrapped well in foil.) • When ready to serve, whip cream with powered sugar and spoon on the top, decorate with fruit.

*Andrea Webster
Chef to the Ambassador of Australia*

BREAD PUDDING   Serves 6 to 8

10 slices whole wheat bread
1 egg plus 3 egg whites
1½ cups milk
¼ cup sugar, plus 2
   teaspoons

¼ cup brown sugar
1 teaspoon vanilla
½ teaspoon cinnamon
¼ teaspoon nutmeg
¼ teaspoon cloves

Sauce:

1¼ cups apple juice
½ cup apple butter
2 tablespoons molasses
½ cup raisins

¼ teaspoon cinnamon
¼ teaspoon nutmeg
½ teaspoon orange zest

Spray an 8 x 8 inch baking dish with vegetable oil. Preheat oven to 350°. • Arrange bread in baking dish in 2 rows, with slices overlapping. In a bowl, beat egg, egg whites, milk, ¼ cup sugar, brown sugar and vanilla. Pour egg mixture over bread. In a small bowl, mix cinnamon, nutmeg, cloves and 2 teaspoons sugar. Sprinkle over bread and egg mixture. Bake for 30–35 minutes,

until golden brown and firm. • To make sauce, combine apple juice, apple butter and molasses in a saucepan. Heat over low heat. Add raisins, cinnamon, nutmeg and orange zest. Bring to simmer and continue simmering for 5 minutes. Serve on the side with warm bread pudding.

Elena Schupp Darden

SCOTTISH CRANACHAN   Serves 4

½ cup old-fashioned rolled
   oats
1 cup heavy cream, chilled
2 tablespoons sugar,
   preferably superfine

2 tablespoons Scotch whiskey
2 cups fresh blueberries or
   other berries

Preheat oven to 375°. • Spread oats in a shallow baking pan and toast in oven, shaking occasionally, for about 12 minutes, or until light golden brown. Remove from oven and cool. Whip cream in a chilled bowl until soft peaks form. Gradually, add sugar and whiskey. Whip until mixture thickens. Fold in toasted oats. • Layer cream mixture and berries in 4 tall stemmed dessert glasses, beginning with a layer of cream and topping with a layer of berries. Refrigerate for up to 2 hours.

Kay Shaw Nelson, Author
"A Bonny Scottish Cookbook"

Les Dames
d'Escoffier

RASPBERRY-PLUM COBBLER   Serves 5 to 6

Filling:

¾ cup sugar
2 tablespoons flour
2½ cups fresh raspberries or
  unsweetened frozen
  raspberries (rinsed and
  well drained)

2⅔ cups pitted, diced red or
  black plums

Dough and garnish:

1½ cups flour
1½ tablespoons sugar
¾ teaspoon baking powder
¼ teaspoon salt
1½ tablespoons chilled
  butter, cut into small pieces

1½ tablespoons canola oil
5 tablespoons skim milk
Small dollops light ice
  cream for garnish (optional)

Preheat oven to 375°. • To make filling, thoroughly stir together sugar and flour in a 1½-quart or slightly larger casserole. Add raspberries and plums, stirring until coated with sugar mixture. • To make dough, blend together flour, sugar, baking powder and salt in a medium bowl. Add butter and canola oil. Using a pastry blender, forks or fingertips, cut in fat until mixture resembles coarse meal. Add milk, tossing with a fork just until evenly incorporated. Pat mixture into a ball and lay between sheets of wax paper. Press into a round large enough to top casserole. Peel off 1 sheet of paper. Center dough over fruit mixture, dough side down. Peel off second sheet of paper. Make several 1½ inch long decorative slashes radiating from dough center. • Bake on center oven rack for 35–45 minutes, or until top is nicely browned, edges are bubbly and a toothpick inserted into dough center comes out clean. Let cool at least 10 minutes before serving. To serve, spoon into bowls and serve with ice cream, if desired.

Nancy Baggett, Author
"Dream Desserts: Luscious Low-Fat Recipes"

C·A·K·E·S

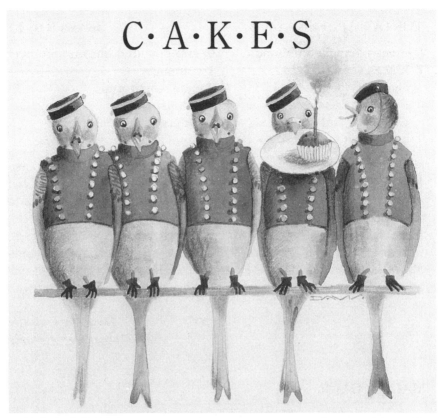

LINZER TORTE

Serves 10 to 12

1 cup butter or margarine
1 cup sugar
1 tablespoon grated orange
  or lemon peel
2 egg yolks
1½ cups sifted flour
1 teaspoon baking powder

2 teaspoons cinnamon
½ teaspoon cloves
¼ teaspoon salt
1 cup ground nuts (filberts,
  almonds or walnuts)
1 cup tart preserves

In an electric mixer, cream butter. Slowly add sugar while continuing to cream. Add peel. Add egg yolks, one at a time, beating well after each addition. • Sift together flour, baking powder, cinnamon, cloves and salt. Add slowly to butter mixture. Add nuts. Mix with your hands until all ingredients are thoroughly combined. • Chill dough for at least 1 hour. • Pat ⅔ of dough into the bottom of a 9-inch springform pan. Spread preserves over dough. Roll out remaining dough and cut into 8 strips ¾ inch wide and place, lattice fashion, over preserves. • Bake at 350° for 50–60 minutes, until edges of strips recede from sides of pan. Remove from pan and cool.

Mrs. Helmut Tuerk
Wife of the Ambassador of Austria

TORTA CAPRESE   Serves 8 to 10

8 ounces blanched almonds	¾ cup unsalted butter, softened
7 ounces semisweet chocolate or 3 ounces unsweetened chocolate and 4 ounces semisweet	1 cup sugar 4 eggs, separated Pinch of salt Powdered sugar Whipped cream, for serving

Preheat oven to 300°. • Butter an 8-inch springform pan and line the bottom with parchment paper cut to fit. • In a food processor, grind the almonds and chocolate together until mixture is very fine. Set aside. • In an electric mixer, cream butter. Add sugar and beat. Add the egg yolks all at once and beat. Add nut and chocolate mixture and beat at low speed. Set aside. • Beat egg whites with salt until firm. Fold into chocolate mixture and pour into prepared pan. Smooth top. • Bake for 45 minutes. Remove from oven and cool before removing from pan. Sprinkle top with powdered sugar and serve with whipped cream.

Donatella Andreani
Wife of the Ambassador of France

MAGGIE CAKE

"This is my favorite recipie"

5 eggs, separated	1 teaspoon baking powder
1 cup butter	1 teaspoon baking soda
2½ cups sugar	4 teaspoons cocoa powder
1 cup buttermilk	1 teaspoon salt
5 teaspoons coffee	2 teaspoons vanilla extract
3 cups flour	

Preheat oven to 350°. Beat egg whites until stiff. • In an electric mixer, cream butter and sugar. Add egg yolks, one at a time, stirring after each. Add rest of ingredients. Fold in egg whites. Make five layers. Bake for 15–20 minutes, cool and frost.

Icing:

3 teaspoons coffee	Dash of salt
1 egg	1 pound powdered sugar
½ cup butter	Small amount cream (optional)
2 teaspoons cocoa powder	Whole Oklahoma pecans
1 teaspoon vanilla extract	

Put coffee, egg, butter, cocoa, vanilla and salt in a mixing bowl and while mixing, gradually add sugar. If needed, add a small amount of cream to produce a spreadable consistency. • Ice cake layers and decorate with whole pecans.

Senator David L. Boren
(Oklahoma)

CHOCOLATE CAKE

½ cup butter
2 cups sugar
¾ cup cocoa
2 eggs
2 cups flour
½ cup buttermilk
1 teaspoon vanilla extract

1 teaspoon baking soda
    dissolved in 1 cup boiling
    water
Powdered sugar
Frosting (your choice) or
    powdered sugar

Preheat oven to 350°. Cream butter, sugar and cocoa in an electric mixer. Add eggs. Alternately add flour and buttermilk. Stir until smooth. Add vanilla and fold in dissolved baking soda. Pour into 3 cake pans and bake for 20–25 minutes. • Remove from oven and cool completely. Frost or sprinkle with powdered sugar.

Senator Hank Brown
(Colorado)

TOM DASCHLE'S FAMOUS CHEESECAKE   Serves 12–14

⅓ box crushed graham
    crackers
8 tablespoons butter, melted
¾ cup sugar
2 8-ounce packages cream
    cheese, at room temperature

4 eggs
1½ cups sour cream
Juice of 1 lemon
1 teaspoon vanilla extract
1 teaspoon almond extract

Preheat oven to 375°. • Combine graham cracker crumbs, melted butter and ¼ cup sugar to make crust. Press into a 10-inch springform pan. • In an electric mixer, cream remaining ½ cup sugar and cream cheese. Fold in eggs. Add sour cream, lemon juice and vanilla and almond extracts. Mix well and pour batter into prepared crust. Bake for 20 minutes. Lower oven temperature to 350° and continue baking for another 25–30 minutes, until cheesecake rises and turns golden brown. • Let cool at room temperature and refrigerate for several hours before serving. May be smothered in berries of your choice, if desired.

Senator Thomas Daschle
(South Dakota)

JUDY'S POPPY SEED CAKE

Cake:

½ cup butter
½ cup margarine
1½ cups sugar
4 eggs separated
1 cup sour cream

1 teaspoon baking soda
2 cups flour
3 teaspoons vanilla
1 2-ounce package poppy seeds

Glaze:

Powdered sugar
Vanilla

Evaporated milk

Cream well the butter, margarine, and sugar. Add egg yolks. Combine sour cream and baking soda. Add to butter mixture with flour, vanilla and poppy seeds. Mix well. Beat egg whites stiff; fold into batter. Pour into greased and floured bundt pan. • Bake at 350° for one hour. Cool for 15 minutes and then remove from pan. Glaze while still warm with a mixture of powdered sugar, vanilla, and evaporated milk. Cool completely and serve.

Mrs. Mark O. Hatfield
Wife of the Senator from Oregon
from her book, "Food for Family and Friends"

ALMOND CHOCOLATE CAKE (ALMONDINA)

Cake:

6 egg whites (reserve yolks
   for frosting)
1 cup plus 2 tablespoons sugar

1 teaspoon vanilla
1 cup plus 2 tablespoons
   grated almonds

Frosting:

3 tablespoons cocoa
¾ cup unsalted butter

1 cup plus 2 tablespoons sugar
6 egg yolks

Preheat oven to 300°. • Beat egg whites until stiff. Gradually add sugar and vanilla, continuing to beat after each addition. Gently blend in almonds. • Pour batter into a large greased and floured pan. Bake approximately 30 minutes. Cool completely. • To make frosting, combine cocoa, butter, sugar and egg yolks in top of a double boiler. Over simmering, not boiling, water beat until frosting thickens to spreading consistency. Remove from heat and cool. • When both the cake and the frosting are cool, frost top of cake. • This cake keeps best in refrigerator, as frosting tends to soften at room temperature.

Ileana M. Munteanu
Wife of the Ambassador of Romania

CHOCOLATE PECAN CAKE

8 tablespoons butter
½ cup dark brown sugar
½ cup shredded coconut
⅔ cup chopped pecans
½ cup semisweet chocolate
  morsels
1 tablespoon milk
1 cup flour

½ cup sugar
1½ teaspoons baking powder
¼ teaspoon salt
½ teaspoon vanilla extract
⅓ cup water
1 egg
Vanilla ice cream

Preheat oven to 350°. • Melt 4 tablespoons butter in a small saucepan. Remove from heat, stir in brown sugar, coconut, pecans, chocolate morsels and milk and blend well. Spread mixture on the bottom of a round 9-inch cake pan. Set aside. • In a mixing bowl, stir together flour, sugar, baking powder and salt. Add remaining 4 tablespoons butter, vanilla, water and egg and beat until batter is thoroughly blended and smooth. Pour over coconut pecan mixture • Bake for 30 minutes, or until a toothpick inserted in the center of cake comes out clean. • Remove from oven and cool in pan for 5 minutes. Turn upside down onto a serving plate, coconut pecan mixture on top. • Serve warm or cold with vanilla ice cream.

Joan Specter
Wife of Senator Arlen Specter (Pennsylvania)

FRESH APPLE CAKE

½ cup canola oil
2 cups sugar
3 eggs
2½ cups flour
½ teaspoon salt
¾ teaspoon baking soda
1 tablespoon baking powder
1 tablespoon cinnamon

1 tablespoon ground cloves
3 cups apples, peeled, cored
  and diced (York or Granny
  Smith preferred)
1–2 cups chopped pecans or
  walnuts
2 tablespoons rum

Preheat oven to 325°. Blend canola oil, sugar and eggs. Add flour, salt, baking soda, baking powder, cinnamon and cloves and mix well. Stir in apples, nuts, and rum. Pour batter into a greased and floured tube pan and bake for 1 hour and 15 minutes.

Senator Harlan Mathews
(Tennessee)

CARAMEL PINEAPPLE CAKE ROLL

2 cans crushed pineapple,
   drained
½ cup dark brown sugar
¾ cup cake flour
1 teaspoon baking powder

½ teaspoon salt
4 large eggs, separated
¾ cup sugar
2 teaspoons vanilla
1 teaspoon grated lemon rind

Icing:
1 cup heavy cream
3 tablespoons powdered sugar

Preheat oven to 375°. Butter a 10 x 15 inch jelly roll pan. Spread pineapple evenly over bottom of pan and sprinkle with brown sugar. • Sift flour with baking powder and salt. • Beat egg whites until foamy and add sugar gradually, beating until stiff. • Beat egg yolks into stiffened egg whites and add vanilla and lemon rind. Sprinkle flour over egg mixture and gently fold in. • Spread batter evenly over pineapple and brown sugar. Bake for 18–20 minutes. Remove from oven and turn upside down onto a damp towel and sprinkle lightly with powdered sugar. Roll up in towel and cool. Remove towel when cool and place cake on a platter. • To make icing, beat cream with sugar until stiff. Cover cake with whipped cream.

Joan Specter
Wife of Senator Arlen Specter (Pennsylvania)

CARROT CAKE

Cake:
1 cup flour
¾ cup sugar
1 teaspoon baking powder
¾ teaspoon baking soda
½ teaspoon cinnamon
½ teaspoon salt

⅝ cup vegetable oil
   (½ cup plus 2 tablespoons)
2 eggs
1 cup grated carrots
1 8-ounce can crushed
   pineapple, drained
½ cup roughly chopped walnuts

Frosting:
6 tablespoons butter
½ teaspoon vanilla
1 3-ounce package cream
   cheese

3 heaping tablespoons
   powdered sugar

Preheat oven to 350°. • Put flour, sugar, baking powder, baking soda, cinnamon and salt in food processor. Process for 5–10 seconds. Add oil and eggs and mix 30 seconds (will be very thick). Add carrots and pineapple and combine thoroughly. Add nuts and mix only enough to distribute. • Pour into greased 8- or 9-inch square pan and bake approximately 1 hour. • To make frosting, place butter, cream cheese and vanilla in food processor and process for about 20 seconds. Add sugar and continue beating. • When cake is cold, spread with frosting.

NOTE: Recipe is designed for a food processor; it can be made, however, using an electric mixer, mixing for longer times.

Senator Carl Levin
(Michigan)

CHOCOLATE DECADENCE   Serves 12

"This cake needs to be frozen first before serving, so allow the time."

Cake:

1 pound semisweet chocolate, broken into squares	4 whole eggs
10 tablespoons unsalted butter	1 tablespoon sugar
	1 tablespoon flour

Topping:

1½ cups heavy cream	Shaved chocolate
1 teaspoon vanilla extract	1 10- to 12-ounce package
1 tablespoon sugar	frozen raspberries, defrosted

Flour and butter an 8-inch cake pan and line with paper. Preheat oven to 425°. • Put the chocolate and butter in the top of a double boiler and heat until the chocolate is just melted. Set aside. • In the top of another double boiler, beat the eggs and sugar until the sugar dissolves and the mixture is lukewarm (do not overcook). Remove from heat and whip until the mixture thickens and has about quadrupled in volume. Fold the flour into the thickened egg mixture. Stir a quarter of the flour-egg mixture into the melted chocolate, then fold the chocolate into the remaining egg mixture. • Pour the batter into the prepared cake pan. Shake it gently to level it. Bake for 15 minutes (the cake will still be runny in the center). Cool a bit, then freeze, preferably overnight, before removing the cake from the pan. • To unmold, carefully dip the bottom of the pan into hot water to loosen the cake. When it moves easily, unmold onto a cake plate. Peel off the paper and discard. • Whip the heavy cream, adding the vanilla and sugar as it thickens. Cover the cake with the whipped cream and decorate the top with shaved chocolate. Refrigerate until ready to serve. • Any time up to 15 minutes before serving, purée the defrosted raspberries in a blender and press through a fine sieve to remove the seeds. Spoon the raspberry purée around the cake just before serving, or spoon some of the purée around individual slices.

Narsai M. David, Author
"Monday Night at Narsai's"

OPERA TÅRTA

"In honor of the Royal Swedish Opera."

Cake:

4 eggs
⅔ cup sugar
3 tablespoons cake flour
½ teaspoon baking powder
3 tablespoons cornstarch

Preheat oven to 350°. Separate 3 eggs, mixing yolks with one whole egg. Add sugar and beat until light and fluffy. • Sift flour, baking powder and cornstarch together. Add to egg mixture. Beat remaining egg whites until stiff and gently fold into egg mixture. • Pour batter into 2 buttered and breaded 8-inch round layer cake pans. Bake in oven for 12–15 minutes. Cool.

Cream filling:

1½ teaspoons unflavored
   gelatin
2 tablespoons cold water
3 egg yolks
3 tablespoons sugar
1 tablespoon cornstarch
1 cup milk
2 teaspoons vanilla extract
1 cup heavy cream, whipped

Soak gelatin in cold water. Mix egg yolks, sugar, cornstarch and milk in top of a double boiler and, stirring constantly, cook slowly until smooth and thick. Remove from heat, add gelatin and vanilla extract. Beat occasionally as it cools. When mixture is cold, fold in whipped cream.

Almond Paste:

1 cup blanched almonds
⅔ cup powdered sugar
1½ tablespoons egg white
1½ teaspoons almond extract
Green food coloring

Grind almonds twice. Mix with sugar, egg white, almond extract and food coloring. Mix until smooth, about 10 minutes. Roll out on wax paper and shape into a large circle. To assemble opera tårta, cut each cake into 2 layers. Spread filling between each layer and on top of the cake and place the layers one on top of the other. Cover top layer with the almond paste and sprinkle with powdered sugar. Refrigerate until ready to serve.

Evelyn DiBona

BUTTERMILK POUND CAKES

1 cup vegetable shortening
2 cups sugar
3 cups flour
½ teaspoon baking soda
½ teaspoon baking powder

4 eggs
1 tablespoon vanilla or
 almond flavoring
1 cup buttermilk

Preheat oven to 350°. • Cream shortening and sugar. Sift flour, baking soda and baking powder together. Add to shortening. Add eggs, flavoring and ½ cup buttermilk and beat for 2 minutes. Add remaining buttermilk and beat for 2 more minutes. • Pour into 2 loaf pans that have been greased and lined with wax paper. Bake for 45–50 minutes. Remove from oven and cool.

Senator Robert C. Byrd
(West Virginia)

CHOCOLATE CHOCOLATE ANGEL FOOD CAKE

Serves 12 to 16

12 large egg whites
1 teaspoon cream of tartar
1¼ cups superfine sugar (or
 granulated sugar, sifted
 twice)

¼ teaspoon salt
1 teaspoon vanilla extract
¾ cup cake flour
¼ cup cocoa powder
¼ cup chocolate syrup

Preheat oven to 325°. • In an electric mixer, beat egg whites for a few minutes. Add cream of tartar and continue beating until egg whites stand in stiff peaks. Combine sugar and salt and slowly add to egg whites while beating. Add vanilla and continue beating until egg whites are stiff and shiny. • Sift flour and cocoa powder together and fold into egg white mixture, trying to deflate egg whites as little as possible. • Spoon ⅓ of batter into an ungreased angel food cake pan. Push mixture into sides to eliminate air bubbles. Drizzle evenly with half of chocolate syrup and plunge chocolate syrup into batter with a spoon or spatula 3 times to achieve marbled effect. Add ⅓ more batter and drizzle with remaining chocolate syrup. Repeat plunging in different places. Cover with remaining batter. • Place pan on middle or lower rack of oven and bake for 50 to 60 minutes. • Remove from oven and immediately turn cake upside down to cool. When completely cooled, run a serrated knife around inside and outside of cake to loosen. Run knife along bottom once sides have loosened. • When serving, use a serrated knife in a sawing motion to cut slices.

Senator and Mrs. John D. Rockefeller IV
(West Virginia)

ALMOND FILLED COOKIE CAKE

Crust:

2⅔ cups flour
1⅓ cups sugar
1⅓ cups unsalted butter

½ teaspoon salt
1 egg

Filling:

1 cup finely chopped
   or grated almonds
½ cup sugar

1 teaspoon grated lemon peel
1 egg, slightly beaten

Grease a 9- or 10-inch springform pan. Combine all crust ingredients in large bowl of electric mixer and mix at low speed until dough forms. Form dough into a ball and refrigerate, if desired. • Preheat oven to 325°. Divide dough in half. Spread half in bottom of prepared pan. In a small bowl, mix almonds, sugar, lemon peel and egg and spread over dough to within ½ inch of sides of pan. Press remaining dough between sheets of wax paper into a circle the size of pan. Remove top layer of wax paper from dough and invert dough onto pan. Remove second sheet of wax paper and press dough into place. • Cover oven rack with aluminum foil under pan to protect oven from spillage. Bake for 45–55 minutes, until golden brown.

Erika Zuntz

MARBLE CHEESECAKE   Serves 10 to 12

12-ounces semisweet
   chocolate chips
2 cups flour
1 cup plus 4 tablespoons sugar
½ teaspoon salt
½ cup butter

1 8-ounce package cream
   cheese at room temperature
1 teaspoon vanilla extract
6 eggs
1 cup sour cream

Preheat oven to 400°. • To make crust, melt chocolate over low heat. Combine 1½ cups flour, 4 tablespoons sugar and salt. Cut in butter until fine. Stir in 4 tablespoons melted chocolate. Press into bottom of 2 springform pans. Bake at 400° for 10 minutes. • For filling, mix softened cream cheese with 1 cup sugar. Blend in remaining ½ cup flour and vanilla. Add eggs, one by one, beating thoroughly after each addition. • Blend in sour cream. • Pour ¾ of cheese mixture in separate bowl and combine with remaining chocolate. Pour half of plain cheese mixture over crusts. Top with chocolate cheese mixture. Cover . with remaining plain mixture. With a spatula, cut through batter to marble. • Place in oven. Reduce heat to 300° and bake for 1 hour. Cool for 3 hours and chill for 8 hours before serving. To cut, use a wet, hot knife.

Mrs. Alvin A. Kraft

"14 CARAT" CAKE

2 cups flour
2 teaspoons baking powder
1½ teaspoons baking soda
1 teaspoon salt
3 tablespoons cinnamon
1⅔ cups sugar

1½ cups oil
4 eggs
2 cups grated carrots
1 8-ounce can crushed
   pineapple, drained
½ cup raisins

Icing:
6–8 tablespoons butter
1 teaspoon vanilla extract
1 8-ounce package cream
   cheese

2 cups powdered sugar (or
   less, if preferred)
A little milk (optional)

Preheat oven to 350°. • Sift flour, baking powder, baking soda, salt and cinnamon together and set aside. • Combine sugar and oil in bowl of electric mixer. Add eggs, one at a time, beating well after each addition. Add flour mixture to eggs and mix well. Blend in grated carrots, crushed pineapple and raisins. Pour into a 13 x 9 x 2 inch pan which has been greased and floured. • Bake for about 50 minutes. Remove from oven and cool. • To make icing, cream together butter, vanilla, cream cheese and powdered sugar. If too thick, add a few drops of milk. Ice top and sides of cake.

Stacey Goodrich

MUSKINGUM CHOCOLATE DEW CAKE

"John Glenn has always liked a moist cake! This cake recipe is one that our children ordered made on special occasions, such as birthdays, etc. For one who really enjoys chocolate, a chocolate icing can't be beaten! Enjoy....."

2 cups sifted cake flour
1 cup sugar
4 tablespoons cocoa
½ teaspoon salt

2 teaspoons baking soda
1 cup cold water
1 cup mayonnaise
1 teaspoon vanilla

Preheat oven to 350°. • Sift flour, sugar, cocoa, salt and baking soda together several times. • In a small bowl, mix cold water and mayonnaise well and add to dry ingredients. Add vanilla and stir well. • Pour batter into 2 8-inch cake pans. Bake for 30 minutes, until a toothpick comes out clean. • Frost with your favorite chocolate icing.

Annie H. Glenn
Wife of Senator John H. Glenn (Ohio)

JOE WHEELER CAKE

1 cup butter
2 cups sugar
4 cups flour, sifted
2 teaspoons baking soda
2 cups buttermilk
4 eggs, lightly beaten
1 teaspoon allspice
2 teaspoons cinnamon
1 teaspoon nutmeg

1 teaspoon cloves
1 box raisins, soaked in
   warm water for 15 minutes,
   well drained and dredged
   lightly with flour
1 cup nuts, chopped (optional)
1 cup citron, chopped
   (optional)

Grease and flour 3 9-inch layer pans. Preheat oven to 350°. • Cream butter and gradually add sugar in electric mixer. Add 1 cup of flour. • Dissolve the baking soda in the buttermilk and add to butter mixture. Add remaining flour and the eggs. Add the remaining ingredients and mix well. • Bake for 25–30 minutes.

Caramel icing:
4 cups sugar
3 tablespoons butter

1⅓ cups buttermilk
½ teaspoon baking soda

To prepare caramel icing, caramelize ½ cup of sugar in a skillet (stir over low heat until melted and brown) and add a little boiling water. Cook for about 10 minutes to a syrup. Add remaining sugar and butter. • Dissolve baking soda in buttermilk and add to skillet. Cook to 234°-238°, stirring constantly. Beat until spreading consistency. • When cake is cool, ice layers, assemble and ice sides.

Mrs. Howell Heflin
Wife of the Senator from Alabama

MARMALADE CAKE

¾ cup butter
1 cup sugar
1 tablespoon grated orange
   rind
1 teaspoon vanilla extract
3 eggs
1–1½ cups orange marmalade

1 cup chopped walnuts or
   pecans
3 cups sifted flour
1½ teaspoons baking soda
1 teaspoon salt
½ cup evaporated milk
½ cup orange juice

Topping (optional):
1 cup sugar
1 cup orange juice

Cream butter, sugar, orange rind and vanilla until fluffy. Add eggs one at a time, beating after each addition. Stir in orange marmalade and nuts. • Sift together dry ingredients and add to butter-marmalade mixture alternately with milk and orange juice. • Turn into a greased and wax paper-lined 9-inch tube pan. Bake at 350° for 1 hour and test for doneness. Cool in pan for 10 minutes and remove from pan. • To make topping, mix sugar and orange juice and cook over low heat until syrupy. While cake is still warm, drizzle topping over cake.

Helen Bing

GOLDEN DATE CAKE

2 cups plus 2 tablespoons flour	1 cup milk
1½ cups sugar	1½ teaspoons vanilla extract
1 teaspoon salt	½ cup unbeaten eggs
3 teaspoons baking powder	1 cup dates, chopped finely after measuring
½ cup shortening	½ cup coarsely chopped nuts

Preheat oven to 350°. • Sift together flour, sugar, salt and baking powder into a mixing bowl. Add shortening, milk and vanilla. Beat vigorously for 2 minutes with a spoon or on medium speed of an electric mixer. Scrape bowl while mixing. Add eggs and dates and beat an additional 2 minutes. Fold in nuts and pour into 2 greased and floured 8-inch layer cake pans. Bake for 35–45 minutes, until wooden toothpick comes out of center clean. Cool completely before frosting.

Fresh orange icing:

3 cups powdered sugar	1½ tablespoons orange rind, freshly grated
⅓ cup shortening	
3 tablespoons orange juice, freshly squeezed	

To make icing, combine sugar and shortening. Blend in orange juice and rind. • Frost each layer and place one on top of the other.

Belinda McKenzie

BANANA CAKE

"Very, very easy!"

¼ cup butter, softened
1 cup sugar
1 egg
1 cup crushed very ripe
  bananas

1½ cups flour, sifted
1 teaspoon baking soda
  dissolved in 1 tablespoon
  hot water

Icing:

1 tablespoon butter
½ cup brown sugar
5 tablespoons evaporated milk

1¾ cups of powdered sugar
½ teaspoon vanilla extract
½ cup chopped nuts

Preheat oven to 375°. • Cream butter and gradually add sugar. Add all other ingredients and mix thoroughly. • Pour into a greased and floured 7 x 11 inch pan and bake about 25 minutes. • Cool on rack. • To make icing, mix all of ingredients in an electric mixer. • Frost cake when cool.

Mrs. Robert W. Oliver

CHRISTMAS CAKE   Serves 12 to 16

"One treat we had throughout World War II was Christmas Cake, albeit with substitutions for the more luxurious ingredients."

3 cups plus 2 tablespoons
  flour
1 pound raisins
1 pound dried currants
4 ounces candied orange peel,
  chopped
4 ounces candied citrus peel,
  chopped
½ teaspoon salt
½ teaspoon nutmeg

½ teaspoon allspice
1½ cups unsalted butter,
  softened
1½ cups sugar
6 eggs, at room temperature
¼–⅓ cup slivered almonds
3 tablespoons brandy
6–8 tablespoons sweet
  sherry or Madeira (for
  basting)

Heat oven to 300° and set the shelf low. Butter a 10-inch springform pan and line the base and sides with a double layer of wax paper. Butter the wax paper. • Sprinkle 2 tablespoons flour on the raisins, currants and candied peels and mix until the fruit is well coated. • Sift 3 cups flour with salt, nutmeg and allspice. • Cream butter, and beat in sugar. Continue beating until soft and light, about 5 minutes. Add the eggs, one at a time, beating thoroughly after each addition. Stir in the flour in 2 or 3 batches. Stir in dried fruit and almonds. Finally, stir in the brandy. • Spoon the batter into the prepared pan and smooth the top, leaving the center slightly hollow. • Bake in the oven until the cake tests done, for 1¾–2¼ hours. If it browns too quickly during cooking, cover the top loosely with foil. • Allow the cake to cool in the pan. Unmold and peel off paper. Baste the top with 2–3 tablespoons sherry. Wrap the cake in cheesecloth soaked in sherry and store in an airtight container for at least 1 month, and up to a year or more, if you wish.

Anne Willan, Director,
École de Cuisine, La Varenne

NUT ROLL   Serves 12

6 eggs, separated
¾ cup, plus 1–2 teaspoons
sugar
1 teaspoon baking powder

1½ cups grated pecans
1½ cups heavy cream
¼ teaspoon vanilla
Powdered sugar

Grease a jelly roll pan or large roasting pan. Line with wax paper and grease wax paper. • Beat egg yolks with ¾ cup sugar until thick and pale. Mix baking powder with pecans and fold into egg yolk mixture. • Beat egg whites until stiff. Fold into egg yolk mixture and spread into prepared pan. Bake at 350° for 20 minutes. Cover cake with a damp towel and chill in refrigerator. • Turn cake onto the damp towel and carefully peel back wax paper. • Whip cream with vanilla and 1–2 teaspoons sugar. Spread on cake. Roll cake carefully and turn out, seam side down, on a serving plate and sprinkle with powdered sugar.

Sarah T. Minikes

BLUEBERRY CAKE

2 eggs, separated
1 cup sugar, plus additional
to top
½ cup shortening
¼ teaspoon salt
1 teaspoon vanilla extract

1½ cups sifted flour, plus 1
tablespoon flour
1 teaspoon baking powder
⅓ cup milk
1½ cups blueberries

Beat egg whites until stiff. Add ¼ cup sugar to whites and beat. • Cream shortening and add salt, vanilla and remaining sugar. Add egg yolks and mix well. • Sift flour, measure and sift again with baking powder. To creamed mixture, add flour and milk alternately. Mix well. Fold in egg whites. Coat blueberries with 1 tablespoon flour and fold into mixture. Pour into 8 x 8 inch pan. Sprinkle with additional sugar and bake at 350° for 50 minutes.

Elizabeth Donahue

ORANGE CAKE   Serves 8

3 navel oranges	2 eggs
1 cup sugar	1 cup flour
10 tablespoons butter, softened	1 teaspoon baking powder
	Whipped cream (optional)

Preheat oven to 375°. • Grate zest from 1 orange. Place zest and ½ cup sugar in food processor fitted with steel blade. Add butter and mix until fluffy. Add eggs and mix well. Add flour and baking powder and process with several bursts of power, just enough to blend. Add juice from 1 orange. Mix quickly and transfer to a well-buttered 8-inch layer cake pan. Place in oven and reduce heat to 350° after 5 minutes. Bake for 25–30 minutes, remove from oven and immediately turn onto a serving plate. • Dissolve remaining ½ cup sugar in the juice of 2 oranges and slowly pour over cake while still warm (see note). Let rest, lightly covered, at room temperature overnight to develop flavor. The cake may be decorated with rosettes of sweetened whipped cream.

NOTE: You may add several tablespoons of orange liqueur to sauce, if desired.

Elizabeth Esterling, Founder
Paris Cooks School

MARGE'S CHOCOLATE DREAM CAKE

1 cup softened butter	1 cup boiling water
2 cups sugar	½ cup Drostë cocoa
3 eggs	2 cups unsifted flour
1 cup buttermilk	½ teaspoon salt
1 teaspoon vanilla extract	2 teaspoons baking soda

Grease a 13 x 9 x 2 inch baking pan. • Beat butter and sugar in large bowl of electric mixer. Add eggs, 1 at a time, and continue to beat until fluffy. Stir in buttermilk and vanilla until blended. • Combine water and cocoa in a small saucepan. Bring to a boil over medium heat, lower heat and simmer for 2 minutes. • Combine flour, salt and baking soda in a large bowl and stir until thoroughly blended. Add buttermilk mixture to flour and beat. Stir in hot cocoa mixture and beat until well blended (batter will be thin). • Pour into prepared pan and bake at 350° for 40–50 minutes, until a toothpick inserted in the center comes out clean. Cool cake in pan on wire rack.

Chocolate frosting:

4 tablespoons Drostë cocoa	2 cups powdered sugar
4 tablespoons melted butter	Half and half

Mix the first 3 ingredients above with enough half and half to make a paste. Beat thoroughly. Frost cooled cake. Cake can also be split into two layers and top and all sides iced.

Marge McMullan

LIGHTHEARTED CAKE

"This cake contains no cholesterol."

2½ cups flour
2 teaspoons baking powder
½ teaspoon baking soda
¼ teaspoon salt
2 cups shredded, peeled
   zucchini squash
1 cup sugar
1 ounce unsweetened
   chocolate, melted
1 teaspoon ground cinnamon

½ cup vegetable oil
¼ cup skim milk
2 teaspoons vanilla extract
3 egg whites or
   ½ cup egg substitute,
   thawed
Vegetable cooking spray
1½ teaspoons powdered
   sugar

Preheat oven to 350°. • Combine first 12 ingredients in a large bowl. Stir well and pour into a 13 x 9 x 2 inch baking pan which has been coated with cooking spray. Bake for 45 minutes or until a wooden toothpick inserted in the center comes out clean. Put pan on a wire rack to cool. Dust with powdered sugar.

Mrs. John K. Walker, Jr.

CHEESECAKE WITH CONFIT OF PARIS MUSHROOMS

Serves 16

Crust:

2½ cups finely ground
   graham cracker crumbs
   (about 9 ounces)
1 cup coarsely chopped
   walnuts

¼ cup sugar
1 teaspoon ground cinnamon
2 pinches salt
6 tablespoons unsalted
   butter, melted

Filling:

3 8-ounces packages cream
   cheese, softened
⅔ cup sugar
3 large eggs, at room
   temperature
¼ teaspoon fine sea salt
3 cups sour cream

2 tablespoons unsalted
   butter, melted
1 tablespoon plus 1½
   teaspoons high-quality dark
   rum
1 tablespoon lemon juice
1 teaspoon vanilla extract

Confit of Paris mushrooms:

2 cups water
¼ cup lemon juice
1½ pounds extra-large fresh
   button mushrooms (the
   whitest possible), washed

1½ cups sugar

To make crust, combine graham cracker crumbs, walnuts, sugar, cinnamon and salt in a large bowl, mixing well. Line the bottom of a 10-inch spring-form pan with the crust mixture, pressing firmly into place. Dribble butter over top and set aside. • Preheat oven to 350°. • To make filling, place cream cheese in large bowl of an electric mixer and beat until creamy. With the machine at medium speed, beat in sugar until well blended. Beat in eggs and salt, then sour cream, butter, rum, lemon juice and vanilla. Pour filling into prepared crust and tap pan solidly on work surface a few times to dispel air bubbles. Bake on middle shelf of oven for about 45 minutes or until top is set enough so that when lightly pressed, no batter sticks to your fingertips and no fingerprints are left behind. Turn off oven and leave door ajar 1–2 inches for 1 hour to finish cooking. Refrigerate for at least 8 hours or overnight for cake to firm. • To make confit, combine water and lemon juice in a non-reactive 2-quart heavy saucepan. Separate mushroom caps from stems and cut caps into ¼-inch slices, placing them in lemon water as cut to prevent browning. Add sugar and bring to a boil. Gently simmer for 1½ hours, stirring occasionally. Remove from heat and serve immediately. (If confit is made ahead, set aside at room temperature for up to 2 hours, then refrigerate.) • To serve, run a thin flexible knife around the edges of cheese-cake, remove sides of pan and slice cake into wedges. Serve on dessert plates topped with some of undrained confit or serve confit in a sauceboat. Refrigerate leftovers.

Kathy Dinardo, Captain
Jean-Louis Restaurant

CHEESE CAKE BARS   Makes about 20 pieces

¼ cup chopped pecans or
   other nuts
5 tablespoons butter, softened
⅓ cup brown sugar
1 cup flour
1 8-ounce package cream
   cheese, softened

½ cup sugar
1 egg
2 tablespoons milk
1 tablespoon lemon juice
½ teaspoon vanilla extract

Mix nuts, butter and brown sugar in food processor. Add flour and continue mixing. Press into a 9 x 9 inch brownie pan. Bake for 12–15 minutes at 350°. • Cream the cream cheese, sugar and egg in a food processor. Add the remaining ingredients and mix well. Pour over the crust and bake an additional 25 minutes. Cut into squares when cool.

Sarah T. Minikes

CHEESECAKE   Serves 10 to 12

2½ cups graham cracker
   crumbs
6 tablespoons sugar, plus
   1½ cups sugar
½ cup butter
1 teaspoon cinnamon
3 8-ounce packages of cream
   cheese at room temperature

4 jumbo eggs, separated and
   at room temperature
1 cup sour cream, at room
   temperature
1 teaspoon vanilla
Powdered sugar

Mix graham cracker crumbs, 6 tablespoons sugar, butter and cinnamon and press into the bottom and sides of an 8- or 9-inch springform pan. Place in freezer. • Mix cream cheese and 1½ cups sugar in a large bowl. Add egg yolks one at a time and beat well. Fold in sour cream and vanilla. Beat egg whites and gradually fold into cream cheese mixture. Pour into cold graham cracker crust. Bake for 1 hour at 300° (or until brown). • Remove from oven and cool completely. Sprinkle powdered sugar over the top. May be served warm or refrigerated until ready to serve.

Lynda J. Robb

CISSEL'S SUPER-DUPER CHEESECAKE   Serves 16

Crust:

½ cup melted butter
   (lightly salted variety)

2 packages cinnamon
   graham crackers, crushed

Filling:

5 8-ounce packages cream
   cheese at room temperature
5 eggs
2 egg yolks
2 tablespoons flour

2 cups sugar
1 cup heavy cream
1 lemon
1 teaspoon vanilla extract

Preheat oven to 450°. • Place graham crackers in a plastic bag and crush. Mix with butter and press into bottom of a 12-inch springform pan. Chill. • Mix cream cheese and eggs, adding one at a time. Add egg yolks and continue to blend. Add flour, sugar and cream and mix. Grate lemon rind and squeeze lemon juice and add both to cheese mixture. Add vanilla and blend well. Pour into springform pan and place on baking sheet. Bake for 15 minutes, until it begins to turn light brown. Reduce heat to 250° and continue baking for 2 hours. Remove from oven and allow to cool. • Refrigerate before serving. • Toppings of strawberries, pineapple or cherries may be added.

Cissel Gott Collins

"Two cakes with traditional Texas ingredients: bourbon and pecans. I've never been able to decide which is better."

BOURBON PECAN CAKE

6 cups chopped pecans
1 9-ounce box of raisins
4 cups flour
1 teaspoon nutmeg
1 teaspoon cinnamon
1 teaspoon ground cloves
1½ cups butter or margarine,
   softened

2 cups sugar
6 eggs
½ cup molasses
1 teaspoon baking soda
1 cup bourbon

Preheat oven to 325°. • Combine pecans and raisins. Dredge with ½ cup flour, stirring well. Set aside. • Combine remaining 3½ cups flour with nutmeg, cinnamon and cloves and set aside. • Cream butter in a large mixing bowl. Gradually add sugar, beating until light and fluffy. Add eggs, one at a time, and beat well after each addition. Combine molasses and baking soda and add to butter mixture. • Add the flour mixture to creamed mixture, alternately with ½ cup of bourbon, beginning and ending with flour mixture.

Mix well after each addition. Stir in pecan mixture. Spoon batter into a wax paper-lined and greased 10-inch tube pan. Bake for 2 hours and 15 minutes, or until a straw inserted in the center comes out clean. • Cool completely in the pan and remove. • Moisten several layers of cheesecloth with remaining bourbon. Cover cake completely with cheesecloth. Wrap in aluminum foil and store in a cool place for at least 1 week. Remoisten with bourbon as needed.

PECAN CAKE WITH PRALINE GLAZE

1 cup raisins	1 teaspoon baking powder
½ cup bourbon	½ teaspoon baking soda
1 cup butter or margarine, softened	1½ teaspoons ground nutmeg
2¼ cups sugar	1 cup buttermilk
5 eggs	2 cups coarsely chopped pecans
3¼ cups flour	

Preheat oven to 325°. • Combine raisins and bourbon, stirring well. Cover and let stand for at least 1 hour. • Cream butter, gradually adding sugar. Beat well. Add eggs, one at a time, beating well after each addition. • Combine flour, baking powder, baking soda and nutmeg. Add to creamed butter mixture alternately with buttermilk, beginning and ending with flour mixture. Mix well after each addition. Fold in pecan and raisin mixture. Pour batter into a greased and floured 10-inch tube pan. Bake for 1 hour or until a straw inserted in center comes out clean. Cool in pan for 10 minutes, remove onto wire rack. Drizzle praline glaze over cake and cool completely.

Praline glaze:

½ cup packed brown sugar	¼ cup heavy cream
¼ cup sugar	½ cup pecan halves
¼ cup butter, softened	

Cream butter and sugars. Stir in cream, add pecan halves. If too thick to drizzle, heat over hot water.

Martha Buchanan

TEXAS HEATH BAR COFFEE CAKE

2 cups flour
1 cup brown sugar, packed
½ cup sugar
1 cup butter or margarine,
    softened
1 cup buttermilk

1 teaspoon baking soda
1 teaspoon vanilla
1 egg
5 ounces frozen Heath Bars
½ cup pecans

Preheat oven to 350°. • Mix the first four ingredients together well. Reserve ½ cup for later use. Add the buttermilk, baking soda, vanilla and egg to the mixture and blend well. Pour into a greased and floured 13 x 9 x 2 inch cake pan. • Crush the Heath Bars and pecans and combine with the reserved ½ cup of flour mixture. Sprinkle over the top of the batter. Bake for 30 minutes. Cool and cut into squares.

Mrs. Ben F. Dixon, IV

APPLESAUCE SPICE CAKE

1 cup shortening
2 cups sugar
2 eggs
1 cup dates, chopped
2½ cups applesauce
1–2 cups walnuts, chopped
4 cups flour

1 teaspoon allspice
4 teaspoons cinnamon
1 teaspoon nutmeg
1 teaspoon salt
4 teaspoons baking soda
4 tablespoons hot water

Preheat oven to 350°. • Blend shortening, sugar and eggs. Add dates, applesauce and nuts. • Sift flour, allspice, cinnamon, nutmeg and salt together. Dissolve baking soda in hot water. Add dry ingredients and dissolved baking soda to egg mixture and mix well. Pour into a greased, 10-inch tube pan or two bread pans. Bake for 1 hour or until cake tests done. Remove from oven and cool on racks.

Senator Donald W. Riegle, Jr.
(Michigan)

C·O·O·K·I·E·S

SNICKER DOODLE COOKIES   Makes about 40 cookies

2¾ cups flour
2 teaspoons cream of tartar
1 teaspoon baking soda
½ teaspoon salt
1 cup butter or margarine

1½ cups sugar
2 eggs, beaten until creamy
2 tablespoons sugar
1 teaspoon cinnamon

Preheat oven to 400°. • Sift together flour, cream of tartar, baking soda and salt. • In an electric mixer, combine butter, sugar and eggs. Add flour mixture and mix thoroughly. Chill for at least 2 hours. • Mix sugar and cinnamon. • Roll teaspoons of dough in sugar and cinnamon mixture and place on ungreased cookie sheet 2 inches apart. Bake for 8–10 minutes.

Senator Dale Bumpers
Arkansas

GINGER COOKIES   Makes about 48 cookies

1⅓ cups sugar
¾ cup butter, softened
¼ cup light molasses
1 egg, slightly beaten
2 cups flour

3 teaspoons baking powder
¼ teaspoon salt
1 teaspoon cloves
1 teaspoon cinnamon
1 teaspoon ginger

In an electric mixer, cream 1 cup sugar and all of butter until very light and fluffy. Blend in molasses and egg. • Sift dry ingredients together and, at low speed, add to sugar mixture. Mix until just combined and refrigerate dough for at least 1 hour. • When ready to cook, preheat oven to 350°. Shape dough into 1-inch balls and roll in remaining sugar. Bake on an ungreased cookie sheet for 8–10 minutes.

The Inn at Little Washington
Washington, Virginia

GRANDMOTHER MERRICK'S   Makes 50 cookies
SOFT MOLASSES COOKIES

⅓ cup shortening
½ cup boiling water
1 teaspoon salt
¾ cup molasses
½ cup sugar
1 egg

2½ cups sifted flour
2 teaspoons baking powder
½ teaspoon baking soda
1 teaspoon ginger
1 teaspoon cinnamon

Preheat oven to 375°. • Place shortening in a bowl. Pour in boiling water and add salt. Stir in molasses and sugar. Add unbeaten egg and beat well. • Sift flour and measure to make 2½ cups. Add baking powder, baking soda, ginger and cinnamon to flour and sift again. Stir into shortening mixture. Drop by spoonfuls onto a greased cookie sheet and bake for 12–15 minutes.

Senator William S. Cohen
(Maine)

SESAME COOKIES   Makes 24 to 30 cookies

½ cup sesame seeds
1 tablespoon butter
1 cup brown sugar
5 tablespoons flour

1 egg, beaten
1 teaspoon vanilla
½ teaspoon salt

Preheat oven to 350°. • Put seeds in skillet and brown slightly in butter. Remove from heat. Add all remaining ingredients and mix well. • Drop dough by tablespoonfuls onto a buttered cookie sheet 2 inches apart. Bake 5–8 minutes. Remove and cool.

Evelyn DiBona

POTATO CHIP COOKIES   Makes 24 cookies

1 cup butter or margarine, softened
½ cup sugar
1½ cups flour

½ cup chopped nuts
1 teaspoon vanilla extract
½ cup crushed potato chips

Preheat oven to 350°. • Cream butter or margarine and sugar. Slowly add flour. Stir in nuts, vanilla and potato chips. Drop teaspoonfuls of dough about 2 inches apart on ungreased cookie sheet and flatten slightly with a fork. • Bake for 15–18 minutes, until slightly browned.

Mrs. Marvin L. Stone

RASPBERRY CRUMB BARS   Makes 30 to 40 bars

¾ cup butter or margarine, softened
1 cup brown sugar, packed
1½ cups flour
1 teaspoon salt
½ teaspoon baking soda

1½ cups uncooked oatmeal
1 10-ounce jar raspberry preserves
½ cup powdered sugar, sifted
1 tablespoon milk

Preheat oven to 400°. • In a large bowl, cream butter or margarine and brown sugar until light and fluffy. Sift flour, salt and soda together and gradually add to butter mixture. Stir in oatmeal. • Grease the bottom and sides of a 9 x 13 inch pan. Press half of the crumb mixture onto bottom of pan. (This is most easily done by breaking crumb mixture into small chunks and distributing evenly over bottom of pan. With a fork push, prod, scratch and press mixture down.) Spread the preserves over the crumb mixture. Sprinkle with remaining crumb mixture. • Bake for 20–25 minutes, until the edges are a deep golden brown and preserves are bubbly. • Allow to cool somewhat. Run a sharp knife between the crust and sides of pan. Finish cooling completely. • Whisk powdered sugar and milk together and scatter over the crumb sheet. Cut into bars. Refrigerate for half an hour to set.

NOTE: Can be kept in or out of the refrigerator.

Anne Mattison

MRS. FIELD'S CHOCOLATE CHIP COOKIES

Makes 9 dozen cookies

2 cups butter, softened
2 cups sugar
2 cups brown sugar
4 eggs
2 teaspoons vanilla extract
4 cups flour
5 cups oatmeal, ground
   to powder in an electric
   blender

1 teaspoon salt
2 teaspoons baking powder
2 teaspoons baking soda
2 12-ounce packages chocolate
   chips
1 8-ounce Hershey bar, grated
3 cups chopped nuts

Preheat oven to 350°. • Cream together butter and sugars. Add eggs and vanilla. Set aside. • In a large bowl, combine flour, oatmeal, salt, baking powder and baking soda. Add to butter mixture and combine thoroughly. • Add chocolate chips, grated Hershey bar and chopped nuts and mix well. • Place golf-ball-sized cookies 2 inches apart on an ungreased cookie sheet. Bake for 6–8 minutes. (They should be soft and gooey.)

Liz Lynch

PUMPKIN BARS

Makes about 24 bars

1 16-ounce can pumpkin
4 eggs
2 cups sugar
1 cup oil
2 cups flour
1 teaspoon baking soda

2 teaspoons baking powder
¼ teaspoon salt
2 teaspoons cinnamon
   or pumpkin spice
1 cup walnuts (optional)

Cream cheese frosting:
1 3-ounce package cream
   cheese, softened
1 tablespoon cream

½ teaspoon vanilla extract
3 tablespoons powdered sugar

Stir together pumpkin, eggs, sugar and oil. • Put flour, baking soda, baking powder, salt and cinnamon into sifter and sift into pumpkin mixture. Add walnuts, if desired, and stir. Pour into a lightly greased, deep cookie sheet. • Bake at 350° for 20–30 minutes. Cool. • To make frosting, mix cream cheese, cream and vanilla. Add sugar and cream well. • Frost pumpkin sheet and cut into bars.

Stacey Goodrich

CRISP LEMON COOKIES   Makes about 40 cookies

*"An ancient recipe found in an old cookbook in a rented house
on Martha's Vineyard years ago."*

1 cup butter, softened
1½ cups powdered sugar,
  sifted after measuring
1 teaspoon vanilla extract
2 tablespoons grated lemon
  rind

1 egg
2 cups flour
1 teaspoon baking soda
1 teaspoon cream of tartar
½ teaspoon salt
Powdered sugar

Preheat oven to 375°. • Cream butter and sugar until light and fluffy. Add vanilla, lemon rind and egg. Mix well. • Sift all dry ingredients except powdered sugar together and add to butter mixture. Blend well. • Drop from a teaspoon on ungreased cookie sheets. Bake for about 8 minutes, until lightly browned. Cool on a wire rack. Using a small sieve, dust with powdered sugar.

Ann Buchwald

HILLARY CLINTON'S   Makes about 40 cookies
CHOCOLATE CHIP COOKIES

1½ cups flour, unsifted
1 teaspoon salt
1 teaspoon baking soda
1 cup solid vegetable
  shortening
1 cup light brown sugar,
  firmly packed

½ cup sugar
1 teaspoon vanilla
2 eggs
2 cups old-fashioned rolled
  oats
1 12-ounce package
  semi-sweet chocolate chips

Preheat oven to 350°. Grease two baking sheets. • Combine flour, salt and baking soda. • In a large bowl, beat together shortening, sugars and vanilla until creamy. Add eggs, beating until light and fluffy. Gradually beat in flour mixture and rolled oats. Stir in chocolate chips. • Drop batter by well-rounded teaspoonfuls onto greased baking sheets. Bake for 8–10 minutes, until golden. Cool cookies on sheets on wire racks for 2 minutes. Remove cookies to wire racks to cool completely.

Hillary Rodham Clinton
First Lady

SOUR CREAM SUGAR COOKIES   Makes 50 cookies

"These are our son Andrew's favorite cookies.
This recipe came from Dan's mother, Vera Coats."

1 cup butter	2 cups flour
1 cup sugar	1 teaspoon baking soda
1 egg	½ teaspoon salt
1 cup sour cream	½ teaspoon nutmeg
1 teaspoon vanilla	Raisins (optional)

Cream butter and sugar together. Add egg, sour cream and vanilla. • Sift dry
ingredients together and add to butter mixture. Chill for at least 2 hours or
overnight. • Place on a greased cookie sheet by large spoonfuls, place a few
raisins in the middle of each spoonful, if you like, and sprinkle with sugar.
Bake at 400° for 10 minutes.

Marcia Coats
Wife of Senator Daniel R. Coats (Indiana)

CREAM CHEESE ULTRA BROWNIES   Makes 24 brownies

"A thick, moist, two-toned brownie with a slightly bittersweet icing."

5 ounces unsweetened
 chocolate
1¼ cups butter
1¼ cups flour
¾ teaspoon salt
⅓ cup sugar, plus 2½ cups
 sugar

1 8-ounce package cream
 cheese, softened
6 eggs
3 teaspoons vanilla extract
1¼ cups chopped walnuts
 (optional)

Icing:

2 tablespoons butter or
 margarine, softened
2 tablespoons light corn syrup
2 tablespoons water

2 ounces unsweetened
 chocolate
1 teaspoon vanilla extract
⅔ cup powdered sugar, sifted

Preheat oven to 375°. • Melt chocolate and butter in double boiler over low heat. Set aside to cool. • Sift flour and salt together. Set aside. • Cream ⅓ cup sugar with cream cheese. Blend in 1 egg and ½ teaspoon vanilla extract. Set aside. • Beat remaining eggs well. Add 2½ cups sugar and 2½ teaspoons vanilla extract and beat until mixture is light in texture and color. Gradually add the chocolate mixture, beating just until blended. Add the flour/salt mixture slowly. Continue beating until just blended. Stir in nuts. • Spread half of this batter in greased 13 x 9 inch pan. Spread cream cheese mixture over the chocolate batter. Dollop the remaining chocolate mixture over the cream cheese mixture. With the tip of a knife, draw through the top two layers to create a swirling effect. • Bake for 35 minutes, or until the edges are light golden brown and the middle is high and dry looking. Do not overbake. Set pan on a rack to cool for approximately 2 hours. • Once brownies, have cooled, make icing. Bring butter, syrup and water to a rolling boil in a small saucepan. Remove pan from heat and add chocolate. Stir until fully melted. Whisk in vanilla and powdered sugar. Spread over brownies immediately. Refrigerate to set icing for at least one hour.

NOTE: Best if made a day or two ahead.

Anne Mattison

CHOCOLATE-CHOCOLATE CHIP BARS   Makes about 70

1 cup butter or margarine
1½ cups sugar
¼ cup water
2 12-ounce packages of
   semisweet chocolate chips
1 tablespoon plus 1 teaspoon
   vanilla extract

2 eggs
2 cups flour
1 teaspoon salt
½ teaspoon baking soda
2 cups chopped nuts (optional)

Preheat oven to 375°. • Combine butter or margarine, sugar and water in a medium saucepan. Bring just to a boil. Remove from heat and stir in 1 package of chocolate chips and vanilla until mixture is smooth. Empty into a large bowl and add eggs. Beat well. • Sift flour, salt and soda together and gradually add to chocolate mixture. Let stand for 10 minutes. Stir in remaining package of chocolate chips and nuts. Spread into a greased jelly roll pan (15½ x 10½ inches). Bake for 20–25 minutes. The batter will be high and the sides should look semi-dry (it will fall as it cools). Cool and, if convenient, refrigerate overnight. Cut into 1½-inch squares.

Anne Mattison

LACE COOKIES   Makes about 25 cookies

1 cup dark Karo syrup
⅓ cup light or dark brown
   sugar, firmly packed
½ cup butter or margarine

1 teaspoon maple extract
1 cup flour
1 cup finely chopped pecans
   or walnuts

In a saucepan, combine syrup, brown sugar and butter. Bring to a boil over medium heat. Remove from heat immediately and add maple extract, flour and nuts. Blend well and drop by teaspoonfuls onto a greased Teflon cookie sheet about 3 inches apart. It is not necessary to grease cookie sheet after first batch. • Bake in a 325° preheated oven for 8–10 minutes. Remove from oven and cool on cookie sheet for 2 minutes. Remove cookies to brown paper and allow to cool completely. Store in an airtight container, placing waxed paper between layers of cookies since they are very fragile.

NOTE: Teflon non-stick cookie sheets are the secret to the success of these cookies.

Barbara Kilcarr

P·I·E·S

PECAN PIE   Serves 6 to 8

¼ cup butter
½ cup sugar
1 cup dark corn syrup
3 eggs, beaten with a fork

2 cups chopped pecans
1 teaspoon vanilla extract
Unbaked pie crust

Preheat oven to 350°. • In a saucepan, melt butter, sugar and syrup. Cool and add eggs. Add nuts and vanilla and pour into pie crust. • Bake for about 40 minutes, until pie center is firm.

Senator Phil Gramm
(Texas)

COFFEE AND CHOCOLATE TART   Serves 8

"Everyone always loves this."

6 ounces semi-sweet
   chocolate bits
½ cup margarine

2 cups Rice Krispies
1 quart coffee ice cream
Grated semi-sweet chocolate

Melt chocolate bits in a double boiler. Blend in margarine. Add Rice Krispies and stir until completely coated. • Butter a 9-inch pie plate and pour in mixture. Spread evenly along bottom and sides. Allow to stand at room temperature for several hours. • Just before serving, fill with ice cream, sprinkle top with grated chocolate and serve.

NOTE: Can be prepared ahead and frozen.

Heidi S. Berry

BLUEBERRY PIE   Serves 6 to 8

2¾ cups flour
1 teaspoon salt
1 teaspoon cardamom
½ teaspoon baking powder
½ cup butter, softened
4 tablespoons heavy cream
  mixed with 4 tablespoons
  water

¼–½ cup sugar (depending
  on sweetness of berries)
1 tablespoon potato flour
1¾ pints blueberries
1 egg, beaten

Preheat oven to 450°. • Mix flour, salt, cardamom and baking powder. Cut the butter into the flour mixture with a pastry blender to the consistency of small peas. Add cream-water mixture and blend until dough forms. Do not use an electric mixer or dough will be tough. Place in refrigerator for 1 hour. • Divide the pastry. Roll out half and press gently into a 9-inch buttered pie plate. • Combine the sugar and potato flour and sprinkle on top of the blueberries, mixing gently. Pour into pie plate. Turn the edges of the dough over the berries and brush the edge with the beaten egg. • Roll out the remaining dough and cover pie, pressing the edges tightly together. Brush the top with the beaten egg. Make a few holes in the top with a fork. Bake 20–25 minutes. • Serve with vanilla sauce or vanilla ice cream.

Mrs. Jukka Valtasaari
Wife of the Ambassador of Finland

APPLE CRUMB PIE   Serves 6 to 8

4 large tart apples
1 8-inch unbaked pie shell
½ cup sugar

1 teaspoon cinnamon
¼ teaspoon nutmeg
¼ teaspoon salt

Crumb topping:
½ cup sugar
¾ cup flour

⅓ cup butter

Preheat oven to 450°. • Pare apples, slice into pie shell and arrange so surface is fairly smooth. Combine the sugar, spices and salt and sprinkle over apples. • Make crumb topping by sifting sugar and flour together, then cutting in the butter until mixture is crumbly. Spread evenly over pie. • Place pie on a metal cookie sheet and bake for 15 minutes. Reduce heat to 375° and continue baking until apples are tender. (If crumbs begin to get too brown, cover with aluminum foil.)

Melissa Lindsay

LEMON MERINGUE PIE   Serves 6

Crust:

1¼ cups graham cracker   ⅓–½ cup butter or
   crumbs (see note)   margarine, melted
3 tablespoons sugar

Filling:

½ cup lemon juice   1 14-ounce can sweetened
1 tablespoon grated lemon   condensed milk
   rind or ¼ teaspoon   2 eggs, separated
   lemon extract   ¼ teaspoon cream of tartar
                            4 tablespoons sugar

To make crust, combine cracker crumbs and sugar in a medium-sized bowl.
Stir in melted butter or margarine until thoroughly blended. Pack firmly into
a buttered 8-inch pie pan, leaving a little for sprinkling on top of meringue.
Chill for 1 hour before filling, or bake in 350° oven for 8 minutes, cool and
chill. • For filling, combine lemon juice and grated lemon rind. Gradually stir
in condensed milk. Add egg yolks and stir until well blended. Pour into
chilled crust. • With an electric mixer, beat egg whites with cream of tartar
until stiff enough to hold a peak. Gradually add sugar, beating until stiff but
not dry. Place on top of pie filling and sprinkle remaining graham cracker
crumbs on top. Bake at 350° until lightly browned, about 15 minutes.

NOTE: Can also use baked pastry crust, cooled.

Senator Robert C. Byrd
(West Virginia)

APPLE-CRANBERRY-RAISIN PIE   Serves 6 to 8

4–5 large tart apples,   1 teaspoon cinnamon
   peeled and sliced   ½ teaspoon allspice
1 cup cranberries   1 teaspoon cornstarch
¼ cup raisins   2 8-inch uncooked pie crusts
½–¾ cup sugar

Mix first 7 ingredients and put in pie shell.
Cover with second pie shell. Bake 45–60 minutes in 350° oven.

Dotty Wexler

TREACLE TART   Serves 8

4 tablespoons Golden Syrup   Grated lemon grind
   (see note)   2 tablespoons fresh white
4 tablespoons butter   breadcrumbs
1 egg, slightly beaten   Squeeze of lemon juice
2 tablespoons heavy cream   1 uncooked 9-inch pie crust

Preheat oven to 350°. • Warm syrup until runny. Add butter and stir until melted and thoroughly blended. Add egg and cream and whisk into syrup. Stir in lemon rind and breadcrumbs. Add lemon juice. Mix and pour into prepared pie crust. • Bake for 30 minutes. • Can be served hot or cold.

NOTE: Lyon's Golden Syrup is a British product and is available in some supermarkets and specialty food stores.

Anne Green

MISSISSIPPI MUD PIE   Serves 8

"Use really good ice cream."

1½ cups chocolate wafer   1 quart vanilla ice cream,
   crumbs   softened
6 tablespoons unsalted   1½ quarts chocolate ice cream,
   butter, melted   softened
2 tablespoons clear crème
   de menthe

Sauce:
1 tablespoon cornstarch   6 tablespoons unsalted butter
¼ cup milk   ½ cup sugar
¼ cup heavy cream   1 teaspoon vanilla
3 ounces unsweetened
   chocolate, coarsely chopped

Mix crumbs and butter and press mixture into bottom and sides of a 9-inch pie plate. Freeze until firm. • Line 8-inch metal bowl with plastic wrap allowing overhang. Stir crème de menthe into vanilla ice cream and pack into prepared bowl. Spread chocolate ice cream into pie crust. Freeze bowl and pie crust until ice creams are firm. • To make sauce, whisk cornstarch into milk in small bowl. Add cream and whisk again. Melt chocolate and butter with sugar in small heavy saucepan over low heat, stirring until smooth. Add cornstarch mixture to chocolate stirring continuously with whisk. Reduce heat and continue to stir until mixture thickens. Remove from heat, add vanilla. Cool to room temperature. • To assemble, invert vanilla ice cream over chocolate ice cream in crust, pressing gently. Remove plastic wrap. Let edge between ice creams soften slightly. Pour sauce into center of vanilla ice cream, allowing excess to drizzle down sides. Serve immediately.

NOTE: This can be prepared up to two weeks ahead. After assembly, freeze pie until sauce hardens to a glaze, wrap and freeze. Fifteen minutes before serving, remove from freezer and place in refrigerator to soften slightly.

Nina Pillsbury

CHOCOLATE, RUM AND PECAN PIE — Serves 8

9-inch unbaked pie shell
½ cup chocolate bits
1 cup white corn syrup
1 cup dark brown sugar
¼ teaspoon salt
5 tablespoons butter, melted
½ teaspoon vanilla

4 tablespoons dark rum (Myers)
3 eggs
1 heaping cup pecans
Whipped cream, with a little sugar and rum folded in

Preheat oven to 375°. • Place chocolate bits evenly over bottom of pie shell. • In a bowl, combine corn syrup, sugar, salt, melted butter, vanilla and rum. Beat eggs slightly and stir into corn syrup mixture until thoroughly blended. Pour into pie shell. Sprinkle pecans evenly over the top. • Place on a cookie sheet and bake in oven for 45 minutes or until set. Serve with whipped cream flavored with rum and sugar.

Mrs. Paul F. Petrus

PEACH PIE SUPREME — Serves 10

Crust:
½ cup unsalted butter
1 3-ounce package cream cheese

1 cup sifted flour
½ teaspoon salt

Filling:
7–8 ripe peaches
2–3 eggs, well beaten
1 tablespoon butter, melted

1 cup sugar
1 tablespoon flour

Preheat oven to 450°. • Cream butter and cheese. Blend in flour and salt. Chill. • Roll out to fill a 10-inch pie pan. • Peel and halve peaches and arrange cut side up in pie pan. Mix remaining ingredients and pour over peaches. Bake for 10 minutes. Lower heat to 350° and bake for 40 minutes, or until custard is set.

Harriet Fraunfelter

BLACK BOTTOM PIE   Serves 8 to 10

"This recipe makes a huge pie."

20 gingersnaps, crushed
5 tablespoons butter, melted
1 cup sugar
1 tablespoon cornstarch
¼ teaspoon salt
2 cups milk
4 large eggs, separated
2 ounces bitter chocolate, melted

1 teaspoon vanilla
1 tablespoon plain gelatin
4 tablespoons cold water
⅛ teaspoon cream of tartar
4 tablespoons dark rum
1 cup heavy cream, whipped and flavored with vanilla
1 teaspoon grated or shaved bitter chocolate

Preheat oven to 275°. • Crush gingersnaps and mix with melted butter. Press into a large (9 x 2 inch) pie dish covering sides and bottom evenly. Bake for 10 minutes in oven. Remove from oven and cool to room temperature. You may turn oven off. • Mix ½ cup sugar, cornstarch and salt in the top of a double boiler. Add milk. Beat egg yolks. Gradually add sugar mixture to egg yolks. Return to double boiler and cook for about 3 minutes. • Divide custard in half. To one half add melted chocolate and vanilla. Spread carefully over ginger-snap crust. Refrigerate. • Soak gelatin in water. Dissolve over hot water. Add to remaining hot custard. Cool slightly. • Beat egg whites until foamy. Add cream of tartar. Continue beating until stiff. Add remaining ½ cup sugar, a little at a time. Beat to stiff meringue stage and fold into custard. Add rum. When custard begins to set, spread gently over chocolate layer in pie pan. Refrigerate. • Top with whipped cream that has been slightly sweetened and flavored with vanilla. Sprinkle shaved or grated chocolate over cream.

Mrs. Howell Heflin
Wife of the Senator from Alabama

UPSIDE-DOWN LEMON MERINGUE PIE   Serves 8

4 eggs, separated
Pinch of cream of tartar
1½ cups sugar
1 cup finely chopped pecans
1½ cups heavy cream, whipped

Juice of 2 lemons
Rind of 1 lemon
1½ cups heavy cream, whipped

Beat egg whites and cream of tartar in an electric mixer until foamy. Gradually add 1 cup sugar, a little bit at a time, until whites are stiff and glossy. Fold in pecans. Line a buttered 9-inch pie pan with meringue, making a well in the center and making sure that meringue extends to the edges as a pie crust would. Bake at 325° for 25 minutes. Remove from oven and push down meringue in the center to form a crust; leave an inch-wide ridge around the edge. Bake for 25 minutes more. Cool completely. • Beat egg yolks until slightly thickened. Add lemon juice, rind and remaining ½ cup of sugar. Cook in a non-aluminum double boiler until thickened, stirring constantly, until mixture coats a wooden spoon. Cool completely. Fold ⅔ of the whipped cream into lemon filling. Pour into meringue shell. Garnish with remaining whipped cream and additional lemon rind, if desired.

Paula Jeffries

VANILLA CHIP FRUIT TART   Serves 10 to 12

Pastry:

¾ cup butter or margarine,
   softened

½ cup powdered sugar
1½ cups flour

Vanilla filling:

1⅔ 6-ounce packages
   Hershey's vanilla milk chips
¼ cup heavy cream

1 8-ounce package cream
   cheese, softened

Fruit topping:

¼ cup sugar
1 tablespoon cornstarch
½ cup pineapple juice
½ teaspoon lemon juice

2 cups assorted fresh fruit:
   sliced strawberries, kiwis,
   nectarines, peaches,
   raspberries or blueberries

Heat oven to 300°. • Beat butter and powdered sugar until light and fluffy and blend in flour. Press mixture onto bottom and sides of a 12-inch round pizza pan. Bake for 20–25 minutes or until lightly browned. Cool completely. • Prepare vanilla filling by placing vanilla chips and heavy cream in a microwave-safe bowl and cook on high for 1–1½ minutes in microwave, until chips are melted and mixture is smooth when stirred. Beat in cream cheese. Spread on cooled crust, cover and chill. • Prepare fruit topping by combining sugar and cornstarch in a small saucepan. Add pineapple and lemon juices and cook over medium heat, stirring constantly, until thickened. Cool. Slice and arrange fruit on vanilla filling and pour juice mixture over fruit. Cover and chill.

Ann Rose

FRESH LEMON TART   Serves 6 to 8

One 10-inch unbaked tart
   shell (use your own favorite
   recipe)
5 eggs
5 small or medium lemons,
   grated zest and juice

1 cup sugar
4 tablespoons unsalted butter,
   melted
5 paper-thin lemon slices
2 tablespoons apricot preserves
1 tablespoon water

Preheat oven to 350°. • Bake tart shell for 10 minutes, remove from oven and cool. • Lightly beat eggs and add lemon zest and juice, sugar and melted butter. Mix well and pour into cooled tart shell. Bake for 30–35 minutes, until lemon curd has set. • When tart cools, arrange lemon slices over top. Melt apricot preserves with water over low heat until preserves have dissolved. Brush lemon slices with this glaze.

NOTE: This tart can be presented more attractively if baked in a pan with a removable bottom and lifted out before serving.

Suzanne Reifers, Food and Wine Consultant
Owner, Suzanne's Restaurant

PUMPKIN PIE   Serves 8
WITH BROILED PECAN TOPPING

Pastry Shell:

1½ cups sifted flour   ½ cup shortening or lard
½ teaspoon salt   3–5 tablespoons cold water

Filling:

¾ cup brown sugar   1½ cups light cream or
½ teaspoon salt   evaporated milk
½ teaspoon cinnamon   3 eggs
1½ teaspoons ginger   1 tablespoon melted butter
¼ teaspoon ground cloves   2 tablespoons orange
¼ teaspoon nutmeg   liqueur (optional)
2 cups canned or fresh
  pumpkin purée

Topping:

⅔ cup brown sugar   ⅛ teaspoon salt
3 tablespoons melted butter   ½ cup chopped pecans
1 tablespoon heavy cream

Make pie shell by placing flour and salt in bowl. Cut in shortening until mixture resembles coarse meal. Add water a little at a time. Blend into a ball. Roll out to 10-inch circle and place in 9-inch pie plate. Flute edge. Chill. • For filling, mix sugar, salt, spices and pumpkin. Beat in cream until smooth. Add eggs, butter and liqueur and beat until smooth. Pour into pie shell. • Bake for 10 minutes in 450° oven. Reduce heat to 325° and bake for 30–40 minutes longer until a knife comes out clean. Cool to lukewarm. For topping, mix all the topping ingredients well. Spread over pie. Decorate with pecan halves. Place pie under broiler 3 inches from heat for approximately 3–4 minutes, until bubbling.

NOTE: The pie can be prepared without topping and served accompanied by whipped cream or ice cream.

Paula Jeffries

CHOCOLATE MERINGUE PIE   Serves 6 to 8

2 egg whites
⅛ teaspoon cream of tartar
½ cup sugar
½ cup chopped nuts
1 cup semi-sweet chocolate bits

3 tablespoons prepared
   coffee
1 teaspoon vanilla
1 cup heavy cream

Preheat oven to 275°. • Beat egg whites with cream of tartar until foamy. While beating add sugar, two teaspoons at a time, until shiny. Spread on greased pie plate, sprinkle with nuts and bake for 50 minutes. • Remove from oven and allow to cool to room temperature. • Melt chocolate with coffee in double boiler. Add vanilla and remove from heat. Beat cream until stiff and fold into chocolate. Pour mixture into meringue shell. Place in refrigerator to cool.

Sally Chapoton

MOCHA PECAN PIE   Serves 6

6 ounces semi-sweet
   chocolate chips
¼ cup Kahlua
3 eggs, beaten
1 cup dark brown sugar,
   tightly packed

½ cup light corn syrup
2 teaspoons vanilla extract
½ cup melted butter or
   margarine
1 cup pecan halves
1 graham cracker pie shell

Melt chocolate in double boiler. Add Kahlua and stir until smooth. Beat eggs, sugar, corn syrup and vanilla and, when well mixed, add chocolate mixture. Stir well. Add butter and stir until well blended. Stir in pecan halves and pour mixture into pie shell. Bake at 350° for 35–40 minutes. Cool on rack.

Elena Schupp Darden

CHRISTMAS RAISIN PIE   Serves 10

Filling:

¾ cup soft brown sugar (generous)

2 tablespoons flour

1½ cups seedless raisins

⅓ cup sultanas or large raisins

½ cup water

2 tablespoons Golden Syrup (see note)

Finely grated rind of 1 lemon

Juice of 1 lemon

½ pound cooking apples, peeled and grated

Pastry:

1¼ cups all-purpose flour

Pinch of salt

2 teaspoons baking powder

⅓ cup sugar

1 egg, separated

1 tablespoon milk

½ cup butter, plus 2 tablespoons

Vanilla extract

Rum extract (optional)

To prepare filling, put all ingredients except apples in a pan, mix and bring to boil and simmer for 10 minutes until raisins are plump and the mixture thickens. Stir frequently. Remove from heat and allow to cool. • To make pastry, sift flour, salt and baking powder into a bowl. Make a well in the center and pour in sugar, vanilla, half an egg yolk (reserve other half), all of the egg white and milk. Stir together until mixed evenly. Add butter in pieces and beat into flour mixture. Knead lightly to form smooth dough, wrap in foil and chill in refrigerator for approximately 30 minutes. • Preheat oven to 375°. • Roll out half of the dough onto a floured surface and line a 9-inch pie dish. Spoon in half of grated apple. Then spread filling over it and add remaining apple. Roll out remaining dough onto floured surface and cover pie. Seal the edges, pierce the top of the dough with a fork and brush with remaining egg yolk mixed with a little milk. Bake for approximately 30 minutes until golden brown. May be served hot or cold.

NOTE: Lyon's Golden Syrup is a British product and is available in some supermarkets and specialty food stores.

Helen Kucharek
Soprano with Pavilion Opera
and English National Opera

DOONESBURY by Garry Trudeau

Index

Breads

Desserts

Eggs and Cheese

Fish and Seafood

FISH

Meat

BEEF

Pasta and Rice

Chicken

Salads and Salad Dressings

Soups

Vegetables